State and Capital in Mexico

Series in Political Economy and Economic Development in Latin America

Series Editor
Andrew Zimbalist
Smith College

†Available in hardcover and paperback.

State and Capital in Mexico

Development Policy Since 1940

James M. Cypher

Westview Press
Boulder, San Francisco, & Oxford

Series in Political Economy and Economic Development in Latin America

Tables 4.2 and 6.3 are used by prmission of *El Economista Mexicano*, Colegio Nacional de Economistas, Mexico City. Table 4.4 is reprinted from *The State and Capital Accumulation in Latin America*, Volume 1: *Brazil, Chile, Mexico*, edited by Christian Anglade and Carlos Fortin, by permission of the University of Pittsburgh Press and Macmillan Press Ltd., London. © 1985 by Christian Anglade and Carlos Fortin. Table 4.5 is reprinted from *Latin American Debt and the Adjustment Crisis*, edited by Rosemary Thorp and Laurence Whitehead, by permission of the University of Pittsburgh Press and Macmillan Press Ltd., London. © 1987 by Rosemary Thorp and Laurence Whitehead.

This Westview softcover edition is printed on acid-free paper and bound in library-quality, coated covers that carry the highest rating of the National Association of State Textbook Administrators, in consultation with the Association of American Publishers and the Book Manufacturers' Institute.

Published in 1990 in the United States of America by Westview Press, Inc., 5500 Central Avenue, Boulder, Colorado 80301, and in the United Kingdom by Westview Press, Inc., 36 Lonsdale Road, Summertown, Oxford OX2 7EW

Library of Congress Cataloging-in-Publication Data
Cypher, James M.
    State and capital in Mexico: development policy since 1940 / James M. Cypher.
        p. cm.—(Series in political economy and economic
development in Latin America)
    Includes bibliographical references.
    ISBN 0-8133-7546-0
    1. Mexico—Economic conditions—1918– . 2. Mexico—Economic policy.
3. Free enterprise—Mexico. I. Title. II. Series.
HC135.C97   1990
338.972—dc20

90-31850
CIP

Printed and bound in the United States of America

The paper used in this publication meets the requirements
of the American National Standard for Permanence of Paper
for Printed Library Materials Z39.48-1984.

10   9   8   7   6   5   4   3   2   1

Por el futuro
Martin, Quinn, y Micaela

Contents

Tables

Acknowledgments

For the past twenty-eight years I have traveled to and periodically lived in Mexico. As an *extranjero* I have enjoyed the advantage of association with nearly every social strata—from *descamisados* in *ciudades perdidas* to members of the elite. These have been my *maestros*, and I owe them a great deal.

Since we met in Mexico in 1975, Ross Gandy, *un Americano exilado*, has provided steady support. He and Juanamaria Cantu have given advice on countless matters of a professional and personal nature. He reviewed the first three chapters of this book and listened and commented as I sketched out what remained. Like Mexico's foreign debt, mine to Ross is unpayable.

In 1981 I became intrigued by the impact of the petroboom and decided to devote a summer to researching its effects. The California State University system provided me with a grant to do so. Further intrigued after that episode, I accepted a position as invited professor of economics at the Universidad Autónoma Metropolitana, Iztapalapa, for the academic year 1982–1983. My intention then was to write this book. I arrived, however, only weeks before that fateful date that still brings shudders to all who know Mexico—August 1, 1982. (Mexico then announced to an incredulous international banking community that it could not meet its foreign debt payments.) A period of intense economic and political turmoil then began. My research plans were rudely inter-rupted by a series of complex events that have taken me years to understand. My year at Iztapalapa was spent observing and puzzling over some of Mexico's more recent mysteries. At Iztapalapa I had a great deal of help. As a member of the faculty research seminar on Mexican political economy I participated in weekly workshops in which my colleagues and I presented our work. A more diverse, intelligent, creative, and combative group of political economists has never been gathered together before, I am sure. For their advice, criticism, and friendship, I thank all the members of the seminar. I owe a particular debt to Gregorio Vidal, the seminar leader, who is a perceptive analyst of the Mexican economy. Other members of the seminar, whose assistance has been of importance to me, are Víctor Soria, Alejandro Toledo, and, most particularly, Daniel Cataife.

It was then that I met Professors Cristina Montaño and Daniel Lund at Iztapalapa's Department of History. To them I owe a debt for many professional and personal favors. I also treasure memories of many idyllic jaunts shared in the beautiful *sierras* of Mexico.

Taking full advantage of a new program of support for research offered by the California State University system, I was able to devote a year of uninterrupted work to this project in 1988. I thank my colleagues and the administration at California State University, Fresno, for this precious year.

Dr. Fausto Burgueño, director of the Institute for Economic Research at the National Autonomous University of Mexico (UNAM) extended an invitation to join the *Instituto* as an invited professor of research in 1988. There I worked under the leadership of Dr. Arturo Guillén, director of the Seminar on Theory and Development. Arturo was a source of constant thoughtful advice on matters large and small, theoretical and empirical. His help was invaluable. Other members of the seminar were always generous with their time and advice. In particular I am grateful for many discussions with Clara Aranda Aranda, Leticia Campos, and Marina Chavez. Being at the *Instituto* enabled me to meet and learn from many of the best students of Mexico's political economy. Of particular help were Alonso Aguilar, Víctor Bernal, Sarahí Angeles, José Rangel, and Elaine Levine.

The administrators and support staff at the UNAM provided me with every possible privilege and courtesy. In particular, the librarians at the *Instituto* did all that they possibly could to track down my numerous odd requests. During the years the Department of Economics at El Colegio de México has provided me with a *credencial* to use their wonderful library.

At Westview Press I have been greatly assisted by the editor of this series, Dr. Andrew Zimbalist. His comments and advice on this manuscript have been invaluable to me. His professionalism and generosity are greatly appreciated. It has also been a pleasure to work with Westview's acquisitions editor, Barbara Ellington, whose tolerance and forbearance I acknowledge.

Shirley Pennell has for many years been a most relied upon resource as secretary. She has helped in countless ways to keep this project moving. At just the right moment it was my great fortune to encounter Jennifer Heyne, who has served as all-around assistant, word processor, and producer of all the tables. Her cheerfulness and efficiency have been of immense help in the last stages of this work.

Last, but very far from least, my wife, Ann Jennings Hoover, has been a constant source of encouragement and support. Her unremitting enthusiasm and confidence in my work have been a most vital, sustaining force.

James M. Cypher

Introduction

A Short Note on Research Methodology

This book is principally concerned with attempting to answer two questions: How important were state programs in facilitating the industrial growth of Mexico from 1940 to 1988? How and why has the nature of state policymaking changed over time? My approach has been to carefully read the literature published by Mexican scholars both on the state and on Mexico's industrialization experience. I have struggled to weave this work into a coherent whole, seeking to use the literature and the insights gained from many Mexican scholars through numerous discussions (along with a certain heterodox body of economic theory) to explain Mexico's changing experience with development policies. In concentrating on the roles of the state and the industrial elite, I hope that I have made some progress in understanding Mexico's development process. Mexican social scientists have often been boldly innovative in their interpretations of Mexico's economy. I hope that this book will increase the level of awareness of their often penetrating, but too often neglected, work.

In many instances I am painfully aware that my results fall short of my objectives. Unresolvable problems arose in my work because, to be blunt, Mexico remains a very underdeveloped country. Libraries and research facilities are less than ideal. Strikes often close universities, making access to libraries and scholars impossible. In most cases books are printed in small runs of 2,000–3,000 copies—finding a copy can be impossible. Diligent researchers can and do miss entire books devoted to their specific theme.

One related issue is worth noting: Examining *internally* generated changes in the economy is something that largely falls outside of the purview of dependency theory. Dependency theory leads social science researchers to look outside of the Mexican social formation for causality while seeing internal matters as largely reducible to effect. This approach has constituted the dominant perceptual framework of social science research in Mexico. Thus, analysis of the transnational corporations was terribly fashionable in the 1960s and 1970s, as was analysis of the debt crisis in the 1980s. This pervasive focus contributed to an intellectual

1

milieu that, until quite recently, too often neglected or slighted empirically oriented research on the internal forces contributing to Mexico's industrialization—particularly the economic role of the state.

From the Outside Looking In

One other issue should be mentioned. This book is concerned with the purposes, objectives, and accomplishments of the Mexican state in a particularly important area. But at the very center of the Mexican state lies *power* carefully wrapped in secrecy. The Mexican state is officially and publicly beholden to no one in terms of explaining its activities. There are no legal checks and balances, either by way of the Senate and the House of Deputies or the Supreme Court. Newspapers lack the resources and often the inclination to pursue stories that bring to light the secret processes by which power is exercised.

How the decisionmaking process functions is open to debate. Some researchers who have explored this matter claim that a small circle of 400–500 state functionaries (the "political elite") make all the policy decisions that matter. Others claim the number is closer to 30. In the summer of 1988 the leader of Mexico's key business association—the *Consejo Coordinador Empresarial* (Business Coordinating Council, or CCE)—claimed that a handful of government functionaries and a group of business leaders ran Mexico. In a statement that continued to resonate throughout Mexico months later, Agustin Legorreta flatly stated (in a moment of unexpected candor) that a "very comfortable little group of 300 people make all the economically important decisions in Mexico" (quoted in Ortiz Rivera, 1988, 14). In one stroke Legorreta boosted the credibility of a small group of researchers who had long claimed that an industrial-financial "oligarchy" (and *not* the state functionaries) ruled Mexico. Wherever the truth may lie in all of this is difficult to know. But one central fact must not be overlooked: Social science research does not thrive in such an environment, and the margin of error, even in the most meticulous work, can be terribly high.

Autobiographies can be an important source of information on the inner workings of the decisionmaking process. Unfortunately, state leaders and private sector magnates have very rarely published disclosing accounts of their power-wielding years. At the top Mexico seems to be very much like an elite club—those who need to know already know, and those who do not, do not. The secrets go to the grave. As the Mexican people say (with a tone of infinite resignation in their voices), "Así es"—that's just the way it is.

In spite of all such problems, however, there are many important and new lessons to be learned from a contemporary study of Mexico's political economy. The problems and possibilities of development for Mexico remain one of the fundamental issues of our time. Only through a careful examination of how Mexico has arrived at its current impasse will policymakers and popular leaders have any hope of overcoming it. In some small way, I hope this book contributes to a needed reconsideration of Mexico's development policies—or, at least, to a better understanding of Mexico's political economy for those who stand on the outside looking in.

1

The Political Economy of the State in Mexico: An Overview

This book analyzes Mexico's state institutions, programs, and policies of industrial development through the prism of political economy. Political economists seek to understand both economic policymaking and the forces behind economic dynamics (cycles, growth, depression, structural change, and so on). Much more than economics (narrowly defined), political economy is concerned with "why" social forces function in a particular way and with "who gets what"—that is, power.

Development economists have been forced to cast their net wider than most because they are concerned with social transformations—by definition "development" demands profound structural change. To be sure, a strong subcurrent in this field has proclaimed that market forces will achieve economic development without the aid of conscious policymaking. And with the recent rise of neoliberalism in the developed nations, the "let the market do it" perspective has become hegemonic within the major development institutions, such as the World Bank and the International Monetary Fund (IMF) (Toye, 1987). Setting aside this recent tendency, which will likely prove to be but a historical aberration, development economics continues to operate within the framework of political economy and thereby retain as its central focus the issue of structural change.

State-led Development

This book examines import-substituting strategies by way of a study of Mexico's development policies between 1940 and 1988. There are at least two common interpretations as to what is meant by "import-substitution" policies—the narrow and the broad. Narrowly defined import substitution is the development by the state of policies designed to close a chronic (or structural) deficit between the export of primary products and the import of manufactured goods. In other words, the narrow definition is

5

constrained to a rather technical balance-of-payments problem that can ostensibly be rectified with marginal changes in tariff patterns and exchange rates.

Broadly defined, import-substitution is a strategy for development which favors the expansion of the internal market, in contrast to orthodox neoclassical doctrines which emphasize development through primary commodity exports (or through following "market forces"). The expansion of domestic industry, then, is to be the motor force of development. The state is to play a crucial role in this process through (among other activities) indicative planning, the construction of state-owned industries in key sectors, the allocation of credit and the shrewd application of temporary protectionist policies in the foreign trade sector. This definition is inextricably tied to the UN's Comisión Económica para América Latina (Economic Commission for Latin America, or CEPAL) created in 1948 and to that institution's principal spokesperson, the late Raúl Prebisch. CEPAL maintained that a complete restructuring of the Latin American economies was necessary. Import-substitution industrialization shifted the central focus of development policy from the international economy to the internal market. Industrialization combined with limited income redistribution, and (secondarily) agricultural modernization became the main policy objectives. Spearheading this structural transformation was the state which would both *guide* and *supplant* the market as circumstances dictated (Prebisch, 1950, 1981). In this book CEPAL's broad interpretation of what constitutes import-substitution industrialization is employed. Such an approach to development is hereafter defined as being "state-led."

For his heresy against the "laws" of comparative advantage, Prebisch was predictably attacked by orthodox exponents of neoclassical economics. On the Left, Prebisch's ideas were taken much more seriously but very critically. The latter's polemic against CEPAL's notion of a semi-independent and humanistically Keynesian path to capitalist development raised the level of discussion regarding the problems of development (Bernal Sahagún, 1980; Rodríguez Garza, 1983).

Explicit in the state-led approach is the reliance upon industrialization as the central focus of the development program. Precisely why industrialization should be the central focus of the development program was never completely clarified by CEPAL. But the following can be surmised: Agricultural wage goods (basic grains and animal products) could be easily expanded given a "surplus" of labor in the countryside and a relatively plentiful supply of land. Small investments in agricultural infrastructure (roads, irrigation, and so on) would yield broad, quick returns. Industry could be promoted by stimulating and deepening simple production processes in wage goods/consumer goods production, such as textiles, food processing, and consumer nondurables. As the industrial labor force expanded, so would the internal market. As the basic goods market was steadily and increasingly supplied by domestic production, the state could shift its policies toward promoting intermediate products—oil, electricity, construction materials, steel, chemicals, and so forth. Later would come capital goods—machinery, machine tools, agricultural implements, trucks, trains and buses, motors, ships, and so on. Agriculture would be swept along by the rising tide of industry, becoming more mechanized, modern, and "efficient." Although the two processes were complementary, industrialization was the cause and agricultural modernization was the effect.

Technology: A Missing Link

Overlooked (or at the very least largely neglected) in the preceding schematic were a number of issues (which will be taken up in the following chapters), particularly technology. Where would the increasingly complex technology necessary to underwrite these great transformations come from? According to institutionalist economists who have long focused on the question of technical change, the relative neglect of the pursuit of technological autonomy was the "Achilles heel" in the "structuralist" approach to industrialization (Dietz, 1988; Dietz and Street, 1987).

As it turned out, at least in the case of Mexico, where state policymaking essentially conformed to the CEPAL approach,[1] the lack of any sustained and serious look at the issue of technological autonomy proved to be a stumbling block in the state's development project. In essence, as the state's policies guided the economy toward relative independence in the production of wage goods/consumer goods and then of intermediate goods, the economy became increasingly dependent on ever-growing amounts of technology embodied in capital goods imports (Boltvinik and Hernández Laos, 1981, 477). Thus, the problem of how to pay for capital goods imports became more acute, leading to profound policy changes that will be discussed in the following chapters.

The neglect of technology is a telling weakness in state-led development. In 1987, for example, Mexico devoted 0.60 percent of its gross national product (GNP) to research and technology. More than one-half of this amount, however, was to pay for *imported* technology. (Korea devoted 2.0 percent of its GNP to research and development; the United States, 2.7 percent) (M. Aguilar, 1988, 83; CIEN, 1988b, 50). If we compare Mexico's expenditures to those of the developed nations, it is more than likely that a disproportionately high share of such research and development (R&D) money was allocated to a small army of clerks, functionaries, and other "unproductive" personnel. Had all the other problems that could have arisen within the context of state-led development been successfully addressed, the neglect of a coherent strategy regarding technology would have been sufficient in and of itself to derail the state-led project.

Thorstein Veblen, and for the most part his institutionalist followers, placed considerable emphasis on the significance of the creation and amplification of a tool-using culture in the making of modern industrial societies. By the term "tool-using culture," the institutionalists mean that a developing society must have imbedded within it a set of social institutions that develop, encourage, and sustain habits of thought and action that inherently approach questions of technical production processes from a critical, aggressive, and dominating perspective. The tool-using culture views every production process as inherently improvable and in the short term sets about to realize the desired change.

Karl Marx made an interesting contribution to the discussion of technical change and economic growth when he drew the distinction between "extensive" and "intensive" forms of labor processes. To Marx, these forms of production help explain the slow transition from pre-capitalist modes of production to a full-blown capitalist society. Under the phase of extensive forms of production, workers deploy the minimum amount of tools and have very low levels of technical training and competence. Many, if not most, workers are first-generation migrants from the countryside and still continue to embrace and express pre-capitalist attitudes toward work and social processes in general. In the extensive phase, profits are derived by way of very low wages, long hours, and the forced speedup of the production process. Labor is offered few, if any, nonwage benefits, such as rights to unionization, disability payment, and retirement. As would be expected, labor tends to respond through a slowdown of production processes, tool breaking, absenteeism, and passivity toward the task at hand.

In the succeeding intensive phase, technical change becomes embedded in the production process and in the wider society. In this phase wages rise and working conditions improve. The overall productive apparatus of society becomes much more tightly integrated, thus making sustained leaps in production a potential possibility and (because the productive apparatus is not planned or controlled) sustained slumps (depressions and recessions) an inevitable eventuality. Although antagonism between labor and capital remains, the labor force is now qualitatively different. It is better trained and much more adaptable, it is capable of completing sustained and repeated technical tasks, and it is aware that the labor process is one of constant small change. The attitude of "We've always done it that way" plays virtually no role in the conceptual apparatus of the work force. The same is true of the capitalists and/or the state managers who run large government institutions, nationally owned (state-owned) industries, and banks.

The institutionalists have taken pains to argue that such changes do not take place overnight or with great ease and fluidity. For institutionalists the movement from the precapitalist forms of production through the extensive stage to the intensive stage is a slow and less than preordained process. Regression, lateral shifts, and dysfunctional combinations of the three logically separable forms of production (precapitalist, extensive and intensive) are conceivable.

Full Capitalism or Disarticulated Production

In Mexico a debate still rages as to where the country should be located in terms of the evolutionary scale sketched here. One widely cited Mexican economist, Alonso Aguilar, dated the transition to full capitalism in Mexico—which presumably meant that Mexico at least entered into the extensive phase of production—to the latter part of the nineteenth century (Aguilar, 1975). In a recent work dedicated to a discussion of Mexico's evolution through these phases of production, Miguel Ángel Rivera Rios maintained that only in the 1960s did Mexico enter into the intensive phase. From his perspective, the intensive phase is yet to be completely consolidated across the economy (Rivera Rios, 1986, Ch. 1). The utility of Rivera Rios's research is that it provides a framework in which the observable unevenness among production processes (and conceptual processes) may be understood. In other words, today within Mexico there are semiconnected sectors of the economy that operate on the basis of intensive forms of production. At the same time there are extensive forms of production in many sectors or in subparts of certain sectors (homework in the textile industry being one current example). Meanwhile, precapitalist forms of production are relatively widespread in the countryside and smaller villages of Mexico and within the service sector (more than one-half of the economy), where the ethos of mercantilism still reigns.

As a first approximation, then, Mexico's economy should be described as one suffering from the effects of a profound disarticulation of non-homogenous forms of production. The pervasive neglect of the creative capacities of the labor force (which are only partially realized when an economy rises to the intensive phase of production) is one of the crucial defining characteristics of the contemporary Mexican economy. The dominant strategy regarding labor is that it should be cheap—in 1988

Mexico reportedly had nearly the lowest paid workers in the world, with an average wage of less than $3.50 per day.

The neglect of technology must penetrate and define (and to a certain degree derive from) the owners and managers of the Mexican economy. In other words, with important exceptions, the dynamics of technical change are not intrinsic norms and rhythms that regulate the very existence of the managerial apparatus of Mexican society (be this apparatus in the financial sector, tourism, industry, agriculture, or government). Rather, such technical change is a somewhat occasional, nonintegrated aspect of Mexican society. Although the direction of current change may well be toward the norms of intensive production, a very considerable residual of precapitalist, mercantilist, and extensive forms of conceiving and doing remains. Labor, for the most part, is simply a cost—and a very cheap one. The expansionary synergism to be found within a form of production that emphasizes labor training and high wages can be glimpsed only rarely in semi-isolated components of the productive apparatus. The inability to create a critical mass of tool-using workers and managers—be they day laborers, skilled workers, or university-trained managers—is both a constraining and defining characteristic of the economy. The inability to recognize the existence of this characteristic, with few exceptions, is a telling indication of the pervasiveness of conceptual and cognitive problems that define and constrain Mexico's opportunities for economic development.

Three Stages of the Mexican State

It is important to distinguish another "evolutionary" process at work in Mexico: the three stages that the state has passed through since the days of the revolution (1910–1917). The following hypothesis is proposed: In viewing the relationship between the State and the economy in the twentieth century, we encounter first a nationalist-populist state (1934–1940), then a capitalist-rentier state (1940–1982), and most recently a neoliberal state (1982–1988). In this view, the element of "reverse evolution" implicit in this terminology is a persistent and increasing one (which is not to argue that such a tendency is irreversible, particularly given the fragmented nature of the socioeconomic "base" of Mexico).

The term nationalist-populist state is intended to convey the following: The state plays a dynamic role in restructuring the economy (and wider society) by way of innovative interventions that are, by and large, constructive, at least in the long term. Few students of Mexico's political economy care to argue that Lázaro Cárdenas's administration (1934–1940) was not the crucial and defining turning point in shifting Mexico's productive apparatus away from colonial and neocolonial forms of production and social organization. It was Cárdenas's administration that forged the idea of the "mixed economy"—a mix of the public and the private in which the autonomy of capitalist forces and forms of production would necessarily be constrained and conditioned by the state, which was the "rector" (controlling and guiding force) of the economy. What Cárdenas and subsequent Mexican leaders attempted to convey with the "rector" concept is best described in this statement from his inaugural address: "The state alone embodies the general interest, and for this reason only the state has a vision of the whole. The state must continually broaden, increase and deepen its interventions" (Hamilton, 1982, 129).

Porfirio Díaz (1876–1911) was the first to utilize the state as a catalyst in prompting capitalist accumulation in Mexico (Ayala and Blanco, 1981). Yet it was Cárdenas who defined the parameters of the contemporary Mexican state through his emphasis on (1) the creation of parastate (state-owned) firms; (2) state banks, which formented new industries and companies; and, above all, (3) the nationalization of foreign capital.

The nationalist-populist state can be viewed as constructive in the following sense: First, the state carried out an *accumulation function*. That is, following Jim O'Connor, the state (once again after Díaz and more directly so) sought to facilitate the private and public accumulation of national wealth (O'Connor, 1973, 6). As the quintessential nationalist, Cárdenas sought the creation of an autonomous national industrial bourgeoisie, whereas Díaz had simply emphasized the need for a nationally integrated economic market and a coherent infrastructure. Second (again following O'Connor), Cárdenas sought to make legitimate the state's power and trajectory vis-à-vis the peasantry and the small emerging industrial working class. This *legitimation function* was fulfilled for the peasantry through a relatively large land reform program. For the working class the state offered the rewriting and enforcement of existing labor laws protecting the right to unionize and the "right" to a "living" wage.

From the 1940s through the 1970s (for reasons advanced in the following chapters), Cárdenas's nationalist-populist project was reoriented toward a capitalist-rentier state. This term is utilized to convey the contradictory nature of the intersection between the state and the national productive apparatus. The "capitalist" elements of the state's project were "progressive" in the sense of developing the forces of production. At the same time, the old "rentier" ethos of the hacendado/merchant capitalist era continued to play a role. Merchant capital—whether it appears as trade capital, bank capital, mining capital, or hacendado capital—seeks its own expansion by way of economic rents and/or unequal exchange. It seeks not to expand, cheapen, or improve its product, but solely to raise its price. Above all, it seeks not to *produce* but rather to *appropriate* a portion of the value of what has been produced. In a word, merchant capital is parasitic. Merchant capital thrives in an economy of pervasive monopolies and cartels. It draws nourishment from the state that accompanies its ascendancy. This state is neither a feudal state nor a capitalist state, but something of both. It is a *transitional* form of the state that first made its appearance in Europe in the fifteenth century. Spain established an economy dominated by merchant capital in Mexico, and the legacy of that era has yet to be completely eradicated.

The Mexican Revolution delivered a terrible blow to merchant capital, but the blow was not fatal. The families who constituted the landed and banking oligarchy of Mexico under Díaz were forced to adjust to a new and more complex reality after 1917. The revolution disrupted and altered the merchant capital ethos, but this ethos had by then penetrated deeply into the ideology of several strata of the society. In spite of the revolution, the state continued to be a reliable source of economic rents. It became a source of personal enrichment for an entire new strata of state functionaries and continued to be an important means by which valuable favors could be extended to members of the old oligarchy.

The modern Mexican economy, and its state, emerged from these complex metamorphoses as a synthesis of diametrically opposed elements. On the one hand, capitalist forces were to be found. On the other, the legacy of the merchant capitalist era had not been completely destroyed. After the revolution, the old landed-banking elite was reconstituted (once again) in banking, in commerce, and in *capitalist* enterprises in agribusiness, mining, and manufacturing. The state now constituted an embodied contradiction. It was capable of both cunning (but parasitic) opportunism *and* herculean efforts aimed at reorienting and expanding the productive apparatus in pursuit of rapid capital accumulation. Historical circumstances dictated which tendency would dominate policymaking.

Many observers have pondered the spectacular growth of the state's external debt during the 1970s and early 1980s. Some have argued, correctly, that the state borrowed to push forward Mexico's program of state-led development. Others, correctly, have pointed to the orgy of waste, fraud, and corruption unleashed by the new funds that poured into Mexico. *Both* interpretations together are correct. Such a result is precisely what the hypothesis of the capitalist-rentier state would predict.

From the onset of World War II through the close of the Korean War, Mexico's program of import-substitution industrialization was underwritten by essentially rentier upswings in the price of exported primary products. These upswings both increased the state's revenues and allowed the landowning agro-export capitalists and financial elements of the business elite to appropriate large short-term economic rents. When this long commodity-based boom collapsed in the early 1950s, the guiding luminaries of the state determined that Mexico could continue to grow by perpetually importing bank capital (for example, acquiring private bank portfolio loans and loans from the World Bank and other multilateral institutions) (Ortiz Mena, n.d.). Antonio Ortiz Mena became the intellectual architect of Mexico's famous model of "stabilizing growth" (which became the wonder of Latin America between 1958 and 1970). He championed foreign borrowing on the questionable grounds that Mexico's internal rate of saving (usually in excess of 15 percent of GNP) was insufficient to provide adequate funds to fulfill the investment needs of the economy. Exactly where and how Mexico would tap its economic surplus in order to return the borrowed capital (plus interest) apparently concerned Ortiz Mena very little. His progeny (who worked the levers of State economic power until they broke in 1982) were even less concerned. Why?

Rentier capital makes money today and worries about the consequences of such moneymaking only when it must. There is no claim here that the stabilizing growth model was built purely upon a speculator's ethos, but rather that the state's project was interpenetrated by both the ethos of rentier capital and pure capitalist forms of behavior and policymaking. There was a fluid mixture of logically opposed element that was so completely integrated and assimilated that policymakers were not forced to face the contradictory nature of their analyses and activities. This would seem to be more than a likely hypothesis to explain an embedded contradiction that became embarrassingly and painfully evident only in August 1982. (The foregoing comments constitute no more than a brief introduction to the capitalist-rentier state form. Chapters 3 and 4 of this book are, in part, devoted to the task of clarifying this concept.)

Having largely self-destructed, the capitalist-rentier form was ripe for replacement. The answer to the question "What next?" quickly came in the form of the neoliberal state constructed by President Miguel de la Madrid Hurtado's administration (1982–1988). The neoliberal state is dedicated to an attempt to turn back the clock to the late eighteenth and early nineteenth centuies when a consolidating form of European capitalism momentarily suggested that the state's function could be that of a "watchman" keeping the competitive rules of the game and enforcing the sanctity of contracts and other property rights (Cypher, 1980). As Karl Polanyi masterfully demonstrated, this brief historical interlude of high *laissez-faire* was mistakenly perceived as a *norm* by some classical economists—a view that was later to be cast into the densest form of dogma by the neoclassical economists of the late nineteenth century (Polanyi, 1944).

Faced with the worst economic crisis that Mexico had known in the twentieth century, de la Madrid Hurtado—trained in the United States by economists who as a group proselytized the free-market nostrums of the classical economists—avidly embraced the neoliberal philosophy that had laid economic waste to Argentina and Chile in the 1970s. The neoliberals viewed the orchestrated ruin of Argentina and Chile as but the short-term costs of "structural adjustment" (Tokman, 1984).

Neoliberal economics—above all the economics of Milton Friedman and Frederick von Hayek—is essentially ahistorical and tautological. Neither historical cases nor analytical critiques pose much of a problem for neoliberals because their economic models are built upon the supposedly inviolable attributes of human nature. The "invisible hand" of Adam Smith *must* work; it therefore *will* work. The only task of the state is to destroy the policymaking and productive apparatus of the state and impose the watchman function.

In analyzing the latest turn of the Mexican state, we are faced with coming to terms with what may well be the most important policy shift in Mexico in the late twentieth century. In 1981 Mexico's state industrialization policies seemed of only minor interest, particluarly in Mexico. By the end of de la Madrid Hurtado's term, as the full force and intention of the neoliberal project became increasingly and more painfully evident, discussions and critiques of the new turn saturated the newspapers, while a spate of more scholarly efforts commenced. The debate over what the state had been and done and over what it should and would be became the number one issue of public debate concerning public policymaking. The neoliberal state has not yet been fully imposed in Mexico. A new administration under Carlos Salinas de Gortari (1988–1994) may be able to gain or retain a considerable degree of latitude in the quest to consolidate the neoliberal state form.

Although the matter of Mexico's fledgling neoliberal state will be examined in the following chapters, it is nonetheless necessary to emphasize that Mexico's newest state form cannot be reduced to a carbon copy of the contemporary Chilean economy or of any other economy. Mexico's unique and long history of state intervention in the economy and its Constitution, which grants broad powers to the state, are two factors that will not be conjured away by an ideologically driven discussion of the merits of free enterprise and unrestricted market behavior. Nevertheless, there are some important parallels with the Southern Cone nations of Argentina and Chile. For example, Mexico is now slowly *deindustrializing*—the new jobs created by the *maquiladora* (in bond) plants, which specialize in labor-intensive fabrication of products intended solely for re-export, were less than the total jobs lost in manufacturing industry during de la Madrid's sexenio (Zuniga 1988c, 14).

Following in the steps of the Southern Cone nations, more than one-half of the firms in the vast state-owned sector of the economy have been or will be privatized. Mexico now welcomes direct foreign investment as never before since the revolution. State funding for Social Security benefits and other forms of social welfare spending has been drastically cut. The state's labor policy now largely reduces to wage cutting and the demand of even greater union subservience to the procapital policies of the state.

It would be idle to speculate regarding the longevity of the trend toward the neoliberal state. Mexico's economic, political, and cultural crisis is currently so profound that the relative weight of clashing social forces cannot be anticipated with any degree of confidence.

Notes

1. This is not to say that Mexico's policymaking was based upon CEPAL's analysis. If anything, the causality probably ran the other way. Mexico's approach to the matter was to a certain degree formed prior to Cárdenas's sexenio and was further consolidated during his presidential years. Raúl Prebisch was quite aware of the innovative programs being attempted in Mexico in the 1930s and 1940s, and he visited Mexico during this period.

There seems to be no unifying or central figure to which we can attribute Mexico's state-guided economic innovations during the 1930s and 1940s. Some key policymakers, such as Eduardo Suárez, Cárdenas's secretary of the Treasury, were strongly influenced by John M. Keynes. (Keynes, not incidentally, was at the height of his apostasy against neoclassical trade theory in these years, maintaining that "national self-sufficiency" was much preferable to the subjection of a nation to the arbitrary swings of an international economy [Cypher, 1988a, 8–10].) High-level Mexican economists have for the most part been able to devote much of their careers to government service. Given such an orientation toward day-to-day policymaking, it is not surprising that no central figure seems to have emerged to give intellectual coherence to Mexico's attempts at state-led growth. Because of this gap it is rather easy, but incorrect, to ascribe to Prebisch an approach that for the most part was chronologically anticipated by policymakers in Mexico. Mexico's approach to government intervention (until most recently) has always been pragmatic, incremental, and nondoctrinaire—all elements that reduce the likelihood that a programmatic scheme such as that produced by CEPAL would ever be published or taken too seriously.

2

Theories of the Mexican State

This chapter begins with a discussion of the *sui generis* nature of the Mexican state, centering the analysis on the concept of the state as rector. This is followed by a review of the literature that attempts to qualitatively account for the rectorship role of the state, briefly enumerating a range of intruments of state policymaking that give concrete shape to the rectorship role. The discussion then descends to the murky realms of theory—here the theory of relative state autonomy and its principal variants in Mexico are introduced.[1] The final encounter is with the theory of state monopoly capitalism.

The State as Rector:
The Sui Generis *Mexican State*

The roots of the modern interventionist-activist state are to be found in the nineteeth century, particularly during the Porfiriate period (1876–1911), which is often mistakenly understood to have been an era of high *laissez-faire*. This notwithstanding, there is little argument that the Mexican Revolution, and particularly the Constitution of 1917, constituted a crucial historical watershed. As Nora Hamilton pointed out in her masterful study of the Cárdenas period (1934–1940), the Constitution "established the basis for an interventionist and implicitly autonomous State, above classes, which would eliminate monopolies, establish Mexican sovereignty over its natural resources, provide the peasantry with access to land and assure the rights of labor" (Hamilton, 1982, 271). But it was only in the 1930s that the definition of the State took its nationalist-populist form. Hamilton believed that this consolidation of the state form was due to conjunctural factors, most particularly the Great Depression of the 1930s, rather than to any legalistic affinity for the 1917 Constitution. According to Cárdenas—and the "Progressive Alliance" of peasants, workers, nationalist businesspeople, and state functionaries who backed him—Mexico could follow neither the path of the "capitalist democracies" nor the road of socialism. Both had revealed fundamental economic, political, and social weaknesses. Mexico was to strike out on its own and create a *sui generis* socioeconomic system that was neither capitalist nor socialist but one preferable to both.

In what is widely regarded in Mexico as the classic study of this metamorphosis of the Mexican state, Arnaldo Córdova answered his own question "What will happen to capitalism?" in the following manner:

> A slogan summarizes this with complete satisfaction: The mixed economy, neither capitalist or communist, with capitalists, but also with the State as owner of its own productive apparatus, and with its powers of guardianship over the rights of workers now defining the existence of the capitalists; and between the capitalists and the State, or if you prefer, together with them, each and every one of the remaining social classes pursuing their own interests, but also collaborating in the common [social] task. Over all of these social elements the State would become the rector, the director of all social activities, the power which constituted the association of all social sectors and which gave life and reason to one unified national project which all social elements must take as their own; as the very incarnation of the interests of all (Córdova, 1974, 180).

Córdova amplified this statement by noting that in the view of the Progressive Alliance, although "the private [business] interests will not diappear, they will no longer be the *sancta sanctorum* of society"; rather, they "will become private interests, 'of a public character'" (Córdova, 1974, 181–182).

But Cárdenas failed to show how business interests (which stood to gain tremendously from the cohesion and direction that Cárdenas was giving to Mexican society) would in fact consent to such unparalleled state leadership once they had accumulated economic power sufficient to challenge the state's autonomy (Córdova, 1974, 183). As will become clear in this and the following chapters, Arnoldo Córdova here located the fundamental contradiction in Cárdenas's nationalist project.

One counterpoint to concentrating business power might have been the *combined* power of peasants and workers. Yet, Cárdenas's approach to constructing the rectorship demanded a *split* in the power of these two fractions, thereby making the state the intermediary in expressing their interests. The peasants were joined into peasant leagues under the Secretariat of Agrarian Reform, while the unions were put under the control of the Secretariat of Labor.

As Nora Hamilton pointed out, the mixed economy and the rectorship were more ideas than realities. Important interests remained and regrouped to challenge *Cardenismo* (Hamilton, 1982, 276). After 1938, when the daring expropriation of the foreign oil industry was consummated (undoubtedly the historical high point of the nationalist project), Cárdenas sought to placate his enemies and critics. No more nationalizations were attempted. Researchers believe that Cárdenas sought to consolidate his gains—at the price of losing the initiative. Although Cárdenas's act of expropriation was not championed by the Mexican business interests, he never carried out any nationalizations against their invested capital. Mexican business interests were not a passive force throughout the Cárdenas period. Then, as now, a favorite weapon for pressuring the state was the business elite's readiness to engage in capital flight. According to Juan Martínez Nava's excellent study, *Conflicto Estado Empresarios* these interests moved more than 1 billion pesos out of the economy between 1935 and 1939—a sum then equal to two and one-half times the annual total deposits within the Mexican banking system (Martínez Nava, 1982, 104).

Eminently qualified researchers of the period, such as Arnaldo Córdova, Nora Hamilton, and Juan Martínez Nava, all seem to concur that the Progressive Alliance never really consolidated its nationalist project for a mixed economy. Cárdenas's project to hothouse capitalist development, side by side with his determination to separate peasants and workers into paternalistic state organizations, held within it the seeds of its own destruction. According to these theorists, what happened in subsequent administrations in the 1940s and 1950s was not really surprising or "counterrevolutionary." The seeds matured and bore bitter fruit. The corporatist tree that sprouted and grew—the Mexican "miracle" as it became known—was not a completely alien by-product of the 1930s.

The Cárdenas period was a watershed rather than a rupture with the past in that a legitimate space was cleared for an activist-interventionist state. But it was nonetheless a project for capitalist development. The idea of a state "above classes" with "its own productive apparatus" functioning in such a way as to force the private sector to "submit" to its direction of economic activity became more remote as Mexico's economic development proceeded.

Yet in both a juridical and historical sense it would be dangerous to overlook or dismiss the aspirations voiced during the Cárdenas period. In Mexico they have, since the 1930s, formed a backdrop for the day-to-day debate over the direction of economic and social policy. Within the framework of the Constitution, one can, for example, champion nationalizations, while citing the "legitimate" revolutionary heritage of the Cárdenas period as a historical precedent. Few nations that have pursued all-out capitalist development have had to confront this type of (often latent) contradiction between policies that nurtured private accumulation and policies that called for revival of Cárdenas's nationalist-populist project. There is no doubt that Cárdenas struck a resonante chord in his vague bid for an economic system that was neither capitalist nor socialist. Finally, even if the nationalist-populist project was largely stillborn, the Cárdenas period left another lasting legacy—the state had a unique role to play as the "rector" guiding the program of economic development.

It is not the objective of this book to attempt to explain the discontinuities between the Cárdenas administration and those of his immediate successors—Manuel Ávila Camacho (1940–1946) and Miguel Alemán (1946–1952). Researchers such as Nora Hamilton have pointed out that these discontinuities are to some degree more apparent than real. That is, after the oil nationalization of 1938, Cárdenas's "revolution" did not advance. As Arnaldo Córdova maintained, the popular voices advocating social change were lost in the labyrinth of government offices that were constructed to "channel" and moderate the aspirations of the underlying population. At the same time, the cluster of basically parasitic interests that had prospered in the pre-Cárdenas period did not disappear, as Hamilton emphasized. The old rentier stratum in banking and landholding was forced to reconstitute itself—it was not annihilated. As the economic role of the state was fundamentally altered and expanded, the state itself became a new avenue for the rapid accumulation of wealth. Personal wealth amassed in a presidential sexenio became one of the few ways in which a bright young *técnico* (technocrat) could achieve fundamental socioeconomic mobility. As long as high-level state functionaries were discreet, corrupt practices were greeted with a nod and a grin. Along with the old rentier elements in banking, commerce, and landholding that were never totally vanquished, a new stratum of rentiers emerged to flourish within the interstices of the state. Alongside the functionalist concept of the state as rector, we find counterpoised the state as a repository and perpetuator of rentier interests. The slippage between the official and the actual image of the state was considerable. These two contradictory yet characteristic elements of the modern Mexican state combine and reproduce themselves in countless ways—in the educational system, the healthcare system, the unions, the peasant organizations, the parastate firms, the economic development apparatus, and the highest policymaking circles of the state.

The Qualitative Nature of the Mexican State

According to standard "value-added" concepts of national income accounting, the Mexican state has not been overwhelmingly large. For example, the public purchases of labor, materials, and services averaged 14.9 percent of GNP in the 1960–1977 period. This was substantially below that of the United States, where state purchases stood at 21 percent of GNP in 1977 (Cordera, 1980, 456, 461).

By other measurements, however, the Mexican state's role in the economy appears much larger. In 1977, for example, 12.4 percent of total demand was claimed through all forms of state taxes. In addition, state borrowing (both internal and external) equaled another 4.6 percent of the gross national product. Finally, the parastate firms (such as Mexico's petroleum giant Petroleos Mexicanos [PEMEX]) had total sales equal to 20.3 percent of GNP. In light of these three components it is possible to affirm that in terms of the *throughput* of the economic system (not value-added), the state's various forms of income accounted for 37.4 percent of the economy's total (Looney, 1985, 154).

No state expenditure/GNP ratio can situate the state in relation to the economy at large because such figures fail to pick up the state's *indirect* role in the economy. The concept of the indirect role of the state entails the state's nonspending programs, such as credit allocation or tariff policies designed to channel economic activities of the private sector in a direction that the state deems desirable. In spite of the intrinsic difficulty entailed in any *quantitative* measure of the state's economic role, commentators have not been hesitant to express *qualitative* judgments. Jorge Tamayo, for example, placed the state—and the parastates in particular—at the center in explaining Mexico's industrialization: "In synthesis we can confirm that, during more than forty years the investments of the parastates have been a decisive factor in the transformation of the productive structure of the national economy" (Tamayo, 1987, 257). Tamayo highlighted the concept of *dynamic efficiency*—the ability of "lumpy" state investments to have synergistic effects during a considerable period of time as linkages create new industries and/or productive processes.

In a 1963 study of the Mexican economy, the management specialist Raymond Vernon concluded that "the Mexican government has gradually placed itself in a position of key importance for the continued economic development of Mexico" (Vernon, 1973, 585). According to Dwight Brothers, another one of the U.S. researchers whose work from the 1960s is still widely cited, "We can say that, in effect, the Mexican economy is characterized by the numerous direct and indirect controls which the State exercises as well as the considerable degree to which the means of production are public property" (Brothers, 1973, 192). In their widely utilized book, *El Poder Empresarial en México*, Salvador Cordero H., Rafael Santín, and Ricardo Tirado concurred: "In sythesis we can say that the direct participation of the State in the industry of the country has been of vital importance for the economy, if not for its volume then for the sectors which it controls" (Cordero H., Santín, and Tirado, 1983, 29).

The most forthright response to this issue was delivered by Rolando Cordera. He rejected all conventional ways of measuring the influence or importance of the state, claiming that the direct formation of capital on the part of the state was the key to calibrating the state's role (Cordera, 1980, 448). Cordera framed the question of the role of the state with particular force and clarity:

> The underlying factor, more often than not, is the strategic *quality* of the State, its indispensable permanent action in the continual recreation of the *material and economic base* of the process of development and its central role as a force that not only synthesizes the contradictions of the society but also, for reasons of history and structure, guarantees the cohesion of the national space (Cordera, 1980, 449).

Cordera was willing to take his critical analysis of the role of the state much further, claiming that the power of the state in the less developed nations was but a mirror image of the *weakness* and incapability of the indigenous business elite in performing its historic task of transforming and rationalizing the means and forms of production. This endemic weakness extended to the business elite's inability to grasp the functional role of the state. Rather than possessing a matter-of-fact view of the state, business saw the state as always tending toward "excesses" that would delimit the legitimate sphere of the private sector. At the same time, the very success of the state brought into stronger relief the business elite's proclivity to engage in what he termed "outrageous rentier" behavior (Cordera, 1980, 449).

In summary, the consensus view of researchers seems to be that the Mexican state's policies were for the most part *functional* in terms of fostering and promoting capitalist development. At the same time, these policies were resisted by the private sector, although the degree of this resistance waxed and waned. Perhaps this resistance was in part the result of a sense of inadequacy in the business elite, which was much more comfortable making money overnight in various forms of speculation than it was in carrying out the disciplined, long-term, and often arduously complex task of making profits by way of industrial production. That the state could often undertake such production, even if at less than maximum efficiency, certainly served to raise the question of what socially useful function the business elements were indeed serving.

Instruments of the State

Before proceeding to other significant issues that directly touch on the political economy of the Mexican state, the following list of the organizations and instruments of the state that are used to pursue industrial development helps to convey an idea of the broad range of state activities.

1. Parastate firms.
2. State investment banks that have been sole owners or co-owners of producing corporations. At many points in the 1940s and 1950s, the state investment banks seemed to have been the most important single tool in promoting industrial development.
3. A bewildering array of indirect state policies designed to promote and stimulate industrialization. Most often mentioned in this regard has been tariff policy designed to give "infant industries" protection from outside competition. Here we also find tax exemption and taxation policies.
4. Credit allocation that is carried out by the central bank and is designed to channel investment funds into "priority" and "strategic" areas.
5. Exchange rate policies and tactics to stimulate imports and penalize exports (or *vice versa*).
6. Indicative planning.
7. An effort (in the 1960s and 1970s) to create industrial parks with state-funded labor training programs linked to this effort.
8. The in-bond *maquiladora* program activated in the 1960s.
9. In the early 1970s the state added a small program in technology, Conacyt, in an attempt to bridge the growing technological lag found in most parts of the Mexican economy.
10. Laws and decrees (such as the famed 1973 law to "Mexicanize" foreign firms, which reduced foreign ownership to minority status) were often promulgated as an integral component of the industrialization effort.

There are two aspects of industrial policies so important and vast that they demand a separate book-length treatment. The state's *labor policy* was consistently one of breaking independent (non-state-controlled) labor unions and destroying all sense of spontaneity and bottom-up forms of union democracy. The effort seems to have been a sterling success. Even the state's worst critics, the business elite, at least give the state credit (if only in a backhanded way) for this industrialization policy. Basically labor policy has been one of keeping labor very cheap, plentiful and pliable. One glaring contradiction here is the overall lack of manpower training which relegates most labor to low levels of productivity.

The second aspect, *agrarian policy*, basically reduces peasants to near-starvation existence by forcing them to sell their wage-good crops (beans, rice, wheat, oats, and corn) at controlled prices near or below the cost of production. As these products are then distributed, often by the state through its buying-and-selling agency Compañía Nacional de Subsistencias Populares (the national company for the subsistence of the masses, or Conasupo), the industrial work force can reproduce itself (with qualifications) by way of cheap food produced by the peasantry. Again, this is the briefest of statements as to what is a complex and nuanced industrialization policy carried on at the expense of the Mexican peasantry. The relationship among the state, the agricultural sector, and the accumulation process are of such complexity as to demand a separate in-depth treatment.

Given the considerable number of instruments created to achieve Mexican industrialization, the question arises whether there was a conscious attempt to integrate all these policies. The answer, it seems, is no. But in presenting the matter so bluntly, one can lose sight of the fact that between absolute order and complete chaos stood a good deal of space in which the state *improvised* its policies. At the margin, of course, it is a simple matter to show significant error in the various policies and inconsistencies among them. For example, it is widely argued that the exemptions from tariffs on the import of capital goods coupled with tax exemptions for investments and accelerated depreciation allowances created an industrial sector that suffered from serious and chronic excess capacity due to a periodic tendency to overinvest in cheap (subsidized) imported capital goods. This in turn meant that the capital-saturated industrial sector failed to absorb most of the labor force that was being released from the agricultural sector as more capitalistic methods of production penetrated the countryside.

Another major inconsistency is worth noting here: Very low taxes on capital, commerce, banking, and landholding along with a low-wage policy meant that the state would have to borrow, abroad and at home, to finance itself (including the parastate sector)., The chronic borrowing forced the state into a very delicate juggling act, which finally became unsupportable in the summer of 1982.

It is not a very demanding exercise to point out other inconsistencies, major and minor, but from such a perspective one can lose sight of the fact that for more than forty years, this contradiction-ridden "system" nonetheless generated, or at least helped to generate, a strong record of economic growth and rapid industrialization. In the early years of the 1940s and 1950s, the "creeping incrementalism" and improvising skills of the state-managers served them well. This was largely because the problems they faced were fairly obvious and the interconnections between a given activity, such as large infrastructural investment, and its effects on the regional or national economy could be traced out with relative ease. But in the 1960s and most particularly the 1970s, matters became much more complex. There were more state policies and projects to consider, the economy had become a relatively elaborate (if still terribly backward) mechanism, and the policymaking instruments of the state (such as the planning efforts) did not grow in pace with the increasing complexity of the economic system.

The Dependency Framework and the Mexican State

Economic development, particularly industrialization, proved to be much more difficult than the structuralist theoreticians at CEPAL had assumed in the early 1950s. Their assumption that the State would be capable of guiding a major transformation of the Latin American economies was called into question by a host of dependency writers in the 1960s. Research into the question of the influence of dependency forms of analysis points strongly toward the conclusion that in Mexico there was no single key dependency writer (or writers) or a definitive work that analyzed the specific policies of the Mexican state from the dependency perspective.[2]

The dependency framework assumes that prime *causality* derives from *outside* the national socioeconomic formation. In essence the dependency writers employ an *instrumentalist* theory of the state. That is, as a first approximation, state policymaking is determined by foreign governments, corporations, and "multilateral" institutions (such as the International Monetary Fund). Internal policymaking is an *instrument* of external forces.

Unquestionably, foreign influence has been an important factor in the determination of state policy since 1940. In Chapters 3–6, an attempt is made to weave into the discussion an account of such foreign influence. From this it is concluded that such influence was often *a* factor but only rarely *the* factor in determining policy.

Dependency analysis dichotomizes national and transnational policy objectives. What, then, if they coincide? Or, alternatively, what if state managers, the Mexican business elite, and transnational capital happen to share a common policy objective? Dependency writers maintain (correctly) that there can be no unity of rivals. But are these three elements always and necessarily rivals? Just as potential rivals can find a *modus vivendi* in a cartel, so, too, can there be a tripartite relationship that is mutually advantageous to the state functionaries, the business elite, and transnational capital.[3]

Peter Evan's research into "dependent development" has shifted the terms of the discussion regarding internal versus external factors. His detailed study of Brazilian industrialization highlighted the role of tripartite elements in the determination of policymaking. He concluded that there was an underlying tendency for state managers and national industrialists to reach an agreement that transnational capital was forced to accept. Transnational capital played an important, fundamental role, but it was nonetheless subordinated to the national coalition (Evans, 1979). Unfortunately, no detailed study matching Evan's work has been conducted on Mexico. Dependency writers in Mexico have yet to articulate a theory of the state or present a coherent body of literature that confirms their views of the determinants of state policy.

Relative State Autonomy

Nicos Poulantzas (Poulantzas, 1978), whose work became prominent in the 1960s, conceived of the state as having some relative autonomy from the economic base, although he considered the economic instance to be determinant in the final regard. He sought to demonstrate that the instrumentalist models (which claimed that the state was but an instrument in the hands of the business elite) were crude and simplistic. They failed to describe a relatively wide terrain wherein the modern states of Western Europe operated at least one-third of the economy. This analysis was part of a broader current that sought to "unpack" the state, taking it out of the "simplistic box" in which many, including the instrumentalists and the dependency writers, had put it. This attempt to view the state as, at least partially, an entity in and of itself with an ability (however constrained) to define goals and to channel and redirect the objectives of pressure groups and vested interests was immediately seen by a wide number of Mexican social scientists as a new and fruitful way of attempting to understand aspects of the Mexican state.

But defining a place for the political instance was not enough. Poulantzas' structuralist model was incapable of explaining when and why the state had relatively more, or less, autonomy. Nor could it explain shifts in either policymaking or the nature of the state apparatus itself. Like the dependency framework and instrumentalist theories, relative autonomy was a static concept that seemed to explain the nature of the "Keynesian" states of Western Europe but certainly failed to anticipate the rise of "austerity capitalism."

Theda Skocpol, concentrating on a study of several states during the course of a considerable period of time, concluded that it was possible for a state to act independently and in opposition to the interests of the socially and economically dominant class (or classes) *but only in a time of crisis*. This meant that "the possibilities of state autonomy [were] limited to specific structural and historical options as a consequence of the previous development of the productive forces" (quoted in Hamilton,

1982, 13). Given a crisis, such as an economic crisis, the state might move to forge or reshape a pattern or structure of accumulation. Furthermore, even within a given pattern (or model) of accumulation, the state had a certain capacity to redefine the power relationships among various interests and thus shape or participate in the making of policy rather than merely implementing it. The state could be pressured, but it could also attempt to create policies and resist and reshape pressure.

Rolando Cordera was one of the many Mexican scholars who made use of Poulantzas' theory to reinterpret the state from Cárdenas onward. Cordera argued for a stage model, claiming that the period from 1940 to 1954 could be described as that of "Primitive Industrial Accumulation" (others have applied stage models claiming that this period was one of "easy import substitution"). While the state's autonomy had been reduced *vis-à-vis* the Cárdenas years, nonetheless;

> the exercise of power on the part of the State continued to be a responsibility which it exclusively held. Furthermore, the very fact that it was the industrial bourgeoisie which held the hegemonic position at the level of the capital-owning class conferred upon those groups which formed the "political bureaucracy" an enormous margin to maneuver and of course access in its "own right" [rather than being subordinated] to the power bloc (Cordera, 1979, 116).

Making full use of a number of concepts employed by Poulantzas, Cordera asserted the autonomy of the state. The "power bloc" of the capital-owning classes (landlords, bankers, and mining, commercial, and agro-export interests) had been weakened by the revolution and *Cardenismo*. This bloc had been split by the emergence of a new, state-created component—the emerging *industrial* bourgeoisie. The industrialist had not yet been completely integrated into a new "power bloc." Cordera maintained that after the mid-1950s the degree of state autonomy diminished substantially as Mexico began to enter a new phase or stage based on "stabilized growth." Yet given an opportune moment, the state could *reclaim* its forfeited autonomy. There was no reason to suggest that *structurally* the degree of autonomy asserted from the agro-export, mining, and banking elite in the 1940s could not once again manifest itself. (The bank nationalization of 1982 seemed to confirm Cordera's view.)

One well-known foreign interpreter of the Mexican economy, E.V.K. Fitzgerald, in a recent and tightly argued article, made pivotal use of the concept of relative autonomy in an attempt to disentangle the conundrum of state power within the modern economy. He started by arguing that the direct antecedents of the Partidad Revolucionario Institucional (Institutional Revolutionary Party, or PRI) in the 1930s created a state

> with considerable relative autonomy from both external (US) and internal (class) pressure.
>   Within this state, a relatively small and stable group of senior bureaucrats ["state-managers"] could make a politico-administrative career without great reference to party politics or direct links to class interests. Consequently ideology, and economic ideas in particular, was to play an important part in determining the form of state intervention in support of capitalist accumulation (Fitzgerald, 1985, 211).

According to Fitzgerald, this newly forged nationalist project, by redirecting the forces of production toward industry and the emerging working class (and redistributing income away from the old agro-export interests and the peasantry), was able to "set the stage for a long period of capital accumulation" (Fitzgerald, 1985, 211).

In the late 1950s, in response to the redirection of the state's project as defined by the stabilizing growth model (discussed in the next chapter), we find some aspects of the state's economic role declining; this was partly due to dominant economic ideas and ideology, as Fitzgerald suggested. By the mid to late 1960s, with the beneficial effects of the stabilizing growth model now exhausted, the state again moved to redefine the underlying policy matrix of the economy but did so with insufficient vigor. Fitzgerald maintained that the state was unable to overcome a pervasive anti-statist bias that had come to dominate public and private sector discourse regarding the role of the state. "The size of the Public sector was seen as the 'dilemma of Mexican development' in the belief that the historic task of state intervention was over and that Mexican capitalists could now manage for themselves" (Fitzgerald, 1985, 214).

President Gustavo Díaz Ordaz (1964–1970) took modest steps to check the relative decline in the state's role. But it was his successor, Luis Echeverría (1970–1976), who faced the task of attempting to redefine Mexico's model or pattern of accumulation. For reasons explored in Chapter 4, neither of these administrations could exercise sufficient autonomy at this crucial historical juncture. In analyzing this bitter experience, Fitzgerald warned that the theory of relative autonomy had to be applied with care, that a mechanistic and functionalist interpretation of the concept would lead to serious misinterpretations. The work of Poulantzas when applied to social formations such as Mexico's allows us to employ certain powerful theoretical conceptualizations. But a full theory of the Mexican state must go beyond these valuable insights:

[Here] is perhaps the core of the problem of state intervention in capital accumulation. In order to undertake the restructuring of the economy, . . . the state requires a certain freedom of maneuvre in order to acquire greater control over available resources. The "relative economic autonomy of the State" involves economic and political costs to the private sector in the long run. However this relative autonomy is a product of history and not the result of an economic strategy; it is not conjured up just because it is "necessary" for accumulation to proceed. In the case of Mexico it was created by the particular circumstances of the reconstruction of state and economy between 1925 and 1940, which provided the basis of a remarkable process of sustained industrialization for the next quarter-century. Despite the need for greater state autonomy, in the 1970s in order to overcome the economic contradictions, there was no commensurate political change (Fitzgerald, 1985, 231).

A Unity of Opposites?
Relative Autonomy and Instrumentalism

Víctor E. Bravo in his book *La Empresa Pública Industrial en México* added a significant contribution to the relative autonomy approach by directing his attention toward the role of the parastate firms. He began by making an argument commonly articulated in Mexico—the state must act as the "general capitalist" in providing both infrastructure and social investments. To do so it must have some relative autonomy because it may have to challenge certain sectoral interests or compete with banks for liquid investment funds. It certainly must tax the property-owning classes to achieve certain long-range objectives. This is not a simple task, for two reasons. First, the state will inevitably make choices that benefit some elements of the property-owning groups more than others. Second, the state has to grapple with the historical fact that there are foreign interests active in the economy. These interests have their own resources and often some of the resources of more powerful states at their behest. The state, then, is caught in an antagonistic relationship of a two-directional nature. This makes the task of acting out the role of the "general capitalist" even more complex than in the developed nations and forces the state to operate under conditions that he described as a "permanent crisis" (Bravo, 1982, 70).

The difficulties, however, do not end here. Bravo maintained that the state must move to assure the realization of "general material conditions" of capitalist socioeconomic reproduction. Yet the state cannot achieve any "absolute autonomy"—except under very particular historical conditions. Therefore, the state inevitably must face—*and respond to*—interests of a *particular* nature. Thus, lobbying, pressure, and threats from industrial associations and sectoral interests are everyday encounters for the state. For Bravo, the state is simply caught between the contradictory role of (1) providing for the general reproduction of the system by acting out the role of the "general capitalist" and (2) responding to particular interests. The first task, to be achieved by way of relative autonomy, is counteracted by the second, which reduces the state's policymaking apparatus to an instrument fulfilling the needs of the most powerful elements of the property-owning classes. The contradiction between the general function and the partial function cannot be overcome within this structure, so the state is forced to oscillate between these two functions as the conjunctures of history dictate. This, clearly, is permanent crisis. The state can break this deadlock only if it is able to develop what Bravo defined as the *"state sectoral function."*

Bravo's State Sectoral Function

The state sectoral function is achieved when the state *consolidates its own material base* by way of ownership of an array of parastate corporations. The parastates are, on the whole, moneymakers, which gives the state a constant source of revenues and an important role in determining key prices within the economy. To Bravo this is the "inner capitalist logic" behind the parastate sector in Mexico. He noted another, quite important consequence of the parastate sector: The parastates can operate in a given branch of industry side by side with domestic and foreign-owned firms and force them to operate efficiently by way of the competition they pose. If the state wishes to emphasize the development of a particular component of the economy, it can lower prices of inputs into this sector and also make cheap credit available. Thus, the "ideal general capitalist" role can be achieved *and* the particular interests can be largely (but not totally) ignored or overcome. Instrumentalism is averted; relative autonomy is maintained. Of particular importance in this regard is the fact that the sectoral function can be used to overcome the weight of foreign capitalist interests (Bravo, 1982, 71).

Perhaps the weakest element of Bravo's analysis is the uncritical reliance on an elite of state managers to achieve the complex tasks sketched here. E.V.K. Fitzgerald warned, in a passage cited previously, that the state managers are hardly a homogeneous group who stand above ideological differences. Under a unusually strong national leader an ethos of nationalism can paper over the ideological disputes that are bound to surface among the state managers. Indeed, Mexico's recent turn toward export-led, free-market models of accumulation certainly did not seem to verify Bravo's view that the parastates would be the instrument by which the "state apparatus increases and perfects its relative autonomy as never before" (Bravo, 1982, 241). Nor would it be possible to find many, if any, who would confirm that the state now has the capacity to "balance the relation of forces within the core of the dominant classes" (Bravo, 1982, 242). The pendulum has definitely swung away from the state sketched by Víctor Bravo, but the objective conditions that gave rise to the type of state he described remain.

Declining Autonomy, Rising Oligarchy?

Carlos Pereyra was widely regarded as a key interpreter of the Mexican state. His thesis was perhaps best expressed in a 1979 article, "Estado y Sociedad"(State and Society) (Pereyra, 1979). In this article, he developed an argument for the "progressive subordination" of the state to private capital. In his view the state can have relative autonomy only if it has the support of the broad masses of the working class and the peasantry. Unlike Víctor Bravo who, unfortunately, seemed to see an elite of state policymakers as a *deus ex machina*, Pereyra argued that in Mexico the capacity of the state managers to challenge the power of international capital and protect Mexico from the centrifugal force of the nonhomogenous private business sector *derived* from the support the state could count on receiving from the underlying population. But, Pereyra argued, to rely on that support the state had to express a nationalist and populist project that delivered (however slowly and irregularly) the image and the actuality of improved socioeconomic conditions to this population.

For the business sector this constituted a potential threat to its interests because if the state had such relative autonomy, it could move, perhaps increasingly, against the interests of private capital. Even if such shifts in power and wealth were not to be *absolutely* threatening to the property-owning classes, they were nonetheless a short-term concern. Meanwhile, the long-term consequences of relative autonomy suggested a slow euthanasia not only of the unproductive rentier but also of productive capital. As the business interests reflected on the growing parastate sector, many imagined they saw the very incarnation of this long-term threat. If the state had the power of the rectorship along with its own industries to give it great independence, and if the state's legitimacy stemmed from the support it derived from the working class and the peasantry, what (in the abstract) was to stop the state at some juncture from simply annihilating private capital?

Pereyra argued that as the private sector's doubts increased, the business interests began to pressure the state—with intermittent success. Although the success of the project to undercut the state's autonomy was not linear, every step in that direction tended to facilitate another because the underlying population became even more distanced from the state. As the populist elements of the state began to decay, the business interests were faced with less and less resistance on the part of the elite state managers. The power of these state managers derived only partly from the parastate forces of production directly under their control. In losing their popular base, they undercut their own autonomy. The resistance put up by the elite policymakers was further diluted because of growing personal links between this elite and those who had historically constituted the capital-owning classes.

Other researchers, tying their analysis more closely to actual events than had Pereyra, tended to confirm his point of view. In a study entitled "Empresarios y Obreros," Eduardo González even isolated a date, 1973, when the business elite shifted from what he termed a *defensive* position to an *offensive* position. He found a "distinct phase" characterized by a "more organized and systematic opposition to the regime and its economic policy" (González, 1981, 654). Carlos Tello (who had held a top position in the economic cabinent of the government in 1973) concurred. Tello maintained that the strongest business groups then "concentrated upon paralyzing the activities of the state and in subordinating it even more to their desires for control" (Tello, 1976, 81).

Complementing the work of Pereyra and others who shared his conceptual approach was a study by Juan Martínez Nava that considered the question from a long-term perspective. Martínez Nava made three central points in his book *Conflicto Estado Empresarios*. First, Cárdenas was accommodating to Mexican business interest on the whole and especially so in the aftermath of the oil nationalization of 1938 (Martínez Nava, 1982, 115). Second, by 1960 it was clear that the successful state-led program to hothouse Mexican industrialization had also created an organized business elite with its "autonomous economic power" and "its own specific political weight." As a consequence, "the dominant (economic) class now had a greater power to condition or influence state action" (Martínez Nava, 1982, 158). By 1975, when the business elite created its capstone institution, the CCE, it had become clear the Mexico had entered a historical period of "dual power." Martínez Nava's systematic proof of the secular decline in the state's relative autonomy was confirmed for the period 1982–1988 (as we shall discuss in the last chapter). The state, it seems, had nurtured a progeny that would devour it.

State Monopoly Capitalism

No discussion of theories of the Mexican state would be complete without a treatment of state monopoly capitalism. Interestingly, Poulantzas' work was partly inspired by his strongly negative reaction to what he saw as the instrumental, mechanistic, and "economistic" roots and characteristics of this theory.[4] Popular in Europe and virtually ignored in the United States, admirers and critics alike felt that this theory had applicability in describing advanced capitalist nations that had fallen under the sway of Keynesianism.

In Mexico we see a unique attempt to apply the theory of state monopoly capitalism to a underdeveloped social formation. This attempt is unquestionably linked to the sizable *oeuvre* of Alonso Aguilar. According to Aguilar, state monopoly capitalism appeared in Mexico in the 1940s and defines the accumulation process up to the present moment. The "why and how" of this theory were tightly expressed in the following statement:

> The system is unable to reproduce the relations of production by way of the old market mechanisms; the State is now utilized even to orchestrate the economic process; now not only by indirect means but by direct and permanent means the State sustains the accumulation process in order to attempt to counteract the contradictions of capitalism and the weakening of the system, using every means within its grasp (Aguilar, 1983, 70).

Although Aguilar readily acknowledged that the new growth of the state required a vast army of state employees to carry on the function of directing and stimulating the economic process, he denied that these new state functionaries exercised any significant degree of autonomy. Because the state was a *class state*, it had to perform within a structure in which the "oligarchy" exercised the decisive degree of influence over how fundamental issues were to be resolved. He rejected the instrumentalist theory of the state but simultaneously granted the state policymakers only a "minimum degree of relative autonomy."

The theory of state monopoly capitalism is ambiguously situated in terms of the debate between the instrumentalists and the autonomy theorists because it approaches the state from a different perspective. The theory suggests a functionalist explanation of the structural relationship among the state, large capital, and the accumulation process. Furthermore, in Mexico this theory is employed within a dependency framework. The theory posits that the modern capitalist state is an outgrowth of the monopoly stage of capitalism. When the contradictions of the monopoly stage become acute, a profound crisis ensues (as in the 1930s). Capitalism exhibits a systemic need for a new structure— state monopoly capitalism—in which state intervention becomes the predominant mechanism driving the process of economic reproduction. The theory seeks to show how the state assists in the reproduction process, how it transfers value created in the state sector to the private sector, and how it forestalls the inevitable outbreak of a profound economic crisis. We can outline the theory in the following manner:

1. State monopoly capitalism signifies a qualitative change in the form in the capitalist relations of production and, above all, in the role of the state.
2. At this historical stage a portion of the productive forces assumes the form of state property. This is due to the fact that these productive forces cannot continue to participate in the accumulation process when they are based in private ownership.
3. The state now attempts to counteract or at least to mitigate the objective contradictions of the accumulation process.
4. Specifically, state monopoly capitalism attempts to counteract the following, as they arise: (a) The falling rate of profit, (b) the tendency of production to outrun consumption, and (c) regional and sectoral disequilibria.
5. A basic activity of state monopoly capitalism is to transfer profits from the public to the private sector. This is accomplished when the state sells products at prices below their cost to the private sector, which uses these products as inputs in their production.

The strength of state monopoly capitalism theory is that it brings the state into the dynamics of the *production* process. This theory argues that the interpenetration of the state sector with the private sector arises from the need to create a new institutional arrangement by which "contradictions" in the accumulation process (which cannot be overcome or temporarily sidestepped by way of reliance on market forces) can be resolved. This is no modest accomplishment.

The weaknesses of state monopoly capitalism are twofold. First, the theory all but denies the state managers any autonomy either (1) in functioning as the "general capitalist" in achieving a small but significant degree of autonomy *vis-à-vis* the advanced capitalist nations (and the "multilateral" institution) or (2) in formulating and implementing programs of economic development. Second, the theory is structurally determined; thus, it cannot explain structural change.

Those who have embraced this theory have not been able to easily explain the rise of neoliberalism in the 1980s. In 1988 Alonso Aguilar attempted to address this issue, after presenting one of the most informative discussions available regarding the de la Madrid administration's program to sell off the majority of the parastate firms. In contrast to the care Aguilar took in analyzing the particulars of this process of privatization, when he shifted to the question of what the new neoliberal program meant for the theory of state monopoly capitalism, his argument turned vague, abstract, repetitive, and, in a word, insufficient. Unfortunately, it bordered on argument by assertion, as can be seen by the following:

> The fact that the State has retreated and reduced the reach of its intervention, above all in the process of production, is not, therefore, a sign that State Monopoly Capitalism has ceased to be—in the sense that now the State does not play a fundamental role in the process of accumulation—but rather it has changed its form of functioning so that now private monopoly capital . . . can consolidate its position, recuperate certain industries, control others and force the State to operate in a form that is more advantageous to it, including at the moment controls over wage increases (A. Aguilar, 1988, 29).

Perhaps it could be argued, in defense of Aguilar's position, that the defenders of state monopoly capitalism theory have not had sufficient time to reassess their position. Many questions remain to be answered. Among them three stand out. First, why did state monopoly capitalism fail to predict the rise of neoliberal economics—a school of thought that centers on the state as the origin of capitalist disorders. Second, given that state monopoly capitalism argues that a key element of the current phase of capitalism is the transfer of value from the public to the oligopoly-monopoly elements of the private sector, why do neoliberals in theory and in practice place such emphasis upon eliminating all state subsidies? Third, as the role of the state is reduced, how can state intervention be a predominant mechanism of the economic system?

The State as a Historical Subject

Despite the best efforts of state managers in nations such as Mexico to modulate and control the rhythmic tendencies of social formations that are dominated by the capitalist mode of production, business cycles, periods of deep stagnation, crises, and the forces of structural change continue to confound these would-be Merlins. The very dynamism and unpredictability of the economic system would seem to argue against any one theory of the state. Yet a case can be made for *combining* the instrumentalist theory, the relative-autonomy-of-the-state theory, and the theory of state monopoly capitalism. In this view, these are *complementary theoretical constructs* that can be alternately employed or emphasized in a given historical conjuncture.

In other words, the state itself has no constant composition in terms of its degree of autonomy or instrumentality or in terms of the precise manner in which it intertwines with the accumulation process. As the latter is subjected to a greater or lesser degree of stress, as the process of socioeconomic reproduction varies in terms of difficulty in time and place, the state is forced to respond. This occurs not in any mechanical and preordained manner but with structurally new combinations of the elements that can be derived from the three principal theories of the state. At any given point in time, one will most likely find elements from all three theories playing a role in defining the nature and parameters of the state construct. Elements of the relative autonomy framework seem to work well in describing the Cárdenas period—as many authors have demonstrated. State monopoly capitalism theory was considered a powerful analysis by many in the 1960s and 1970s because it served to highlight and explain central aspects of state behavior that the relative autonomy model relegated to a secondary or lower level of importance. The rise of the neoliberal model brings the instrumentalist theory into the foreground. The Mexican state, as will be demonstrated in the concluding chapter, has become inordinately solicitous of the interests of the large "groups" of national economic power that believe their profits can best be expanded by a state that redirects the accumulation process toward the external market.

It is no simple task to move adroitly among these three theories, plucking the most significant elements from them to present a model of the state. This is a difficult task in a period of relative stability in the accumulation process and is perhaps impossibly complex in a period of crises and profound structural change such as Mexico underwent in the 1980s. Making the task even more trying is the fact that although the social formation of Mexico is now *dominated* by the capitalist mode of production, a significant degree of disarticulation exists within the core of the productive apparatus. The half-life of the rentier ethos of merchant capitalism seems to be long in Mexico. The rentier elements participated in the debt buildup of the nation from the 1950s onward. They were well represented in the great stock market boom of 1986–1987. They continue to exercise power in the state policymaking apparatus, as can be seen by the fact that the tourism complex is gaining on industry as the prime focus of development policy. It remains an open question whether these rentier elements have increased their role in the economy over time or whether the recent surge in speculation and unproductive activities is simply the result of a profound economic crisis. In other words, the question remains whether forming a conjunctural synthesis of the three dominant theories of the state is sufficient given that all have arisen from discussions of the nature of the state in *purely capitalist modes of production*. Whether one needs a particular theory of the state in conditions of what might loosely be defined as "peripheral capitalism" remains an unfinished discussion. The answer to this lies in building a careful set of historical case studies of Mexico's state activities since the 1930s. This, rather than quick translations of the latest in in-vogue theory from Europe, is more likely to take us to the core of the matter.

As a matter of first approximation in the Mexican case, the following forms of the state were suggested in Chapter 1: first, a nationalist-populist state in the Cárdenas years; second, a capitalist-rentier state from roughly the early 1940s through the early 1980s; and, third, a neoliberal state from that time until the present (1989). Complementing this division is the following application of corresponding theoretical models of the State: first, relative state autonomy; second, state monopoly capitalism; and third, instrumentalism. But this latter tripartite division, as has been emphasized in this section, is but a crude approximation dealing only with the *dominant form* of the state model in the given period. None of these state models of accumulation is employed here to the *a priori* exclusion of the others. We are dealing with the relative weights of combinations, a fact that only becomes manifest when we turn to concrete historical situations.

It is, of course, of great importance to show the turning points at which one form gives way to another. This has been attempted only partially here in considering the metamorphosis of the state form during the late 1970s and early 1980s. Nora Hamilton, Arnaldo Córdova, and others have more than begun the task of attempting to explain the earlier turn away from Cárdenas's populism. For this reason, and because of its timeliness in terms of contemporary political economy, this book has concentrated on the latter turning point.

The heterodox and historically determined view of the state advanced here differs from those who have endorsed one theory above all others but coincides with the observations of some careful interpreters of the state. In a important work on the Mexican state, Douglas Bennett and Kenneth Sharpe concluded that

> Assuming the State to be an "independent" variable creates the risk of falling into a kind of voluntarism which fails to understand the real limits placed on the ability and will of the State to act. Assuming the State to be a "dependent" variable risks a determinism which is both blind to historical possibilities and provides only a mechanistic explanation of state action. The State must be conceived of as both a historical product and as a creator of history (Bennett and Sharpe, 1982, 205).

Rolando Cordera interjected a similar note of caution:

As has happened in other countries that have undergone capitalist development, the State in Mexico has played a central role in the definition of the direction and rate of the economic process. Nevertheless, this role has not always been the same, nor has it arisen from the same motivations. In other words, the relationship is structural and necessary; but at the same time it is a social-historical relationship, that is, it is subject to the contradictory movements of its very mode of production—as much in the economic "base" as in the super-structure, as much in the economic as in the political (Cordera, 1979, 102).

Having reviewed a representative sample of the almost innumerable works produced in Mexico on the state, it is now time to move from the abstract to the specific, keeping in mind that the state is not a *deus ex machina*, an "independent" variable, or a marionette "dependent" one. Rather, the state is a historical subject of deep, but comprehensible complexity.

Notes

1. The discussion of theoretical conceptualizations of the Mexican state has been delimited to those works primarily conducted by Mexican political economists. Those desiring a broader discussion of the state drawing from the fields of public administration and political science should review Gilberto Ramírez and Emilio Salim C.'s *La Clase Política Mexicana* (The Mexican Political Class) (Ramírez and Salim C., 1987). These authors summarized the work of non-Mexican researchers in Chapter 3.

2. In his dependency focused study of Mexico, *Acumulación Capitalista, Dependiente y Subordinada* (Capitalist Accumulation: Dependent and Subordinate), Carlos Perzabal devoted less than fifty pages of his book to an empirical analysis of Mexico's economy and barely mentioned the state; the remainder of the work was devoted to reassertions of the standard *obiter dicta* of the dependency school (Perzabal, 1979).

The closest one may come to finding a work on the state centered in dependency framework is Fernando Carmona's well-known study, "La Politica Económica" (The Political Economy) (Carmona, 1978). In it he noted that it was impossible to analyze the fundamental elements of Mexico's development policy without a theory of the state because the state had been the "executing arm of this policy" *but* in a country that lacked "structural independence" (Carmona, 1978, 183). Unfortunately, Carmona did not go too far beyond this point, although he was often forceful and persuasive.

In another publication, he broached the question of the relative autonomy of the state (a matter taken up in the following section of this chapter): "It is enough to appreciate the general results of the action of a State such as Mexico during the post-war period to conclude that such relative autonomy is in reality smaller than ever, especially when confronted with the monopolistic oligarchy or hegemonic finance capital. Here we find deepening of structural dependence which demonstrates the clear lack of autonomy from international monopoly capital" (Carmona, 1980 199). Unfortunately, the argument tends to be circular, assertive, and descriptive. The conclusions come before the proof; regrettably, there is no proof.

3. In their excellent study of the Mexican auto industry, Douglas Bennett and Kenneth Sharpe acknowledged many of the criticisms of dependency theory (Bennett and Sharpe, 1985). Nonetheless, they attempted a nuanced defense of this theory. Clearly, the dependency framework functions adequately to describe certain important sectors of Mexico's economy. The quarrel with dependency theory is not with its ability to *describe* some aspects of the economy but rather with its ability to *theoretically define* and account for the entire dynamics of the Mexican economy (Cypher, 1979).

4. According to Poulantzas, capitalism was in the *stage* of state monopoly capitalism. His quarrel was with a version of this theory that sought to subsume the state as a semiautonomous political instance within the economic "instance." Poulantzas claimed the dominance of the political over the economic instance under certain conditions, but he agreed that the state was the prime organizer of the accumulation process (Poulantzas, 1978, 16, 21, 42, 45, 105, 110, 115).

3

The State and the Macroeconomy in the "Miracle" Years: 1940-1970

Undoubtedly, in the end, the myth of industrialization came to embody the secret of controlling the popular movement, the origins of which are to be found in the Revolutionary period; social reform, a strong government, a powerful state, presidentialism, corporatism binding the popular masses, the institutionalization of class and social conflicts, and a "popular" Constitution all combine in the project that is to pacify all and resolve everything: industrialization.

—Arnaldo Córdova, (1977)

In this chapter the major initiatives that the state developed to promote industrialization during the so-called miracle years from 1940 to 1970 are discussed and analyzed. Incorporated into this discussion is an analysis of the socioeconomic interests that define how the question "Industrialization for whom and for what?" will be answered. Finally, the question of why the "miracle" had disintegrated by the late 1960s is examined through an analysis of three major attempts by Mexican economists to formulate a response.

This period can be subdivided into (1) the war years, 1940–1946; (2) the decade of the agricultural boom, 1946–1955; and (3) the stabilized growth period, 1958–1970. Because there were strong elements of continuity in the first fifteen years, Mexican researchers have often combined the first two subperiods, using terms such as "the stage of primary industrialization" and "the easy import-substitution stage." For broad purposes this is a useful approach, yet the subdivision made above permits one to focus more narrowly on fundamental conjunctural turning points.

In the stage of primary industrialization, the state clearly set about to build an industrial base, but the means for achieving this were never subject to preconceived deliberations of either a theoretical or tactical nature. What stood out in this conscious attempt to use the state to transform the economy was a pervasive, opportunistic resiliency. Some have termed this effort *ad hoc* policymaking, whereas others have called it *improvisation*. Given the increasing role of the state and the impressive performance of the economy one must beware of the temptation to attribute to the state a degree of order, purpose, and intention it never possessed. The economy at this point was not complex, and policymakers could more often than not grope their way toward reasonable solutions— something that would defy them later when the circumstances changed but the methods did not.

Nacional Financiera (the national development bank, or Nafinsa) engaged in internal calculations designed to prioritize investment projects and introduce a much higher degree of systematic analysis into the core economic institutions of the state. But business interests reacted fearfully and successfully pressured the state to abandon its quasi-planning operations. Thus, there were attempts to shift beyond the pervasiveness of improvised policies, and for a time some of them succeeded–but none lasted for long.

The War Period: Peasants Versus Agribusiness, 1940–1946

Although data sources from the sexenio of Ávila Camacho (1940–1946) are not completely reliable, it is nonetheless certain that the war period brought an economic boom, of sorts, to Mexico. The gross national product grew at the rate of 6.1 percent per year, with per capita income rising more than 22 percent in the sexenio (Ramírez, 1988, 54). This burst of prosperity was unevenly felt, however, with inflation and a no-strike pledge during the war working in tandem to undercut workers' real income, which fell some 33 percent during the period (Ramírez, 1988, 54; Niblo, 1988, 24).

The overall impact on the underlying population was much worse than these figures suggest, for they leave out the peasantry, which along with other classes in the countryside accounted for 65 percent of Mexico's population. Basic food production essentially stagnated throughout the Ávila Camacho sexenio. Cyclical movements were of great importance, particularly the shortfall of 1943, which brought back fear of famine in some parts of Mexico. During the war, the Ávila Camacho administration imposed price and wage controls. But price controls were selective and fell on a narrow range of basic goods, including foodstuffs. So, the peasantry was faced with more-or-less frozen prices in selling its crops (there were minor adjustments) while general prices soared an average of 18 percent per year. Along with the fact that the overall level of output for basic foodstuffs was nearly stagnant, Ávila Camacho's administration permitted a fundamental and irreversible change to take place in the countryside.

The *ejido* movement (the traditional semicollective farm units that had flourished under Cárdenas) and land reform were set aside in pursuit of capitalist agribusiness methods in the countryside that could exploit the export boom in fibers and edible oils caused by World War II. Once the floodgates were opened to capitalist farming methods to meet the wartime needs, competition also spilled over into lands producing basic foodstuffs. Here, too, capitalist agribusiness methods could be used to feed the growing cities and/or to export basic foods. Although the actual data sources are weak, it seems that the peasantry fared even worse than did the industrial working class because of the "scissors" effect of price controls on their output and the soaring prices of their inputs. (Large farming interests could avoid the scissors effect either because they were more efficient or because they could produce for the export market and avoid price controls. The peasantry tended to produce for the local market, in small volume, and without commercial relations to import-export companies. In short, a dual market in agricultural commodities emerged.) Meanwhile the peasants were being bought out or simply crowded out of land they acquired in earlier periods.

As a U.S. ally during World War II, Mexico fit into that country's war planning operations primarily as a source of edible oils but also as a source of fibers, minerals, and strategic minerals. The mining sector, largely controlled by transnational corporations, was able to meet the surge of wartime demand from excess capacity.

The war boom was compacted into the four-year period 1940–1943. A sample of crops grown to meet wartime demand (cotton, henequen, cotton seed, sesame seed) increased in output volume by nearly 80 percent in these years (Niblo, 1988, 18). Meanwhile, war demand for major minerals and strategic minerals was such that "there was scarcely a mineral produced in Mexico that did not at least double in output between 1939–1940 and 1942–1944" (Niblo, 1988, 21). The volume of industrial output increased by the impressive (but nonetheless significantly smaller amount) of 39 percent in these years (INEGI, 1985, vol. 2, 501). What is most interesting is that in the subsequent three-year period, 1943–1946, with the war boom winding down, Mexico's industrial production surged ahead and increased by 19.5 percent.

In agriculture, however, the peasants had little means or capacity to expand production. The United States (through programs of both the Department of War and the Department of Agriculture) was anxious to get quick results that would jump agricultural exports. It allocated tractors and other capital-intensive forms of mechanized farming to Mexico while sending teams of technicians and farm advisers. Meanwhile, a twelve-year boom in state-financed agricultural infrastructure construction commenced. The number of irrigated hectares soared from 126,000 in 1939 to 816,000 in 1945 (Niblo, 1988, 23). Complementing this was a new emphasis on road building to get the crops to railheads and ports. Roads completed rose from 9,000 kilometers in 1939 to 17,000 in 1945 (Niblo, 1988, 23).

The Drive to Industrialize

The boom in agricultural and mining exports was not matched by a flood of imported consumer goods or machinery. Machinery was allocated to Mexico strictly on the basis of U.S. needs in the war effort. Mexico was paid in unspendable dollars for its exports, with the dollar deposits building up in the banking system. This monetary influx contributed to the inflationary tendencies to some degree. But more importantly, national industry could not expand in pace with either the mining or the (capitalist) agriculture export sectors. Industrial output rose 63 percent from 1940 to 1945, but prices of industrial products rose about 150 percent (INEGI, 1985, vol. 2, 501; Niblo, 1988, 21). That output jumped by as much as it did was a tribute to the ingenuity of the national industrial sector, which primarily relied on increasing work shifts and "artisan" workshops (using semicapitalist methods) to fill the need for manufacturing products. This was "extensive" expansion based on labor-intensive forms of production.

Behind the scenes Nafinsa was moving to undertake some of its largest-ever investments in steelmaking (and related industries), fertilizers, railroad cars, diesel trucks, and cement (Nafinsa-CEPAL, 1971, 283). Nafinsa's strategy was to build an array of sources to provide "intermediate" inputs into the process of industrial production. Nafinsa's technocrats argued for the creation of a technically efficient group of industries to produce a requisite range of intermediate products needed to support the industrialization drive. (These projects were beyond the reach of the "new group" of industrialists, who rode the long wave of expansion created by the war and the postwar agricultural boom. Only the older, wealthier financial-industrial groups could afford to fund such projects. But these groups were notorious for their aversion to risk and their preference for quick returns. Only Nafinsa could take the risks.)

Yet Nafinsa's program was modest in that a "thin" cadre of technicians provided the skilled labor needed to run these new projects. Had Nafinsa tried to create a machine-building sector, it would have run into a skilled labor shortage. Mexico did not have the educational infrastructure to support a "deeper" form of industrialization. There is no way to assign a numerical value to Nafinsa's strategy, but given the historical conditions, it appears to have been correct and of key importance.

Given (1) that it was agribusiness and mining that were the growth industries during the war, (2) that from 1946 through 1955 Mexico could ride the agricultural boom caused by reconstruction from the war in Europe, and (3) that the boom in primary products was brought on both by the Korean war and the U.S. military's massive stockpiling of primary products, the question arises as to why Mexico was so determined to build an *industrial* base. The answer is not without irony because the fundamental transition to industry commenced in the midst of a prolonged agricultural export boom. The ideology of the revolution, the legacy of the Cárdenas years, and Mexico's long history with the fleeting nature of agricultural export booms under Porfirio Díaz had all combined to create a consensus among those who wielded policymaking power that Mexico had to cut its ties of dependence based in agro-export production. This consensus arose because these booms generated instability within the economy, while export-based production left the nation at the mercy of distant forces that could neither be controlled nor influenced.

Using one of the few historical sources available regarding how the Mexican business interests viewed this matter, Rogelio Hernández Rodríquez analyzed a series of letters (some addressed to President Ávila Camacho) written by the prominent businessman Antonio Ruiz Galindo. Ruiz Galindo was a strong champion of import-substitution industrialization on the grounds that Mexico possessed a potentially vast internal market that could expand based upon the complementary relationship between increases in aggregate demand (driven by private business investment, state investment, and wage increases) and internal increases in supply. The broadly Keynesian views presented by Ruiz Galindo were widely shared by others in business as well as by key economic policymakers in Ávila Camacho's government. There is every reason to believe that Ruiz Galindo was speaking not merely for himself and that his attempt to influence the president was not in vain (Hernández Rodríquez, 1984).

From the war period we can derive some lessons regarding policymaking in Mexico. As mentioned, Mexico was flooded with dollar deposits in the banking system because it could not readily exchange its dollar receipts, gained from export earnings, for U.S. imports. This caused consternation among the economic policymakers at the Secretary of the Treasury and the Banco de México (Bank of Mexico) who wanted to reduce inflationary pressures (and redirect purchasing power away from luxury consumption). Following a method adopted in the United States, a wartime excess profits tax was proposed.

It was felt that an excess profit tax could be used to channel funds to Nafinsa by way of the tax. (The Treasury and the Banco de México are major participants in the board of directors of Nafinsa.) This, like subsequent efforts, met a wave of organized protest from the business elite. Having failed, the economic policymakers then considered selling government bonds to the private sector—another scheme the latter apparently frowned upon. Finally, in a classic example of *improvisation*, the policymakers simply demanded that the reserve requirement of the private Mexican banks be put at 33 percent as of August 1943. (The reserves went to the Banco de México, which then channeled funds to Nafinsa.) In 1944 this requirement was raised to 50 percent (a figure that was kept for decades with minor changes). Of course, this was an exceedingly high reserve requirement, but it did serve to drain the banking system of its excess liquidity and probably helped control the inflation, which roared along at an 18 percent annual rate through the sexenio (Ramírez, 1988, 54).

Now, however, the central bank had the liquidity, and from there it was an easy (but unplanned) step to channel the funds to Nafinsa and into other government developmental projects, such as irrigation projects and infrastructure (Niblo, 1988, 33). So a new development policy was created, not because the state set about to channel credit throughout the economy but because there was a *short-term* need to control inflationary pressures. This is the type of behavior that researchers have in mind when they refer to the *improvised* nature of Mexico's state industrialization policies.

State and Industry During the War Period

Ávila Camacho immediately took steps to change the nature of the relationship between the state and the business elite that Cárdenas had established. The latter's excess profit tax was repealed, and a new and much less threatening version of the law governing nationalizations was promulgated. Along with grouping workers and peasants into state-controlled unions and peasant organizations, Cárdenas had grouped all businesses into a "business chamber" known as the Cámaras Nacionales de Comerico y Industria (the National Chambers of Trade and Industry, or CANACOMIN). The idea was to place business associations *under* the state, which would allow business groups to have a *defined* space for dialogue within the apparatus of the state. Business associations were denied the possibility of influencing policy through an open debate (such as through a privately paid publicity campaign using mass communications to gain public influence). Many business interests readily accepted this new corporatist scheme. Some probably did so out of commitment to a new nationalist project under the leadership of Cárdenas, others because they were small or medium-sized interests who were not capable, individually or collectively, of challenging the state on policy issues.

Not all business interests entered into the new arrangement, however. The Confederación Patronal de la República Mexicana (the Employers Association of the Federal Republic, or Coparmex), founded in 1929, stood outside of the Cárdenas scheme and attacked it for its "socialist" objectives. According to Luis Bravo, Coparmex arose as a "defensive" employers organization and was "promoted by a wave of anti-business radicalism which swept through Mexico" (Bravo, 1987, 93). Coparmex represented old money in Mexico, which meant that it primarily represented old renter capital that had been accumulated in hacendado agriculture, oligopolistic commerce, and, of course, banking. Coparmex represented "merchant capital," above all, but the largest Monterrey-based industrialists were also strongly represented. This was less of a contradiction than might appear on first sight because these industrial magnates were normally the scions of banking–trade–agro-export families from the region. These bankers and industrialists formed the first national economic groups. (Nora Hamilton's study of the Garza Sada's four groups provided an excellent historical analysis of Mexico's most powerful Monterrey-based family [Hamilton, 1982, 306–316].) Given their preindustrial ideological orientation, it was inevitable that they would mount a battle against "statism" at the first opportunity (as we shall see).

Historians have argued that Ávila Camacho broke apart CANACOMIN in 1941 because he feared that the united forces of business and commerce could overwhelm the state (Torres, 1979, 285). Maintaining Cárdenas's corporatist arrangement but returning to a division that extended back to 1917, Ávila Camacho dissolved CANACOMIN. Its two constituent elements, the Conferedación de Cámaras Industriales de los Estados Unidos Mexicanos (the Mexican Industrialists' Association, or CONCAMIN) and the Conferación de Cámaras Nacionales de Comercio (the National Trade Association, or CONCANACO), representing large industrial and trade capital, respectively, were separated. Most importantly, under the organization of CONCAMIN, a semiautonomous "chamber," the Cámara Nacional de Industria de la Transformación (the National Chamber of Manufacturing Industries, or Canacintra), would be created.

Canacintra was the organization of the new group, or the "group of the 40s," which, according to researchers, was the locus of the new national industrial faction of the business elite (see Zabludovsky, 1980, regarding the importance of the new group). What was new regarding this faction was twofold. First, its members were new *national* small and medium manufacturers without ties of origin or finance that linked them to transnational mining or agro-export interests. (They produced a wide range of products such as steel, electric motors, consumer durables, lumber, cement, and machined metal products.) Second, they were an indirect product of the state's industrialization programs. They championed these programs because it was in their interest to do so. For Canacintra, unlike Coparmex, statism was not a threat but a means of attaining necessary external support in launching and maintaining businesses.[1] More important, perhaps, than the subsidies and protection this group would receive as a result of the state's industrialization policies was the new market that the state constituted as it commenced its massive investments in infrastructure, industry, and capitalist agriculture.

Ávila Camacho's regime was clearly key in locating the origins and particularities of Mexico's new national industrial elite. The state in this period was "reinventing the bourgeoisie"—a fundamental function in a state-led model of development. As the faction of the 1940s grew and prospered under the direct support given to it by the state, it came to have a presence in both CONCAMIN and CONCANACO that went beyond its representation in Canacintra (Conchiero and Fragosa, 1979, 136). As late as the 1970s and again during the aftermath of the bank nationalization in 1982, the faction of the 1940s called for unity between business and government and an end to the divisiveness that had been promoted, above all, by Coparmex. The distinction that researchers such as Elvira Gutiérrez Conchiero and Juan Manuel Fragosa (Conchiero and Fragosa, 1979) drew between the faction of the 1940s and older groups of capital during the stage of primary industrialization was meaningful until the late 1960s. In the 1980s there was a blurring of the two polar groups—the 1970s were a period of transition.

There are dangers in taking the "reinventing of the bourgeoisie" argument too far, for it emphasizes the functionality of the state's redirection under Ávila Camacho. There is a risk in ignoring the fact that the war also gave rise to a boom in the rentier ethos. The war boom created scarcities—some genuine, some contrived—that companies and state functionaries could manipulate to their advantage. Mexico was changing, deeply, permanently, and quickly, under the "opportunity" created by a distant event—World War II. The nationalist-populist dreams and aspirations of the revolutionary cadre who had backed Cárdenas were dissipated in a new environment in which opportunism and parasitic behavior could flourish. Stephen Niblo, in a detailed study of the period, noted that "a new life style . . . came to establish the meaning of modernity for many." Mexico was now beset by a "wave of promoters and speculators." And "through it all a new individual meaning of development emerged much closer to a *nouveau riche* model of conspicuous consumption than to the radical populism of the pre-war period" (Niblo, 1988, 27).

Antonio Ruiz Galindo complained in a letter to President Ávila Camacho that Mexico could not develop by constructing luxurious "apartment buildings, . . . nor by the raising of ostentatious mansions, personal recreation complexes or ornate decorations." He drove his point home by emphasizing that "this is capital that is subtracted from that available for the urgent work of development" (Hernández Rodríquez, 1984, 39). It would be difficult to improve upon Stephen Niblo's final assessment of the period:

> The highly regressive impact of the War boom on patterns of income distribution established a pattern that was to be the wave of the future. In a reversal of the distributive patterns of the early Cárdenas years, the acceptance of a kind of prosperity based upon mass contributions to the most privileged created a different kind of Mexican Revolution. A revolutionary elite grew in close association with government policies. War contracts, tax breaks, falling real wages, a regressive tax structure, and monetary favors all constituted the increased role of the State in the process of capital accumulation (Niblo, 1988, 34).

Nafinsa and State Policies to Promote Industrialization

Nafinsa's story has been well told on more than one occasion (Bennett and Sharpe, 1982; Blair, 1964). Nafinsa was created in 1934 and restructured in December 1940 to emphasize the promotion of industrialization. After another restructuring in 1947, Nafinsa became the chief contracting agent for public foreign loans. Under the more *laissez-faire* government of Miguel Alemán (1946–1952), it was to moderate its aggressive policies of constructing state industrial firms. Nafinsa was redirected to emphasize infrastructural programs that would be noncompetitive with the private sector.

Calvin Blair, in his classic 1964 study, "Nacional Financiera," presented a compelling argument that Nafinsa was destined to be reined in by Alemán's administration. Blair was probably guilty of sizable exaggeration when he claimed that "in the realm of economic power Nafinsa may have a slight edge" over the *entire private sector* (Blair, 1964, 201). That he would dare make this comment in what was clearly a well-researched study was a general indication of how far one careful observer might go in assessing Nafinsa's role. Such a statement helps us to understand why the private sector was fearful of Nafinsa and successfully pressured President Alemán to reduce and alter its role.

Nafinsa was directed to pursue the following objectives as the result of its 1940 restructuring: (1) promote industrialization, (2) promote the production of intermediate and capital goods, (3) invest in infrastructure, (4) help stimulate and develop indigenous entrepreneurial talent, (5) build confidence within the Mexican private sector, and (6) reduce the role of direct foreign investment in industry (Blair, 1964, 200). Blair maintained that Nafinsa went through three periods: (1) the experimental period, from 1934 to 1940; (2) the period of "uninhibited industrial promotion," from 1940 to 1947; and (3) a subsequent period, from 1947 to the early 1960s, promoting infrastructure and heavy industry. During the second period, we see the beginnings of an attempt to systematically approach the question of economic development and industrialization. It is here that we find the origins of Mexico's version of import-substitution industrialization.

Nafinsa's economists were essentially persuaded by arguments in favor of comparative advantage. After the war, however, they argued that Mexico would be subjected to devastating international competition from a recovered Europe and a U.S. economy that was undergoing an amazing increase in its manufacturing capabilities. Protectionism should be chosen, not on the basis of an economic philosophy but rather on the basis of expediency. It was all a matter of pragmatism. The war had made the importation of most manufactured goods impossible. Consequently, Nafinsa had funded and/or created new industries. Toward the end of the war, creating state-owned firms was prioritized on the grounds of defending investments that had already been made. Nafinsa argued that Mexico should be protected, restructured, and industrialized but that it would resume "free" trade once a new industrial base had been built. Inertia, however, seems to have overtaken Nafinsa at some point. Protectionism became institutionalized, even as it was argued by many of Nafinsa's policymakers that protection should be a short-term phenomenon.

At several points Blair mentioned that Nafinsa was guided by an optimism in support of improvisation more than by any theory or analysis as to what Mexican development patterns should be (Blair, 1964, 215, 219). Nafinsa's was a much more incrementalist and nonprogrammatic approach to development than that offered by CEPAL. In making its investments, Nafinsa emphasized "linkage effects." (Backward linkages went from the project toward raw material production, mining, and agriculture, and forward linkages went from the project toward processing, refining, marketing, and distribution. The theory behind this was that by selecting projects with a high degree of linkages, subsidiary or "linked" industries would be stimulated.) This is all well known today, but in the early 1940s it constituted innovative policymaking (Blair, 1964, 226).

Blair expressed ambivalence in his assessment of Nafinsa's methods of selecting projects and evaluating their performance. He clearly emphasized the "systematic" nature of Nafinsa's investments in the following statement:

> Nafinsa established in 1941 a department of promotion and began to make systematic studies of industrial development projects. With a predilection for manufacturing, it promoted enterprises in practically every sector of the Mexican economy over the course of the next seven years. The roster of firms aided by loan, guarantee, or purchase of stocks and bonds reads like a "who's who" of Mexican business (Blair, 1964, 213).

But when turning to a more focused look at Nafinsa's activities in promoting heavy industry, which were strongly linked to the creation of very large parastate firms in the 1940s, Blair maintained that Nafinsa's criteria were mixed and not reducible to a program of providing subsidized inputs (such as petroleum products) to private industry:

> Nafinsa's interest in heavy industry reflected a complex of overlapping motives. The motives were not always consistent with one another, and there was no formula for priorities or relative weights. In the deliberating process within Nafinsa qualitative assignments of priorities were made in response to technical judgments and to economic and political pressure.
> Import replacement continued to be a major overall objective. But even the promotion of an obvious import-replacing industry sometimes required the stimulus of a special event (Blair, 1964, 225).

Many of the disputes to which Blair refered never went beyond the closed confines of the state apparatus. Some well-known cases, however, pointed to a consistent pattern of oligopoly resistance to the new firms that Nafinsa (and other development banks) created. For example, in the 1940s Nafinsa successfully promoted the vast Altos Hornos steel complex in the face of determined opposition by the Monterrey-based private steel industry. The private sector falsely claimed that the new steel complex would create excess capacity. (A dispute over petrochemicals is discussed in Chapter 5 and a similar case concerning synthetic fibers in Chapter 6.)

Nafinsa, in addition to promoting parastate firms, extensively engaged in lending long-term capital to the private sector and in forming partnership investments with both the private sector and international firms. (Historically, investment funds had been primarily raised outside of banking channels from retained earnings by family-dominated "groups," many of which were the most powerful elements in CONCAMIN, CONCANACO, and Coparmex.) By 1961 Nafinsa's investments were supporting 533 industrial firms, and its long-term investments were twice as large as the sum of such loans deriving from the private banking system (Blair, 1964, 195). (Nafinsa continued to be a prominent development agency through the 1980s, but its "golden age" came in the 1940s and early 1950s when the private sector's reluctance to commit funds to industry was particularly acute.) Considerable space has been devoted to Nafinsa because this development bank seems to express most clearly the efforts by the state to promote a national development project in Mexico. Blair was far from being alone in his emphasis on Nafinsa—many other researchers have emphasized its pathbreaking role, most recently Douglas Bennett and Kenneth Sharpe (Bennett and Sharpe, 1982).

The new group of nationalist industrialists that prospered as a direct and indirect result of Nafinsa's activities found Nafinsa to be a necessity. Yet the business community in general was afraid of Nafinsa for two reasons. First, Nafinsa wanted to use the parastate firms as a "yardstick" to measure the efficiency of private firms. Second, Nafinsa's firms would be capable of engaging in "unfair" competition with the monopoly-oligopoly firms that were accustomed to what can only be described as huge or "abnormal" rates of return on their investments (Blair, 1964, 233–234). Blair maintained that in this struggle private sector interests were able to curb Nafinsa. The most powerful business associations, such as Coparmex, and the most powerful financial and industrial groups (such as those owned by the Garza Sada family) used their personal influence and institutionalized "advisory commission" positions of "consultation" with the government to undercut Nafinsa's program. In general terms Matilda Luna and her colleagues noted this shift:

> The great economic expansion in Mexico in the 1950s and 1960s increased the economic, political, ideological and cultural influence of the business sector. As a result, the social pact, almost imperceptibly and certainly without any violent ruptures, underwent several fundamental modifications: the influence of business in the appointment of officials increased and consultation with business leaders on these matters became mandatory; business acquired veto power over policies it did not approve of; the core of the state apparatus itself came to be dominated by technicians and experts whose rationalistic discourse of efficiency gradually moved toward the orthodox pro-business policy; and the nation's financial apparatus became a privileged arena for the formulation of general development policies by pro-business elites (Luna, Tirada, and Valdes, 1987, 16–17).

Nafinsa, particularly from 1940 to 1946, was a means of creating a new group of industrialists subordinated to the state, which thereby afforded it some autonomy in the area of industrial development. At the same time, the fact that President Alemán could reorient Nafinsa in 1947 (away from its aggressive support for industrialization toward more indirect forms of infrastructural investments, particularly support of capitalist agriculture) demonstrated the staying power of the old financial and industrial groups and the very limited (and even declining) autonomy that the state was able to exercise. That the rules of the game that governed Nafinsa's participation could change so drastically implied that there was no determinant, behind the scenes, "logic of capitalism" (such as the state monopoly capital model implies) working to delineate Nafinsa's "correct" role in the economy.

Creating "New" and "Necessary" Firms

During Ávila Camacho's period, there was a noticeable tilt toward protection of Mexico's industrial base. Tariffs jumped in 1941, and protectionism again rose in 1944, when import licensing was introduced. (This gave policymakers near absolute control over the quantity of imports.) Nevertheless, it was industrial promotion rather than control over the balance of payments that was central to Ávila Camacho's regime (King, 1970, 16–28).

Second in importance after Nafinsa, but not separate from it, was the 1941 legislation known as the Ley de Industrias de Transformacion (the Manufacturing Industries Law). This law exempted "new" and "necessary" industries from a wide range of taxes, import licensing fees, and quotas. The law was extended in 1945, giving new and necessary firms exemptions of federal taxes for up to ten years. (Necessary firms were defined as national manufacturers that were needed to satisfy existing internal demand.) Between 1940 and 1950, the largest manufacturing firms in Mexico took advantage of the law. The 570 firms that qualified (some were new, whereas others fit the loose definition of necessary) owned 68 percent of the entire manufacturing capital of Mexico. Nafinsa-owned or -financed firms were at the top of this impressive list of beneficiaries. Nafinsa's firms accounted for fully 30 percent of the entire manufacturing capital in this period (Navarrete, 1967, 22).

Ávila Camacho's Keynesian-influenced secretary of the Treasury, Eduardo Suárez, attacked the law on the grounds that it was vague in wording and applied in an undiscriminating manner. He argued that it lacked forms of control and sanctions—the Treasury refused to support the program (Navarrete, 1967, 21). That on this and other occasions there could be such high level resistance to key aspects of the economic program put forth by Ávila Camacho supports the hypothesis of the *improvised* nature of the economic program of the 1940s. Incrementally, an important process of industrialization was being facilitated by a series

Table 3.1:   Real Growth of the Mexican Economy: 1946-1952
(real cumulative growth -- in percent)

Δ Gross Domestic Product	39.9
Δ Agriculture (including livestock)	43.4
Δ Industry	51.7
Δ Petroleum	81.0
Δ Construction	45.3
Δ Manufacturing	50.5
Δ Services	34.6
Δ Exports	72.4
Δ Gross Investment*	38.9

* estimated

Source: Nacional Financiera, *La Economía Mexicana en Cifras* (México: Nafinsa, 1978), pp. 25-28, 229.

of state activities (only the most important ones have been mentioned here). But the state had no clear programmatic prescription for development, nor did the new group of industrialists or any other.

The Agricultural Boom, 1946-1955

Miguel Alemán's sexenio was framed and defined by an export boom in agricultural commodities driven first by reconstruction from World War II and then by the commodities boom sparked by the Korean war. Alemán was known as an industrializer; yet agricultural exports, supported by vast state investment in irrigation (and related infrastructure), were the main force behind the boom. From 1946 to 1955, the value of agricultural output grew at the real annual rate of 9.0 percent—slightly outpacing real manufacturing growth of 8.2 percent per year (Solís, 1986, 97, 170).

Table 3.1 presents aggregate data that chronicle the economy's expansion. Using the sexenio-based figures, however, is somewhat deceptive in this case. It appears that industry, not agriculture, was the leading sector of the economy. Excluding 1952, however, the rate of growth in agriculture was slightly greater than that of manufacturing industry—45.7 percent versus 44.1 percent.

Under Alemán the last vestiges of support for a serious land reform program were swept away. Henceforth, although the total amount of land distributed in any sexenio would wax and wane, the peasants would be given only very marginal land, which was often desert and wasteland. In Alemán's sexenio, land under cultivation jumped appreciably—a 25 percent increase in nonirrigated land and a 30 percent increase in irrigated lands (INEGI, 1985, vol. 1, 348). He increased the percentage share of total state investment directed toward agriculture by roughly 25 percent and devoted more to agricultural investment than to industry (Hansen, 1971, 62). Mexico had the advantage of a large system of rivers in the north that with dams and canals could be diverted to a immense area of land on which multicrop production could be practiced annually. The state's investment program was redirected away from land reform and toward infrastructural investments (most particularly irrigation projects and associated investment in electricity and road building), which had the direct effect of lowering agricultural production costs. Exports of goods and services increased by 72.4 percent during the sexenio; the expansion in foreign trade was nearly double that of the entire economy. Led by a boom in cotton production, agricultural exports climbed from 44 percent of total exports in 1946 to 56 percent in 1952 (Torres, 1984, 143–145). Alemán veered away from Ávila Camacho's industrialization program because world prices for agricultural commodities were high from the late 1940s through the Korean war.

Along with abandoning land reform for the unrestrained promotion of capitalist agriculture in the countryside, the Alemán administration reduced the degree of independence that existed in the official unions grouped under the Confederación de Trabajadores de México (the Mexican Workers Confederation, or CTM). A 1947 decree gave the secretary of Labor the "right" to refuse to acknowledge the legitimacy of union elected officials. This in essence gave the state the power to impose union officials. Materially, workers did better on average than they had under Ávila Camacho, but their wages lagged well behind the 39.9 percent increase in gross national product during the sexenio; real wages for urban workers rose only 6.7 percent (King, 1970, 26).

With Alemán continuing and deepening the antipopular policies of Ávila Camacho, state controls on foreign investment were weakened— an act which was severely criticized by the remnants of loyalists to Cárdenas. Alemán was further attacked for allowing a large number of his cabinet secretariats to be filled by prominent business leaders from the old group—a situation out of the ordinary in Mexico, where career state managers normally occupied such positions. Consistent with all of this, he is generally seen to have opened the floodgates of corruption (Cline, 1963, 157-159).

Under Alemán, Nafinsa was curbed and redirected toward infrastructural programs that supported the central project of accumulation— capitalist export-based agriculture—while protectionism was further boosted in the aftermath of the balance-of-payments crisis of 1948, which forced a devaluation of the peso. When the tariff law was revised in 1948 to increase the degree of protection, Regulation 14 of the law exempted the importation of capital goods from the tariff rates. Many subsequent commentators have seen this exemption as a key flaw in the protection program because Mexico could not be expected to develop an independent, sophisticated capital goods industry as long as machinery and related products could be freely imported. Further, it has been argued that firms were led to overinvest in capital and consequently to neglect more labor-intensive forms of production. At the time, of course, Regulation 14 was viewed as a necessity lest machinery imports should be inordinately expensive and thereby cut off Mexico's incipient industrialization. Critics have deplored the subsequent lack of policymaking innovation in this particular area (Nafinsa-CEPAL, 1971, 189–197).

Alemán's Agriculture Boom and the Theory of the State

Alemán's administration emphasized foreign borrowing and a free hand in printing money, which brought the problems of foreign indebtedness and inflation into the foreground. Falling global agricultural and commodities prices and the draining effect of payments on foreign borrowing and chronic inflation combined in 1954 to create another balance-of-payments crisis that precipitated a devaluation of the peso. To many observers this crisis brought to light the false underpinning of the brief prosperity experienced in Alemán's era.

An agriculture boom based in massive state subsidies for water, roads, and electricity and reliant upon (1) inflated prices in global markets, (2) subsistence wage payments and (3) imported farm machinery could not stimulate a complementary industrialization process based on the growth of internal markets. State managers clearly lacked the vision and power to construct and enforce an agricultural policy that did more than opportunistically ride the export boom. Much more capital-intensive methods were utilized, warranting the term *capitalist* export-based agriculture (in contrast to agro-export methods). But the state did not exercise sufficient control over the agriculture boom in terms of integrating the stimulus received by agriculture into the rest of the economy.[2] Although capitalist farming methods spread rapidly, restructuring the Mexican agricultural sector, the macroeconomic effect was limited largely to increases in short-term land rents. There was little regard for the long-term need to forge definitive, complementary relationships between national consumer and capital goods industries and modern mechanized agriculture. Nor could agriculture-based growth be tied to a stable internal market if wages were to be held to a mere 7 percent real increase.

The Capitalist-Rentier State Form

Under Alemán the capitalist-rentier state was consolidated and went on to dominate state policymaking through 1982. The degree of relative state autonomy diminished while instrumentalist aspects of the state came into the foreground. At the same time Mexico's version of state monopoly capitalism began to make a shadowy appearance. Regarding the latter, state investments jumped approximately 100 percent (in real terms) from 1946 to 1950, with emphasis placed upon petroleum and petroleum products (fertilizers and chemicals), electricity, and irrigation (Cabral, 1981, 81–84). The state shifted from prioritizing the creation of parastate industrial firms to providing cheap inputs (below market cost) to the largest elements of the private sector.

One well-known researcher in the area of business-state relations, Gina Zabludovsky, confirmed the commonly asserted view that instrumentalist links grew at a rapid pace during Alemán's administration. One case in point was the creation in 1949 of the Consultative Committee on Economic and Fiscal Policy. Members included representatives of the presidency, the Treasury, the subsecretary of the economy, CONCAMIN (large industrial capital), CONCANACO (large commercial capital), and the Asociación de Banqueros Mexicanos (the Mexican Bankers Association, or ABM). The function of the committee was to review all government initiatives regarding the economy so that the state would have formal access to the views of the business elite. The existence of this committee did not actually demonstrate instrumentalism, but it did cast doubt on the nature of the state's autonomy, as Zabludovsky clearly implied (Zabludovsky, 1984, 24).

In 1950 a dispute arose between the Alemán administration and the business elite. Alemán's regime, utilizing its institutional powers, passed legislation—the Ley de Atribuciónes al Ejecutivo en Materias Económicas (the Presidential Law of Attribution in Economic Affairs)—strongly opposed by the organized business groups. This law gave the government power to set priorities in the production, distribution, and sale of all products (through price setting, rationing, or the control of foreign trade). Protest from business ended in 1951 when the law was suspended. Making a 180 degree turn, the state then passed legislation that gave it in conjunction with the elite business organizations the capacity to regulate prices (Zabludovsky, 1984, 26). This resolution to the dispute suggested that state autonomy was declining.

The Alemán period was one in which the business associations set out to reformulate the business-state relationship as well as business's relation to society at large. The latter consisted of utilizing U.S.-style probusiness advertising to alter the public's perception of business behavior. The former was signified by the growth of new business associations such as the Mexican Highway Association, which was created to maintain a permanent relationship with a government that had embarked on a massive highway building program. Represented in this association were the steel industry, the rubber industry, the transnational auto companies, cement contractors, and several members of the old, preindustrial, banking elite. In the new business associations Zabludovsky found a renewed source of *amiguismo* (cronyism—although she used the term "personal contact"): "With the integration of the business elite into new national private associations, there arose a new type of organization that can be distinguished from the 'chambers' because of its voluntary association, the small number of members and the maintenance of relations with the government based upon personal contacts" (Zabludovsky, 1984, 23–24).

Conchiero also noted the new relationships emerging and highlighted the fact that state functionaries could now easily move from the political realm to private industry based upon contacts made with (and assistance given to) the new private associations. Although she emphasized the "faction of the 1940s," Conchiero's comments clearly had more general application:

> The relations between the state bureaucracy and the faction of the 40s have taken two principal forms that have given rise to two groups of the bourgeoisie: One consists of those that by way of the opportunities presented to public functionaries can accumulate capital and thereby enter into business activities and in this way identify with concrete capitalist interests of this faction, and be transformed into members of the bourgeoisie. The other is the opposite, that is, members of the bourgeoisie being incorporated into the bureaucracy through occupying positions which place them next to decision-making power (Conchiero and Fragosa, 1979, 140).

Thus, a blending occurred of interests of those at the apex of the pyramid of private sector economic power with top policymaking individuals in the state apparatus. This blending did not commence with the Alemán administration, but it was consolidated and institutionalized during this period. This phenomenon was also noted by Roger Hansen (Hansen, 1971, 219–220), who summed up the extreme nature of the metamorphoses achieved in the complementary regimes of Ávila Camacho and Alemán this way:

No other Latin American political system has given as much material reward to its commercial, agricultural and industrial elites. The taxes and wages they have had to pay have been low, their profits have been high and the growing public infrastructure that serves as a base for its productive activities has developed in pace with its needs. . . . It is difficult to imagine a combination of policies devoted to supporting the profit-making activities of the private sector larger than those established by the Mexican government after 1940. In this sense, and in spite of the continued prominence of Public sector activities the Mexican government is "a businessman's government" (Hansen, 1971, 117).

The End of Primary Industrialization, 1953–1955

In 1953, real growth of the economy was virtually zero (as a result of the end of the Korean hostilities), with annual exports declining 17 percent. The slump engendered a balance-of-payments crisis in 1954. Mexico was forced to devalue the peso—an activity the Mexican elite saw as a sign of weakness. In 1955 the rate of inflation was 17 percent, a level not seen since the days of World War II (INEGI, 1985, vol. 1, 311; vol. 2, 751). Real wages increased almost 8 percent in 1953 while the profit rate dropped by roughly 16 percent (Bortz, 1987, 153; Solís, 1986, 302). In the four-year period 1953–1956, total real wages increased 12.7 percent (Bortz, 1987, 153).

In 1953 the Ruiz Cortines administration (1952–1958) attempted to control the inflation through credit restriction. Simultaneously, it directed state investments toward the subsistence sector of agriculture (the peasantry). The latter policy was inspired by the idea that a revived countryside would have the mass purchasing power needed to stimulate the internal market for manufactures. This policy was strongly opposed by the various industrial associations, which complained that the policy of import substitution and state assistance for industrialization had been abandoned. Their reaction was to cut private investment and engage in capital flight.

Before Adolfo Ruiz Cortines's new plan to revive the *campo* could be tested, his administration reversed itself in 1954 and opted for a sizable jump in state spending—spending jumped 44 percent, unadjusted for inflation (Pellicer de Brody, 1978, 148–149; INEGI, 1985, vol. 2, 628). Government investment increased 29 percent in real terms to counteract the slump. The jump in state spending seemed to momentarily staunch the economy's wounds; real gross domestic product increased a remarkable 10 percent in 1954. Because the big jump in state outlays was again oriented toward industrial promotion, it constituted a futile attempt to reassure the business elite. Then, attacked by the private sector, the government drastically retrenched. In 1955 government investment fell by 9 percent. Again in 1956 it declined an additional 2 percent (INEGI, 1985, vol. 2, 606, 751).

Using "errors and omissions" in the balance-of-payments account as a proxy, we can see that capital flight was the response of a business elite that had been showered with what Roger Hansen argued were favors of a magnitude unknown in Latin America. In 1954 the amount attributed to "errors and omissions" was three times that of 1953. In 1955 this figure was three and a half times greater than that of 1953. In both 1954 and 1955 capital flight equaled approximately 15 percent of the value of total exports (Brothers and Solís, 1966, 84).

In these years the government response was to borrow heavily abroad. In 1955 long- and short-term borrowing amounted to a total equal to 29 percent of the value of the export of goods and services. Although private sector investment slumped, the Ruiz Cortines administration at this point opened the floodgates to foreign investment. During Alemán's administration foreign investment had averaged $48 million per year (in current U.S. dollars). In the three-year period 1954–1956, the annual average jumped to $108 million (INEGI, 1985, vol. 2, 612).

The picture that emerged was one of economic chaos: profits falling, wages (surprisingly) rising, inflation out of control, two devaluations (1954 and 1955), surging capital flight, quick increases in foreign investment, and extreme vacillation in the government's program. Roger Hansen described the depth of the private sector's dismay over the balance-of-payments crisis and the economic stagnation: "It is probable that in no other time since the PRI assumed power has there been such frank and severe criticisms voiced regarding the existing system of government" (Hansen, 1971, 71). Neither the private sector nor the government seemed to know what to do as the stage of primary industrialization ground to a halt.

One contradiction in Ruiz Cortines's strategy was that the big jump in state outlays had been partially financed by tax increases on *exports*. Exports in value terms increased 10 percent in 1954, but tax income on exports increased 55 percent and accounted for 21.5 percent of total state tax revenues (INEGI, 1985, vol. 2, 632). In 1955 income from export taxes again jumped by 50 percent, although exports (in current prices) increased by 20 percent. Given the deep deficit in the current account (defined as commodity exports plus services income minus commodity imports plus service payments) during those two years, the jump in the export tax was a serious error. It is difficult to escape the impression of the state apparatus floundering. The *improvised* approach that had now become institutionalized provided no policymaking guide at this juncture.

While the Ruiz Cortines government stood firm against those who urged exchange-control instruments to stop capital flight, it did increase import tariffs 25 percent in 1954 and put even tighter controls on the import of consumer goods. (The private sector had maintained that currency exchange controls threatened the "freedom" of the private sector and might reduce its "incentive" to invest—not a terribly convincing claim then or now.)

As mentioned, direct foreign investment now became an important stimulus to the economy. This was coupled with deep reliance on long-term borrowing from multilateral development institutions such as the World Bank. The business associations strongly supported the new opening to foreign capital and apparently did not oppose the concept of debt-financing the state's investment program. The alternative to the latter was an increase in taxes, which would have had to fall on the swollen incomes of the business elite. Thus, a short-term gain for the business elite—avoidance of a major tax increase—was traded off for a long-term problem—endemic debt financing, which became the strategic element of the stabilized growth model. The Ruiz Cortines administration apparently understood the dangers in this policy (at least to some degree) because it struggled to raise the income tax. These efforts were squashed by the industrial, banking, and commercial chambers in one of a series of strong clashes between the state and the private sector during these crisis years (Pellicer de Brody, 1978, 157).[3] Meanwhile, in 1954, after a series of consultations with the chambers, a 30 percent investment tax credit was passed, cutting deeply into the revenue sources of the state.

Another example of the increasing involvement of the business associations in high policymaking was the creation of the Consejo de Fomento y Coordinación de la Producción Nacional (Coordinating and Development Council for National Production) in 1953, which had tripartite membership: government (3 members), business (18 members), and labor participation (4 members) (Hernández Rodríquez, 1988, 47). It apparently was a prime conduit carrying the chambers' views on a host of issues—tax policy, foreign investment policy, tariff policy, support to basic industries, and so on—into the highest policymaking circle of the state (Pellicer de Brody, 1978, 162).

It is commonplace to note that Ruiz Cortines began to control the rate of increase in the money supply after 1954 and instituted other *related monetary and fiscal policy changes* of a fundamental nature. This is often seen as much of the essence of the qualitative shift in policymaking that took place in 1954–1955. But more important is the fact that it was the *nature* of the underlying relationship between the private sector and the state that had changed.[4] The private sector was able to exercise *increased* power in a crucial historical moment of economic crisis, forcing the state to increasingly rely on indirect policy instruments (such as monetary and fiscal policy) and to raise its necessary investment funds through borrowing (and from the promotion of direct foreign investment). Henceforth, the state's increasing reliance on *circulation* (borrowing and monetary policy) would indicate that the business elite had successfully redefined the terms of its struggle against the state in the course of the Ruiz Cortines sexenio.

The Making and Unmaking
of the Mexican Miracle, 1955-1970

During and after the years of the stabilized growth model (1958–1970), critics and admirers of the program were willing to agree that *in its own terms* the model was a success; the terms being the maintenance of steady growth, control of inflation, and stability of the peso. The available literature on the period is now rather dated. The evidence available suggests that the foundations of the stabilized growth model were very weak, leaving cumulative (but hidden) problems stemming from the model to surface in the 1970s and later.

The period was flanked by a serious recession in 1958–1959, when real growth of the GDP fell to zero (with population growing nearly 3 percent annually), and by a drop in the growth rate to 3.4 percent in 1970–1971. Between those two dates GDP growth in real terms averaged 6.5 percent, while inflation averaged a mere 2.8 percent per year (Ramírez, 1988, 54). From 1959 through 1969, annual real increases in industrial workers' wages were slightly less than 5 percent, which was exceptional by most standards (Bortz, 1987, 153–154).

Behind this facade of apparent prosperity were major problems directly arising from the policies pursued in the stabilized growth model. The model was built on the assumption that Mexico suffered from a shortage of domestic saving (an argument that has never been convincingly presented) and that Mexico would have to make up the shortfall in savings by borrowing abroad. (Total government debt rose from 10.2 percent of GDP in 1958 to 20.9 percent in 1967. External debt rose from 6.2 percent of GDP in 1958 to 9.0 in 1967. Thus, internal borrowing was larger and grew faster [Ortiz Mena, n.d., 28]. Nonetheless, the foreign debt had to be paid in dollars—an important distinction.) Antonio Ortiz Mena, secretary of the Treasury under presidents Adolfo Lopez Mateos (1958–1964) and Gustavo Díaz Ordaz (1964–1970), was the architect of the model. Ortiz Mena maintained that Mexico would have no present or future problem with external borrowing because Mexico had a surfeit of investment projects that would yield a high rate of return. The only constraint to growth was the supply of savings. Future payment of the interest and principal on the debt would come from the expanded economy to be created by a high rate of investment (Ortiz Mena, n.d., 24–37).

In theory, if the rate of return on investments was high enough (using rate of return in a social sense of generating a high rate of growth of gross national product), debt repayment would constitute no serious problem. But financial specialists such as Ortiz Mena often tended to overlook the essence of the growth process when adding and multiplying figures relating to savings and investment rates. Would Mexican businessmen and state managers be capable of sequentially making long-term investments that had both a high private and a high social rate of return?

Mexico was moving into the "intensive" stage of accumulation in which production depended upon high capital investments per worker and in which rising productivity per worker was necessary if investments were to pay (and pay back the accumulating foreign debt). In order to realize increases in productivity, a highly trained work force was needed that would labor side by side with an efficient management cadre. Further, it was not enough to make things efficiently and in a fundamentally new way—the products had to be sold at an increasing rate and at a price that covered costs. The latter, then, depended upon a growing mass market that was driven by wage and salary increases. To make Ortiz Mena's simple investment-driven model work, a number of conditions had to be met simultaneously. First, there had to be, an essentially new labor force adequately trained to meet new conditions of production. Second, there had to be new management cadre capable of integrating men and machines and able to understand and develop appropriate and (largely) indigenous technical change. Third, there had to be an abrupt break with the tradition of keeping wages at the subsistence level or below it. This was quite a list of demands for any society, and for Mexico it proved to be too much.

Pitfalls of Investment-led Growth

If we take the decade of the 1960s as a point of reference, we can see that the stabilized growth model was driven by investments in the public and private sectors. Investment in real terms grew at an annual rate of 10 percent—twice as fast as wages and one-third faster than the growth in GDP (INEGI, 1985, vol. 2, 611). Although a well-known argument in economic theory holds that disproportionate increases in investment based upon (1) the need to catch up from past periods of low investment, (2) the need to restructure and deepen capital goods for the industrial base, (3) the expectation of future consumer demand, and (4) exports need not be destabilizing, it remains a delicate task to show how, in fact, these complex relationships will function harmoniously to maintain steady growth. The latter is a necessity in meeting the debt payments that have underwritten this type of investment boom.

The state played a key role in the investment-driven model in two ways. First, the state allocated credit (perhaps at below market rates— this seems to have been a state secret). Second, the state subsidized the use of primary industrial inputs such as petroleum products, electricity, and transportation as well as cement, steel, lumber, and mining products. All this was accomplished through the pricing system of the parastate firms. It has been argued that the state first adopted this scheme to keep inflationary pressures down (Pellicer de Brody, 1978, 184). Like so many other improvised policy shifts, this one became permanent and directly tied to stimulating investment (rather than controlling inflation). As this policy became understood in the 1960s, the theory of state monopoly capitalism was readily applied to account for those state pricing and investment policies designed to maintain a growing supply of intermediate products for private industrial use. This policy of subsidizing the costs of production was the *push factor* of state activity in that the private sector was being *pushed* toward capital-intensive investments by the state.

Of lesser importance was the *pull factor*. The state continued to create new industries that pulled investment into new areas. From 1958 through 1966, for example, the state directly accounted for 39.2 percent of all investment (King, 1970, 48). Investment (public and private) grew at an annual average rate of 9.1 percent from 1958 through 1967—much faster than the 6.4 percent real growth of the entire economy (Ortiz Mena, n.d., 10). The state put an increased emphasis on investment for industry during these years. Francisco Vidal Bonafiz argued that Nafinsa was particularly active in these years. Its role was complemented by the Sociedad Mexicana de Crédito Industrial (Mexican Industrial Credit Corporation, or Somex), the development bank that the state acquired in 1963. Somex was quite important in creating new state investments and parastate firms in auto parts, petrochemicals, machine tools, and electronic equipment (Vidal Bonafiz, 1985, 59–86). Given these push and pull factors, the state constituted a prime moving force behind the private sector's investment boom in the miracle years.

But a number of problems came to the foreground. There was nothing in the institutional arrangement adopted to prevent an overaccumulation of capital from occurring and everything to encourage such a result. This is exactly what happened, according to several researchers, most particularly Julio Boltvinik and Enrique Hernández Laos (Boltvinik and Hernández Laos, 1981).

Chronic excess capacity (the proof of overaccumulation) necessitated high cost production, which in turn tended to lower the rate of return on capital. In the private sector the rate of profit slid steadily from 1957 to 1971 (Solís, 1986, 302). The matter of capacity utilization hinged, of course, on pricing practices. Mexico's oligopolies, monopolies, and cartels ensured that prices would be quite high, thereby reducing production below what it might have been. (Likewise, low wages undercut the growth of the internal market.) In 1970, according to one study, 1.7 percent of the industrial companies in Mexico accounted for 53.7 percent of total industrial production, and 4.6 percent of these firms accounted for 73.6 percent of production (Gollas, 1979, 272).

What of the government's rate of return? Here, apparently, the data are not sufficient to determine either a static or time-trend rate of return.[5] The parastatals had long had a higher capital intensity than had the industrial sector as a whole. Given that prices were set below production costs in the most important parastate firms, the state also engaged in the overaccumulation of state capital relative to the existing and future market. With a low rate of private and social return, past debts could not be paid, except by eliminating outlays earmarked for investments that would be necessary to maintain future growth. The only "solution" was a Ponzi scheme of increased borrowing to finance both previously accumulated debts and future growth. But this, of course, doomed the model somewhere in the future.

Along with near pervasive excess capacity that came to haunt the Mexican private sector (and most assuredly the public sector), a range of production-based questions arose. In order to maintain long-term growth Mexico needed to drastically alter its labor training program— something that was done in fits and starts in the 1960s but always insufficiently in terms of sustaining the growth model. In manufacturing, productivity increased at only a 3.6 percent rate from 1960 to 1968— well below the investment rate and significantly below the increase in real wages (Huerta, 1986, 215). This strongly implied that neither the industrial labor force nor industrial managers were equal to the task of efficiently matching the new industrial capacity with trained, capable labor. Overinvestment in capital goods was steadily combined with underinvestment in management skills and labor training. Víctor Bravo argued persuasively that "authoritarian" management patterns in the parastatals undermined the efficiency of technicians in the state sector, causing the state sector to perform below its potential (Bravo, 1979).

In this context the question of technology policy arises. Unless the state is willing and able to carefully invest in a research and development program to complement the industrialization drive, a nation will have to pay dearly for imported machinery and related licensing and royalty fees. This is not, of course, an all or nothing proposition because an underdeveloped nation cannot sidestep its technological dependency. But important steps can be taken to limit the drain caused by borrowing to invest and subsequently diverting scarce borrowed funds toward payments for inappropriate technologies. Mexican universities and the private sector are notorious for their neglect of this issue. In the 1980s, for example, Mexico devoted six times *less* of its GDP to research and development than did Korea (Guadarrama, 1988, 70).

Industry and Debt in the Stabilized
Growth Model: Central Contradictions

In terms of altering the structure of the economy toward industry, the stabilized growth model achieved considerable success. According to some measures of the sectoral distribution of the GDP, manufacturing industry increased from 21.1 percent of total production in 1955 to 26.5 percent in 1967 (Hansen, 1971, 59). Other sources place manufacturing industry's weight in GDP at 18.3 percent in 1956 and 22.8 percent in 1970 (Solís, 1986, 171). In either case manufacturing industry's relative share of total product increased by roughly 4 percent points at the cost of agriculture declining by roughly 5 to 5.5 percent. The new growth model paid scant attention to agriculture, and it was merely a matter of time before domestic production of wage good foodstuffs would have to be supplemented by the importation of food. (Once world prices for agricultural products declined after the Korean war, Mexico's agricultural export policy collapsed. After the period of policy chaos, that covered the years 1954–1957, a new policy of relative neglect of agriculture prevailed through the 1980s.)

Yet basing an industrialization drive on foreign borrowing introduced several problems that eventually could not be ignored. First, foreign loans and credits obtained with difficulty were used primarily to import machinery and equipment to support the industrialization effort. (This normally meant that an oversupply of such capital goods would be imported because the state's subsidies—accelerated depreciation, investment tax credits, exemptions of the tariff laws, and subsidized inputs from the parastates such as PEMEX—all encouraged the private sector to accumulate machinery and neglect more labor-intensive methods of production.) But state policies were not the only factor contributing to capital imports because firms undoubtedly increased their capital stock in order to (1) increase market share, (2) compete with new foreign firms, and (3) weaken labor by substituting capital at the point of production. Second, foreign loans financed imported technology in the form of royalties, patents, licensing, and service fees. Third, foreign loans paid for food. Fourth, hard currencies were sought and utilized by those who intermittently engaged in capital flight.

With such apparent weaknesses in Ortiz Mena's miracle model, the question to pursue is why the model was followed to its "logical" end. The answer is that the model was another example of an improvisation intended to solve a conjunctural problem that arose between 1953 and 1958 (that is, the collapse of the export-led agriculture boom).

Had the state been a purely capitalist state rather than taking the capitalist-renter form, considerable attention would probably have been directed toward the more subtle weaknesses of the model. Riddled as it was by *amiguismo* and by state managers who found it to be a lucrative means of personal "primitive accumulation," the state could not borrow extensively without substantial portions of these funds being diverted to personal ends. In this sense a portion of top state managers used the state to appropriate wealth.[6] The essence of the rentier ethos was to appropriate but not *produce* wealth. A capitalist state engaged in two functions: accumulation and legitimation. The capitalist-renter form added two other functions: *personal* accumulation and widespread misman- agement of state employees and businesses. Rentier interests lived in the world of the short run and within the confines of the sphere of money and commercial capital. The question of technology, capital-labor ratios, social rates of return, long-term investment strategies of the parastates, control of capital flight, and so on were beyond the interests and capabilities of the balance-sheet mentality of rentier policymakers such as Ortiz Mena.

There is no attempt here to imply that a purely capitalist state would necessarily have solved the accumulation problem, nor to beg the question by assuming that to construct a developed economy one first must have a capitalist state. The latter would abstract from the very problem of development and essentially assume it away by suggesting that devel- opment would have to be preceded by a social agent that was already *developed*. Rather, it is here affirmed that the state, even if it can exercise a certain degree of autonomy (from, in this case, the old agro-export, banking elite) and serve as a catalyst in the development process, must nonetheless be organically linked to and derived from the very society that objectively demands a structural transformation. The old institutions, habits of thought, and behavior do not die simply because they are antithetical to emerging social objectives—not, at least, in the short run.

The Parastate Industries in the Miracle Years

In 1964, when the government first began to report the total sales of the parastate firms (majority-owned companies and "decentralized" state industries such as PEMEX, the state-owned rail company, the electricity company, and so on), the amount was equal to that taken by the state in all forms of taxation and other revenues, excluding borrowing (INEGI, 1985, vol. 2, 632–634). Parastate sales were equal to 11.6 percent of the GDP. Clearly, the parastate sector, midway through the years of the stabilized growth period, had reached considerable size. Although researchers rarely mention the role played by the parastate firms in the miracle years, aside from noting that they functioned to provide cheap inputs to the private sector, it should here be noted that the number of parastate firms increased from 146 in 1955 to 336 in 1970. The strongest growth came between 1966 and 1970 when 87 new state firms were created (Vidal Bonafiz, 1985, Appendix 1). The firms created and purchased (from the private sector) during this period were of varying size—making number counting only the crudest of methodologies. The largest were (1) a foreign-owned electric power company acquired in 1960 through nationalization, (2) a foreign-owned truck and bus complex, Diesel Nacional (National Diesel, or DINA), and (3) the investment bank, SOMEX, which owned more than thirty manufacturing companies. SOMEX owned a number of auto-related corporations. With DINA and these auto parts companies, the state attempted (through joint ventures with foreign auto producers) to build a national auto industry.

López Mateos was the president who revived hopes of a national project for development through his emphasis on "Mexicanization"—the majority ownership by Mexicans of industrial, and particularly mining, companies. In 1961, he modified the mining laws to assure national majority ownership in that sector. In 1962 he issued a decree that national policy would be to build an integrated automobile industry (Vidal Bonafiz, 1985, 68). A genuine attempt was made to utilize the producing and buying power of the various state-owned motor and auto parts firms to assist in the development of the auto industry (Blair, 1964, 228; Camarena, 1981, 30). According to Douglas Bennett and Kenneth Sharpe, "The López Mateos administration brought with it a concern for strong state action to re-stimulate import substitution" (Bennett and Sharpe, 1982, 198). According to Olga Pellicer de Brody, "From late 1959 onward the Mexican government adopted new measures in economic policymaking that basically entailed greater participation by the Public sector in the economy emphasizing industrial activities" (Pellicer de Brody, 1978, 287).

Timothy King's study of Mexican industrialization also emphasized López Mateos's renewed stress on import substitution, noting that he aimed for a national materials component of 60 percent in the manufacture of autos. López Mateos also issued a list of manufactured products that he wished to see developed, noting that in these areas protection and subsidies would be readily available (King, 1970, 42). King noted that the administration "took steps in both the electronics and the car industries to promote 'integration'—in other words government powers were used to ensure that some high percentage of the costs of materials came from domestic sources" (King, 1970, 42).

Another area of state involvement was the petrochemical industry. New parastate firms were created and sizable sums of state funds invested. Yet in spite of the sectoral stress on new national industries, the pervasive logic of the strategy followed by López Mateos and Díaz Ordaz in regard to state investments and industrial policy was to emphasize the production of intermediate products (oil, electricity, fertilizer, steel, cement, chemicals, trucks, and so on) sold at near or below production costs. This was intended to raise the profit margin of domestic and transnational firms, that would thereby be encouraged to expand their investments in the future.

As the parastate firms grew rapidly there was an attempt to impose greater order on the various components of the state apparatus. In 1962 a new law to control the investments of the state was passed that attempted to unite the plans and projects of the office of the presidency with those of the Treasury, the secretary of Industry and Commerce, and Natural Resources (Pellicer de Brody, 1978, 283). In 1965 President Díaz Ordaz followed with an augmentation of this legislation designed to place the Secretariats of the Presidency, Natural Resources, and the Treasury in charge of producing an integrated investment plan for the twenty largest parastate firms. The program was to include not only considerations of future capital expansion but also integration of pricing policies, financing arrangements, expenditures, and so on. In these two pieces of legislation the state was attempting to unify and coordinate its largest parastate firms in order to determine and direct the impact that the state sector would have upon the economy.

The 1965 effort to impose greater rationality on the parastate sector arose for pragmatic reasons. Timothy King noted that in 1964 there was a near doubling of private sector borrowing. This occurred because several of the major state agencies were quickly moving to complete state projects at the end of the sexenio. Following the boom in state sector investments, the private sector rushed to expand as well—a response that tended to deny the "stabilizing" premises of the stabilized growth model (King, 1970, 42). This burst of activity was followed in 1965 with a considerable cut in state investments (-7 percent).

This "political business cycle" served to undercut the stabilized growth model. The prerogatives of presidentialism stood at odds with Ortiz Mena's objectives of steady growth in the state sector. (Typically a new president enters office without a clear plan. Thus, outlays are low in the first year. By the sixth year state investments reach a fever pitch as the president rushes to finish "his" projects.) Clearly, the state firms needed coordination, and the state needed an investment plan.

For all of this, however, the attempts to impose order and stimulate certain sectors were neither well conceived nor well executed. The improvised, hesitant nature of these efforts stood out, as Pellicer de Brody noted: "The growth in manufacturing activities in these years, although surprising, was without question anarchic, in spite of the timid attempts and good intentions of those in charge of industrial policy to impose order" (Pellicer de Brody, 1978, 290).

A similar overall evaluation of the period came from the researchers of CEPAL in their 1979 study *Principales Rasgos del Proceso de Industrialización (Principal Characteristics of the Industrialization Process)*. Duly noting the strong growth in the economy, particularly in manufacturing industry, they nonetheless adopt a critical view throughout the book. For example, they attacked the import-substitution policy of the 1960s for its lack of "any general program where a concrete declaration of the viable social objectives meriting attention are to be addressed within the adopted growth model" (CEPAL, 1979, 40). In an earlier work they were particularly critical of the fact that the various *indirect* forms of state policymaking (such as fiscal policy and tariff policy) had absolutely no systematic and controlled connection to the policies pursued by other parts of the state apparatus, such as the parastate firms (Nafinsa-CEPAL, 1971, 165–166). The overall image of the period was one of very general emphasis on manufacturing industrialization *within an environment lacking systematic efforts to coordinate state activities, define objectives or evaluate and learn from past efforts.*

Not all research into the period was so condemning of the state's role. For example, Leopoldo Solís noted that a number of studies claimed to have found a new efficiency in state policymaking in terms of mounting strongly countercyclical programs when the economy headed toward a slowdown. But Solís rejected such an approach, claiming that the state in fact engaged in a political business cycle during the period of the sexenio. It actually destabilized the economy. Further, although he conceded that one can find a "certain compensating effect" in economic policymaking, the state simply lacked a sufficient degree of coordination within its apparatus to perform the function of the countercyclical stabilizing agent (Solís, 1986, 295).

There was a rather crude functionality to general state policies, that from a certain perspective suggested a high degree of rationality. Some, researchers stress this to the exclusion of more tightly focused critiques. For example, Miguel Ángel Rivera Rios reflected on the decade of the 1960s and found a definite *pattern* to the state's activities. He stressed the size of the state's investment in industry and the aforementioned pricing policy designed to support private sector profits (Rivera Rios, 1986, 45).

As is often the case, what was found to be true about the period seemed to be determined in part by the questions raised and the type of evaluative criteria employed. For example, those who viewed the matter from a distance and in very broad terms found the state's role to be functional and to confirm the hypotheses of state monopoly capitalism. Others, such as CEPAL, made more detailed examinations and argued that the state was faltering and blundering on a sizable scale. Yet, as has been argued in Chapter 2, the state was neither a carefully designed machine to facilitate growth nor a bastion for the exercise of directionless bureaucratic caprice, but something of both. It was a historical subject burdened with accumulated and institutionalized weaknesses and subjected to a new compulsion to realize a growth project that exceeded its capacity.

Business-State Relations in the Stabilized Growth Period

During the stabilized growth period there were two serious clashes between the state and the business elite. The first occurred as a result of three actions by López Mateos. First, he stated that he identified with the extreme Left of the Mexican Revolution. Second, he quickly recognized the Cuban revolutionary government in 1959. Third, in late 1960 he nationalized a foreign-owned electric power corporation. Massive capital flight ensued—Roger Hansen placed the flight at 1.5 percent of the GDP (Hansen, 1971, 221). The administration was faced with a coordinated campaign of public resistance on the part of the key business associations (CONCAMIN, CONCANACO, and Coparmex). López Mateos acted almost immediately to reassure the business associations that he had no more nationalizations in mind and that his was a probusiness government. In a systematic study of this confrontation, Juan Martínez Nava concluded that the event demonstrated a new capacity among the largest business groups to act in unison to openly define the limits of state intervention.

In 1961, real private investment fell 12 percent, causing total investment (private and government) to stagnate (Ceceña Cervantes, 1982, 336). According to Martínez Nava, this struggle to define the path of accumulation was highly significant. The business associations had become sufficiently sophisticated to combine their economic power and define their own autonomous political project. Relative state autonomy from the financial and landholding oligarchy of the groups was clearly on the decline:

> after decades of being the principal beneficiary of the accelerated growth and industrialization of the country, [the business elite] had consolidated autonomous economic power that now signified their own specific political presence. With this there had arisen a greater capacity for the economically dominant class to condition or influence state activity: in the case of Mexico there is a new and growing evidence of the influence of the socioeconomic structures over political structures and over the state itself.
>
> These structural conditions . . . have now resulted in a decline in the margin of the relative autonomy of the Mexican state (Martínez Nava, 1982, 158).

In 1964, López Mateos attempted to engage in a much needed tax reform. He sought to reduce the chronic and structural reliance on borrowing used to finance the state's large investment program. He was defeated, primarily by the organized power of the business elite (Fitzgerald, 1985, 225). It has been argued on more than one occasion that Mexico has had the most regressive tax system (and the most lightly taxed business elite) in all of Latin America. Whether this is accurate, it is certainly evident that the Mexican state's autonomy seemed to evaporate whenever the question of tax reform was raised.

Table 3.2 clearly demonstrates that capital was strongly favored in the stabilizing growth period, with capital's share of the income tax falling from roughly 50 percent in 1955 to 14 percent in 1966. (As can be seen in Table 6.3 of Chapter 6, capital's share of income has been larger than that of labor's.) The British economist Nicholas Kaldor, commissioned by the Mexican government in the 1960s to conduct a (still only partially released) study of the Mexican tax system, concluded that given the government's declared "revolutionary" aims, the Mexican tax system was without parallel among societies with similar goals for its favoritism toward the business elite (cited in Hansen, 1971, 266).

Some have seen within the fiscal policy of all-out favoritism to the wealthy a deeper design. If taxes were to be set so low (in Ortiz Mena's model because "high" taxes would reduce domestic savings), the state would have to borrow internally and abroad in order to finance the industrialization project. But this meant, according to some observers, that the state would constantly be permitting the atavistic Mexican banking elite to exercise an *implicit veto* over the state's projects by

Table 3.2: Direct Taxes on Labor and Capital Incomes: 1955-1966
(millions of current pesos, or percent)

Year	(1) Direct Taxes on Labor Income	(2) Column 1 as a % of all Personal Income Taxes	(3) Direct Taxes on Capital Income	(4) Column 3 as a % of all Personal Income Taxes
1955	336	48.0	364	52.0
1956	423	50.2	419	49.8
1957	512	52.3	467	47.7
1958	598	56.3	452	43.1
1959	684	60.2	452	39.8
1960	844	58.9	588	41.1
1961	972	59.5	661	40.5
1962	1,369	63.8	761	35.5
1963	1,740	69.7	713	28.6
1964	2,137	69.7	892	29.1
1965	2,646	78.7	710	21.0
1966	2,893	82.9	500	14.3

Source: Based on and calculated from data presented in Centro de Estudios Contables, "Es Justo Nuestro Sistema de Impuestos?" in Leopold Solís (compilador), *La Economía Mexicana*, vol. 2 (México: Fondo de Cultura, 1973), p. 62.

refusing to fund the internal portion of the government's debt (Hernández Rodríquez, 1988, 43). Whether this was a consciously developed policy is unknown. But the *structural* effect of such low taxes on capital's share was to give the business elite and particularly the banking faction of that elite a uniquely powerful role to play in either supporting or opposing changes in the industrialization policies.

Theoretical Interpretations of the Stabilized Growth Period

When in the early 1970s, it became clear that stabilized growth was no longer attainable and that a new era of macroeconomic instability had arrived, an attempt was made to determine where the flaws in the model were located. From this discussion, it is possible to identify three dominant theoretical interpretations of the period. The first has been labeled "external imbalances"; the second "underconsumption"; and the third, "the falling rate of profit." No one theory adequately accounted for the collapse of the stabilized growth model.

External Imbalance

One view, widely shared among researchers, maintained that the key to the crisis was to be found in the state's ability or inability to maintain a stable balance of payments on the foreign account. Failure to do so drew down the nation's foreign exchange and eventually led to a devaluation of the currency. This caused inflation in the price of imported goods and led to internal restrictions of credit to combat the imported inflation. The most vigorous attempt to explain Mexico's economic recessions and the structural crisis that commenced at the end of the 1960s by way of an analysis of fluctuations in foreign trade was made by Rene Villareal in his book *El Desequilibrio Externo en la Industrialización de México (External Deficits and the Industrialization of Mexico)* (Villareal, 1976). Variants of Villareal's thesis were relatively widespread in the literature on Mexico's industrialization, giving rise to what has here been termed the "external imbalances" thesis. (See, for example, Hernández Laos, 1985; Casar and Ros, 1984; Trejo Reyes, 1987; and Villareal, 1982.)

The argument of this thesis was relatively straightforward: Mexico's version of import-substitution industrialization concentrated first on the national production of simple consumer goods and then later on the production of intermediate goods, which the new parastatals produced and sold at subsidized prices to the private industrial sector. Meanwhile, imports of capital goods were encouraged by way of exemptions in the tariff laws and tax incentives that encouraged the rapid mechanization of production processes. Inevitably, the *benefit* of the value of the new national goods produced (in terms of eliminating these goods from the import side of the foreign trade account) was *less than* the increasing amount of machinery and equipment imported to sustain the industrialization drive.

Furthermore, the argument went, given the shortage of internal savings, the foreign trade sector faced a structural problem: The stimulus of imported funds had to be balanced against the future outflow of interest and principal payments on the foreign debt, which was accumulating to keep the rate of investment high. The encouraging of direct foreign investments led to the future outflow of repatriated profits and royalty payments.

This argument, however, was suspect. The amounts involved did *not* appear to be large enough to have undermined Mexico's long period of growth. In 1970, for example, 1.67 percent of Mexico's total income went abroad to pay for interest, principal, royalties, and repatriated profits on its foreign debt and foreign investments (Boltvinik and Torres, 1986, 31). New debt was constantly acquired between 1956 and 1967. But new foreign borrowing annually ranged between .01 and .025 of total GDP (Nafinsa-CEPAL, 1971, Table 28). In viewing data such as these, it is difficult to attribute the downfall of stabilizing growth to external financial factors. They were, of course, contributing elements in that

Mexico needed to increase its exports of manufactures in order to counter the debt-related outflows. This, however, did not occur.

In viewing the trade in manufactures, there can be little doubt that Villareal and others pinpointed an acute weakness in Mexico's form of capital accumulation. As can be seen from Table 3.3, after 1962 Mexico failed to significantly reduce its reliance on the importation of capital goods and consumer durables (column 3). Nor was Mexico able to proportionately increase its manufacturing exports to cover its steady reliance on capital goods imports. Rather, as can be seen in column 5, manufacturing exports as a share of GNP fell steadily from 1955 through 1968.

Yet problems arose even within the context of this argument. Given (1) that the foreign trade sector was not abnormally large (imports, for example, were 9 percent of GNP in 1962—a relatively modest figure) and (2) that the merchandise deficit in the account on commodity trade and services was not extreme (for example, the deficit in 1967 was 0.16 percent of GDP), it is not immediately obvious that the shifts in macroeconomic performance were adequately described by an argument that took the foreign trade sector as its point of departure. Until the mid-1960s Mexico could well afford its reliance on foreign machinery because agricultural exports kept the merchandise trade deficit low. When Mexico became a net importer of agricultural commodities from the 1970s onward, however, the reliance on capital goods imports created a more immediate problem. But this situation tended to shift the locus of the breakup of the stabilizing growth model from the area of external imbalances to that of *internal imbalances between the industrial and agricultural sectors.*

Furthermore, it remains an unproven assumption that Mexico suffered from a chronic, endemic savings shortage during this period. Mexico certainly suffered from an inadequate financial structure in terms of having large, efficient, and readily accessible capital markets. Most investment was conducted by utilizing internally generated retained earnings either from industrial and trade companies or from the large banking groups that generally financed their own nonbanking corporations. The act of saving and investing was conducted by a small, interlocked group of the business elite. Dwight Brothers estimated that 65 to 80 percent of private investment in Mexico in the 1950s and early 1960s came from retained earnings of the groups—they did not circulate through an "open" market for credit via the banking system (Brothers, 1973, 206). The private banks offered practically no credit to agriculture; between 1947 and 1952, for example, roughly 90 percent of credit to this sector came from the state (Torres, 1984, 80). There was a virtual absence of adequate financial institutions available to productively utilize

Table 3.3: Industial Import Coefficients* and Manufacturing Exports

Year	(1) Consumer Non-durables (IC)*	(2) Intermediat Goods (IC)*	(3) Consumer Durables & Capital Goods (IC)*	(4) Total Manu-factures (IC)*	(5) Manufacturing Exports as a Share of GNP (IC)*	(6) Manufacturing Exports as a Share of Manufacturing Production
1929	0.35	0.56	0.96	0.56	n.a.	n.a.
1939	0.22	0.56	0.90	0.46	n.a.	n.a.
1950	0.07	0.42	0.74	0.31	3.3%	17.7%
1951	0.07	0.50	0.76	0.37	2.9%	16.0%
1952	0.07	0.46	0.74	0.34	2.5%	13.3%
1953	0.08	0.42	0.72	0.33	2.4%	13.5%
1954	0.06	0.39	0.68	0.29	2.7%	15.0%
1955	0.06	0.41	0.70	0.31	3.0%	15.9%
1956	0.07	0.43	0.71	0.34	2.8%	15.0%
1957	0.06	0.40	0.68	0.32	2.5%	13.4%
1958	0.06	0.40	0.69	0.31	2.6%	13.8%
1959	0.07	0.34	0.64	0.28	2.4%	12.1%
1960	0.06	0.35	0.67	0.30	2.5%	13.0%
1961	0.05	0.33	0.69	0.29	2.6%	13.4%
1962	0.06	0.31	0.63	0.27	2.7%	13.8%
1963	0.06	0.31	0.59	0.26	2.7%	13.8%
1964	0.06	0.31	0.58	0.27	2.4%	11.7%
1965	0.06	0.29	0.55	0.26	2.0%	9.4%
1966	0.06	0.27	0.51	0.25	2.2%	9.9%
1967	0.06	0.24	0.53	0.25	1.8%	8.3%
1968	0.05	0.24	0.52	0.24	2.0%	8.9%
1969	0.05	0.22	0.50	0.23	2.1%	9.5%
1970	0.04	0.21	0.47	0.20	n.a.	6.0%

Year						
1971	0.04	0.21	0.44	0.19	1.6%	n.a.
1972	0.04	0.21	0.46	0.19	1.8%	n.a.
1973	0.05	0.23	0.49	0.22	2.0%	n.a.
1974	0.06	0.26	0.53	0.26	2.1%	n.a.
1975	0.04	0.22	0.55	0.25	1.4%	n.a.
1976	0.04	0.20	0.51	0.22	1.9%	n.a.
1977	0.03	0.20	0.45	0.19	1.9%	11.5%
1980	n.a.	0.25	0.55	0.31	1.8%	8.4%

* Import coefficient, IC = M/(M + Q), where M = Imports, for sector of origin, Q = total domestic production for sector of origin.

Sources: Julio Boltvinik and Enrique Hernández Laos, "Origen de la Crisis Industrial," in Rolando Cordera (compilador), *Desarrollo y Crisis de la Economía Mexicana* (México: Fondo de Cultura, 1981), p. 477; Nafinsa-CEPAL, *La Política Industrial en el Desarrollo de México* (México: Nafinsa, 1971), Table 10; René Villareal, "De la Industrialización Sustitutiva a la Petrodependencia," in Hector González (compilador), *El Sistema Económica Mexicano* (México: La Red Jonas, 1982), p. 36.

savings from the middle classes, medium-sized business interests, or intermediate-sized agricultural producers.

Neither the government nor the banking leaders moved to create a competitive and efficient system of financial markets. That the government did not do so would fit with the argument that several researchers have made regarding the structure of economic power in Mexico. Prominent works in this area have generally claimed that the banking elite (usually defined as finance capital) was the *dominant faction* of the business elite and that the large banking interests had a considerable degree of influence in diverting the state from an attempt to rationalize the antiquated and monopolistic national banking system (Conchiero, 1978; Hernández Rodríquez, 1988). Finally, the low savings argument failed to consider the role played by conspicuous consumption. The lack of adequate financial instruments and methods to lure savings into the banking system would accentuate the expenditure of these funds on ostentatious forms of consumption. Although there is no question that difficulties with the balance of payments were an element in explaining Mexico's problems with capital accumulation, the assumptions built into the external imbalances argument are too weak to serve as a complete explanation for the breakdown of the stabilized growth model by the late 1960s.

Underconsumption

The underconsumption interpretation of the structural crisis of the 1970s concentrated upon internal factors of a much broader nature, particularly the role of effective demand. Underconsumption analyses have a long legacy in the history of economic thought, with the twentieth-century variants of this theory emphasizing that the more equally income is distributed, the higher will be the portion of income spent on consumption. According to this argument, in contrast to the Ortiz Mena formulation, high savings constituted a brake on capital accumulation because a high-saving society was one with a high degree of income inequality. This meant that the society would quickly "overinvest" (because the domestic market is limited) and then would subsequently reduce investments in future years, thereby lowering effective demand. The underconsumptionists emphasized the very high levels of income inequality existing in Mexico. They stressed that the amount of income received by the bottom 40 percent of the population was steadily declining. As Table 3.4 demonstrates, the underconsumptionists were partially correct. The bottom 40 percent suffered declines in their income share, but the next 40 percent experienced increases—with the top 10 percent experiencing steady decline through 1970. The data, then, were mixed and not sufficient to bolster the underconsumptionist argument.

Table 3.4: Mexico, Distribution of Income (% Share)

Income Groups (Deciles)	1950	1963	1968	1970	1977	1983*
I	2.43	1.69	1.21	1.42	1.08	1.3
II	3.17	1.97	2.21	2.34	2.21	2.7
III	3.18	3.42	3.04	3.49	3.23	3.8
IV	4.29	3.42	4.23	4.54	4.42	5.0
V	4.93	5.12	5.07	5.46	5.73	6.3
VI	5.96	6.08	6.46	8.24	7.15	7.9
VII	7.04	7.85	8.28	8.24	9.11	9.8
VIII	9.63	12.38	11.39	10.44	11.98	12.6
IX	13.89	16.45	16.06	16.61	17.09	17.1
X	45.58	41.6	42.05	39.21	37.99	33.5
Xa (second 5%)	(10.38)	(13.04)	(14.90)	(11.52)	(12.54)	---
Xb (top 5%)	(35.10)	(28.56)	(27.15)	(27.69)	(25.45)	---

* Preliminary results

Sources: Instituto Nacional de Estadística, Geografía e Informática (INEGI), *Estadísticas Históricas de México* (México: Secretaría de Programación y Presupuesto [SPP], 1985), p. 233; INEGI, *Encuesta Nacional de Ingreso-Gasto de los Hogares* (México: SPP, 1986).

There seemed to be an *element* of underconsumption in the pre-1970 experience *and* an element of income redistribution. Which effect was more powerful? The bottom 40 percent lost 2.12 percent of the total income from 1950 through 1970, while the next 50 percent (groups V–IX in Table 3.4) gained 7.75 percent. Even though the new middle class (V–IX) had a lower propensity to consume than did the bottom 40 percent, the modest standard of living of the lower part of this middle class combined with high aspirations in regard to consumption patterns would tend to support the argument that *in toto* Mexico did not have an underconsumption problem (in a *relative* sense) during these years. In an *absolute* sense (in the sense that even in 1970 the top 10 percent received 39.4 percent of the income), it could be argued that had there been even more of a decline in the share of this group from 1950–1970 Mexico would have had a much greater and more sustainable growth experience. In this latter sense the underconsumption argument was more defensible, but even here it failed to show why a structural crisis should appear when the distribution of income was, in the aggregate (and relative) sense improving.

Although termed underconsumptionist, the analysts who belonged to this group put emphasis on the dependency arguments regarding a chronic outflow of the economic surplus due to (1) direct foreign investment, (2) technology dependence, and (3) foreign borrowing (bank loans). In addition, the theory of oligopoly played a major role in attempts to explain the breakdown of the stabilized growth model. One of the most widely read interpretations that attempted to explain Mexico's economic crisis from this perspective was written by José Ayala (along with four co-authors) in a well-distributed and discussed book, *México, Hoy* (Mexico Today) (Ayala, 1979, 19–96). By utilizing the dependency framework the underconsumptionist could explain why balance-of-payments problems (such as the drain from profit, interest, and technology payments) were likely. At the same time the undercomsumption argument suggested that growth would inevitably end in the ditch of stagnation due to weak demand for the internal market. The oligopoly argument added a third important component to the theory: As growth proceeded there was a tendency for the larger corporations and companies to absorb the smaller. According to Ayala's data, in 1960, 1.8 percent of the industrial firms accounted for 77.8 percent of the value of industrial production, whereas in 1970, 1.6 percent of the firms accounted for 72.9 percent (Ayala, 1979). According to oligopoly theory, the high degree of industrial concentration meant that firms would have the power to push up prices. The higher prices would then limit the growth of the market. This in turn would reduce the tendency of the oligopoly firms to domestically reinvest their profits for further growth. When this argument was combined with underconsumption and dependency considerations, Mexico faced a "self-limiting growth model."

Further limiting capital formation were the transnational firms that were directing their investment toward a very narrow market consisting of the upper middle class and the elite. These firms did not adapt their productive apparatus to the needs and peculiarities of the nation but rather sought to sell their already existing products in an "external" (for example, Third World) market. Thus, direct foreign investment would have limited spillover effects because only a small amount of investment was needed to meet a limited market. Meanwhile, the oligopoly structure would permit very high profits, which could be withdrawn from the nation.

Here was a more inclusive argument than that presented by the external imbalances thesis, especially because it could be seen to complement this thesis. There were, however, five problems with the underconsumption model, which were associated with Keynesian-type models in general. First, the underconsumption argument was at best only partially born out by the data. As mentioned previously, in the relative sense Mexico's income distribution could be seen as *improving* in the aggregate. (This should not be seen as a cavalier argument disdaining the wretched and often worsening conditions of the bottom 40 percent of the population. Unquestionably, the underconsumptionists' deep and continued concern with the need to link growth models to a modicum of social justice provided a welcome antidote to more me-chanistic analyses that overlook this issue.)

Second, there was no conscious theory of the state employed. That is, the underconsumptionists did not explore and utilize the literature regarding the relationship between the state and the dominant economic powers to show how policymaking was derived. The state was again a "black box"—presumably a neutral and transparent entity that at one moment could build a self-limited model and in the next build a populist model based on income redistribution.

Third, the production process, and contradictions arising within the production process, played no role in the model, which was demand driven and determined. Supply was not discussed. As in other Keynesian models, production problems were assumed away, along with the labor process, labor unions, technology, and related considerations.

Fourth (deriving from the third point), the question of sectoral imbalances determining or helping to determine the accumulation process was not examined. For example, in the above critique of the external imbalances assumption of undersaving, emphasis was placed on the sectoral imbalance between (1) a state program that sought to transform the manufacturing sector and (2) a banking system left in a preindustrial mode.

Fifth, in emphasizing the need to alter income distribution, proponents of this interpretation insufficiently acknowledged how the distributional breakdown between capital and labor affected the accumulation process, particularly in a nation such as Mexico. Redistributing income, John M. Keynes argued, would raise the level of consumption and thereby raise profit expectations leading to increases in production, investment, and growth *if* the increase in demand was not absorbed by price increases from oligopoly firms. But income redistribution—however moderate and gradual—cut both ways. That is, although we could emphasize, as did Keynes, the demand-enhancing aspect of income redistribution, we would also have to note that if capitalists' incomes declined due to income redistribution, this could only mean that the mass and rate of profit had declined. This tended to discourage investment and production, and in Mexico even the hint of such a step could and did encouraged devastating capital flight. Thus, although the Ayala version of the underconsumption argument was preferable over that of the "external imbalances" thesis, there were very strong arguments against a complete acceptance of this theory.

The Falling Rate of Profit

Only a small number of articles and books written on the breakdown of the stabilized growth model adopted a framework of analysis different than the preceding interpretations. Of interest in terms of its power to explain the twists and turns of the economy prior to 1971 was a body of work developed by economists who have published in the journal *Teoría y Política*. This group, rejecting dependency analyses and criticizing underconsumption theory, presented a forceful interpretation of the period.

In a concise treatment, Joaquin Vela González began his study with the assumption that a capitalist economy could not avoid economic crisis—there was no "model" of accumulation that could be maintained (Vela González, 1983). Business cycles, crises, slumps, panics, and so on were all endemic to capitalist economies. This was true for the two hundred fifty-year existence of capitalism as a system, so Mexico could hardly be expected to avoid these cycles no matter how *sui generis* the economy might have been. Next, he argued that Mexico only entered into the stage of full capitalism in the mid-1950s. Prior to that Mexico was still dominated by "extensive" forms of backward production—with the accompanying institutions and social-behavioral patterns and perspectives that one would anticipate from a mode of production that was evolving toward a "pure" capitalist form.

This argument could be deduced by observing cyclical behavior prior to 1958. These cycles were fundamentally induced by recessions in the United States, showing that Mexico had a disarticulated economy that depended on "external" export stimuli coupled with "extensive" production methods within the internal market (Vela González, 1983, 75–76). But

> the crisis of 1958 represents a point of transition between the extensive and intensive phases of the development of capitalism in Mexico. The fall in the growth rate and in the rate of investment, that indicated the crisis and the recession in this and the following year, were directly influenced by the termination of the growth of the merchant-capital sector (la ecónomia mercantil) and the halt in the growth of the new industries that had been created by the import-substitution program. In this context Mexico felt for the first time the effects of the falling rate of profit on internal investment. Over and above these effects the conjuncture of 1958–59 was determined by the world recession that had a considerable impact on the United States economy. . . . We will term this a crisis of *transition* given that the endogenous elements that derive from the innate tendencies of capital accumulation have now acquired a unprecedented weight (Vela González, 1983, 76).

After 1960 Mexico entered into a new phase that was driven by both the state (which was more oriented toward facilitating accumulation) and the influx of capital from abroad. When in 1971 the boom in the industrial sector ended, with manufacturing production having jumped 111 percent between 1960 and 1969, *exports did not decline*, which indicated the *endogenous* nature of the slump (Vela González, 1983, 84).

In what was the major effort by the *Teoría y Política* group, Miguel Ángel Rivera Rios extended and deepened many of the arguments just summarized in *Crisis y Reorganización del Capitalismo Mexicano* (Rivera Rios, 1986). Rivera Rios argued that as the economy shifted into the "intensive" stage, capitalists had to adopt new, often capital-intensive methods of production. This was particularly true when Mexican capitalists began to develop investments in intermediate and capital goods industries where the efficient level of production demanded very large outlays for fixed capital that could not be recouped for long periods of time. Here the risk of overexpanding a given market was higher due to the fact that the recoupment period was so long and the mass of capital committed was often "lumpy" (an entire plant often had to be bought). It was difficult to know how "rational" the investment decision would turn out to be. As the market grew, the various competitors attempted to increase their share under the grow-or-die syndrome. But by how much? If the various participants overinvested, in the sense that *collectively* they bought too much equipment given the absolute size of the market, a pullback in investment would ensue. But given the time lags, they could not individually know that a mistake had been made—potentially a very big mistake—until it was too late.

Given the new intensive stage and the support that the state was making to the accumulation process (in terms of low prices of industrial inputs and subsidies to encourage rapid capital accumulation), it was only a matter of time, Rivera Rios argued, before the innate "contradictions" inherent in the competitive struggle to capture markets would manifest themselves in an endogenous business cycle brought on by the falling rate of profit, which itself was but an expression of the overcapitalization of various key industries.

This rather standard treatment of the overaccumulation process was buttressed by an "uneven development" theory. Here Rivera Rios and Vela González argued that when the state shifted toward the underwriting of heavy industry, it all but totally neglected agriculture. Public expenditures for agriculture, including infrastructure and irrigation, fell from 20 percent of total state investments in 1940–1949 to 9 percent in 1960–1970 (Rivera Rios, 1986, 50). As a consequence, the growth in agricultural output eventually began to lag far behind that of the rest of the economy. In 1960–1965 real agricultural output increased at a 6.2 percent annual rate, but output subsequently fell to 1.2 percent in 1965–1970 and 0.58 percent in 1971–1976 (Guillén, 1984, 101).

Inefficient *minifundistas* (small landowners) stayed on the land, limiting the supply of qualified industrial labor. Simultaneously, their inefficient methods—unchanged because of a lack of commitment on the part of the state in developing "traditional" agriculture—caused domestic food production to lag behind consumption. This forced food imports, that eventually increased the cost of "reproducing" the industrial labor force. This increase in the reproduction costs of labor was reflected in wage increases, that further squeezed the profit rate. According to Rivera Rios' estimates, the profit rate fell, on average, 25 percent from the period 1963–1967 to 1970–1976 (Rivera Rios, 1986, 177). Writing from a much different ideological perspective, Leopoldo Solís showed a somewhat similar decline (Solís, 1986, 302).

Although (1) the implicit "instrumentalism" and functionalism of the treatment of the state in this groups' work was considerably less than adequate, (2) the discussion of the creation and changes in state policy was all but non-existent (an important oversight because in this formulation the state was held to be fundamental to the accumulation process), and (3) the distinction between "extensive" and "intensive" phases was a bit mechanical in the historical application, nonetheless this group's work was a refreshing attempt to deal with production processes and the internal contradictions of the accumulation process. The emphasis on the uneven development of industry and agriculture was particularly important.

The work of this group was, to a degree, complementary to the external imbalances thesis and the underconsumption thesis. Although their critiques of underconsumption were often well taken, it serves little purpose to dispense with all demand side (or Keynesian) considerations in order to advance a "supply side" or sphere-of-production argument. That the latter took logical precedence over the former could be cogently argued; yet this still left "aggregate demand" a role to play in the determination of the economy.

Finally, none of the theories, unfortunately, devoted much specific attention to the state as such—its policies, the struggle for autonomous policymaking power, the shifts in the relationship between the business elite and the state and so on. This was all the more curious because all of these theoretical formulations granted that the state played a fundamental role in the accumulation process from 1940 to 1970.

Notes

1. Sanford Mosk in his *Industrial Revolution in Mexico* viewed the new group as being of utmost importance in analyzing business-government relations (Mosk, 1950, 21–62). Many came forward to challenge Mosk's position. His work was

summarily dismissed in Robert Shafer's *Mexican Business Organizations* (Shafer, 1973, 108–113). Many in Mexico argued that Mosk had made too categorical a distinction and had ignored the influence that the PRI exerted on Canacintra. But Shafer's denial of Mosk's research was less than convincing.

Mosk argued that the new group could be distinguished in five ways. First, the size of its manufacturing concerns was much smaller than those owned by either the older groups or foreign investors. Second, these new manufacturers had no direct or indirect links to the private banks; they needed state intervention in order to gain access to adequate credit. Third, they adopted a Keynesian position regarding unions and wages—high wages meant an expanding market. Fourth, they believed that industrialists and the government should work together to carry-through a state-led program of industrialization. Fifth, the internal market should be the province of Mexican industrialists—foreign investors should be discouraged in every way.

Mosk believed that the new group was in a period of ascendency and would dominate CONCAMIN while displacing Coparmex. He was too optimistic. The new group was in the ascendency in the 1940s, 1950s, and 1960s. By the 1970s, however, a process of assimilation had blurred the distinctions among the business associations. Many of the most successful business leaders from Canacintra had prospered, joined CONCAMIN, and adopted an ideology that approximated Coparmex's.

The principal business associations can be arranged in terms of their ideological alignment, with their date of creation in parenthesis. Beginning with the "radical" organizations that are outspoken proponents of *hyper-laissez faire*, one first encounters Coparmex (1929) and then the Confederación de Cámas Nacionales de Comerico (Confederation of National Chambers of Commerce, or CONCANACO) (1917). Still very much on the Right, but less so that the preceding associations, one encounters CONCAMIN (1918), the Associación de Banqueros Mexicanos (Mexican Bankers Association, or ABM) (1924–1982), the Cámara Americana de Comercio (American Chamber of Commerce) (1951), and the CCE (1975). Somewhat more accommodating to the PRI's views, but nonetheless highly critical of statism, is the influential, little-know, thirty member Cámara Mexicana de Hombres de Negocios (Chamber of Mexican Businessmen, or CMHN) (1964). The only organization that would deserve the label of "moderate" is Canacintra (1942), because it has generally supported state-led development.

2. Agro-export capital relied upon labor-intensive production methods having little or no regard for technological advancement or capital-intensive methods of production. Traditional export products such as sugar, coffee, henequen, and beef were generally produced with such backward production methods.

Cotton, wheat, and a broad range of fresh produce were cultivated, primarily in the northwest, as a result of Alemán's vast state investments. Here capitalist (capital-intensive, "scientific," and "modern") methods of production prevailed in terms of machinery, cultivation, fertilizers, pest-control, packaging, and shipping.

3. As an example of the difficulty the state has had in constructing an income tax system it is worth recalling how the secretary of the Treasury conducted

the processes of the restructuring the tax system in 1947. The Treasury went directly to the chambers (CONCAMIN and CONCANACO) for ideas and for basic research on how to carry out the tax reform. On its own the Treasury conducted a survey sampling personal income in order to compute tax rates. But then the secretary, Ramon Beteta, stated, "In an additional effort to inspire confidence in the taxpayers, the Secretary of the Treasury authorized the trade and industrial chambers (CONCANACO and CONCAMIN) to *receive* the declarations of income, and to have them make the assessment and aggregation of the data in order to assure those who were sampled that the collected data would not be used against them" (Hernández Rodríquez, 1988, 46–47, italics added).

According to Rogelio Hernández Rodríquez, who examined this telling incident, "With such a decision Beteta recognized the role of the business elite as the valid interpreters of the society. . . . Here is a case of tax reform where according to Beteta confidence in carrying out the basic research could not be left in the hands of the state: the business associations had converted themselves into channels of opinion that the state recognized. It was only natural that the business elite converted such activities into a custom" (Hernández Rodríquez, 1988, 47).

4. The tendency to examine monetary and fiscal policy changes to the exclusion of other explanations of macroeconomic fluctuations was represented in Hector Guillén *Origenes de la Crisis en México* (Origins of the Crisis in Mexico) (Guillén, 1984).

5. Although state-owned firms are in the public sector in Mexico, it is often as difficult (if not more so) to locate meaningful data regarding the parastates as it is for the private sector. (For a brief discussion of this issue, see Aguilar "Capital Monopolista y Empresas Estatales" [1983, 20–46].)

6. According to Jesús Silva Herzog, one of Mexico's highest level state functionaries in the 1930s and 1940s, "Politics degrades and corrupts everyone. . . . State functionaries are rarely considered honest, they are only interested in their own gain. . . . Being a state functionary is the easiest and most profitable profession in Mexico. . . . There are many public functionaries who have made their fortune in only a few months" (quoted in Hansen, 1971, 165; also see 164–172).

4

La Docena Trágica: *1970-1982*

The twelve-year period that followed the stabilized growth era is known in Mexico as *la docena trágica* (the tragic dozen). During two successive presidential sexenios, socioeconomic problems reached an acute level. The numerous attempts on the part of the state to address these problems were judged a "tragic" failure. It was a dramatic period of experimentation with development programs that were only partially thought out, were briefly implemented, and then were abandoned. Luis Echeverría's turbulent sexenio (1970-1976) was marked by (1) two serious slumps (1971-1972 and 1975-1976), (2) massive capital flight, and (3) an open struggle between the state and the business elite that signified a permanent turning point in the relationship between the state and large capital. Echeverría's successor, José López Portillo (1976-1982), began his sexenio bound by a three-year International Monetary Fund austerity program. This was followed by (1) the petroboom (1978-1981), (2) the dependence on massive international borrowing to buoy a declining economy in 1981-1982, and (3) the bankruptcy of the state that precipitated the bank nationalization of 1982.

Although unable to restore Mexico to its former status as a model developing nation, these administrations did ironically achieve some of their principal objectives. Echeverría espoused what he termed "shared growth"—increasing wages and peasant incomes at the same rate as the economy's growth. On the whole, wages kept up with prices for the poorest elements in society, while for the more skilled, such as industrial workers, wages rose considerably. López Portillo took seriously the concept of full employment. In spite of the fact that Mexico's population growth in previous years had been more than 3 percent per year, the López Portillo administration managed to keep the rate of unemployment from growing. Both presidents viewed their administrations as "populists." In the sense that both men consistently sought to protect wages and promote employment for social elements that had been largely excluded from the benefits of the growth of the Mexican economy from 1940 to 1970, there was an important degree of truth in their claim. There have been many attempts to demonstrate the failures of the period, but one should not loose sight of the fact that on the whole the vast majority of the Mexican people received a greater share of the benefits of growth than they had previously. This was no small achievement, particularly when measured against the unmitigated failures of the subsequent administration headed by Miguel de la Madrid Hurtado (1982–1988). Nor were all these benefits to be found in increased incomes. Both presidents increased educational outlays and devoted a growing share of their budgets to housing, government distribution of food, health care, and sanitation—all elements of the "social wage." The label "tragic" projects a one-sided criticism of these administrations.

The crisis years of the Echeverría administration presented an "opportunity" to revive the powerful state of the Cárdenas period through a definite rupture with the patterns and norms established in the stabilized growth era. But, as Arnaldo Córdova emphasized (see Chapter 2), to achieve such a rupture would demand the full participation of the underlying population in the construction of a renewed populist state project. Echeverría, however, never sought the reincorporation of the masses into the struggle to redefine the growth model. A modern-day Ahab, Echeverría was determined to steer his own ship of state; the crew could pull on the lines and receive good rations, but the voyage was to be charted by the captain and his officers. Refusing to make a genuine Left turn, Echeverría and López Portillo set the stage for social forces that would steadily and quickly pull the nation to the Right. A historic opportunity was missed. At the epicenter of this historic struggle was the state—its policies, its role, and its power were in the process of fundamental transformation.

Echeverría and the Macroeconomy

In suppressing a growing student movement (that sought to challenge the hierarchical decisionmaking process that had become institutionalized throughout the government, economy, and society in the stabilized growth years), President Díaz Ordaz's unexpected, uncontrolled use of state violence brought on a crisis of state legitimation in 1968. The "massacre of 1968" revealed a surprising degree of savagery and exposed the contempt and fear the PRI held for a populist movement.

Upon taking office, President Echeverría sought to deal with this crisis through a populist posture that emphasized the need for income redistribution. He claimed that growth and income redistribution were compatible (Tello, 1979, 41). Yet neither he nor his cabinet ever demonstrated that income redistribution and growth *were* compatible, given Mexico's economic structure and political system.

With Echeverría one finds the beginnings of a shift within the economic policymaking elite toward what might be defined as "hyper-Keynesianism." That is, Keynes's emphasis on the *possibilities* (and necessities) of income redistribution were coupled uncritically with his emphasis on aggregate demand as the determining force in establishing the profit level. According to this curious brand of Keynesianism (sometimes known in Mexico and elsewhere as the Cambridge approach), income redistribution would increase mass purchasing power that would increase internal sales and in turn increase the overall level of profit. Because, it was argued, Mexico had very high levels of unused industrial capacity, an increase in aggregate demand should be met with an increase in aggregate supply. Inflation would not be a serious problem. Wage increases could be funded from a government deficit, foreign borrowing, or both. The fondness for deficits among the Cambridge devotees exceeded that championed by Antonio Ortiz Mena in the stabilized growth era. (See, for example, Eatwell and Singh, 1981, for a classic statement of this position.)

This theory gained increasing force throughout the twelve years, especially when the Cambridge-trained economist José Andrés de Oteyza became the secretary of industrial development under José López Portillo. Keynes, of course, had Britain primarily in mind in his discussion of income redistribution. In the Mexican case, the question immediately arose as to where the increase in wages was to come from. Normally wage increases occurred when the government raised the minimum wage (the benchmark for all wage and salary rates). It is also approximately the *average* wage rate (because many workers were paid somewhat below this "legal" minimum rate). Business elements responded to government-decreed wage increases with price increases. These increases led, particularly in Echeverría's sexenio, to price controls over as many as 300 basic consumer goods. But the business elite was free to raise prices on all other goods and to cut investment and production where the elite's production encountered price controls. Such actions created "shortages" in basic goods, leading to pressure to increase prices to eliminate what were usually contrived shortfalls in supply. As a result, the unions and Echeverría's government pushed to increase the minimum wage. Here, Keynes's virtuous circle became a vicious circle of wage and price increases. Furthermore, investment funds were shifted out of basic goods production into other activities, such as speculation and capital flight, or into the expansion of luxury goods production. In Mexico, wage increases were understood to lead to cuts in the profit level. Because the state was at the epicenter of the distributional struggle, the business associations pressured the government whenever the issue of redistribution was raised.

Table 4.1: Mexico, Main Economic Indicators: 1970-1976
(real cumulative growth--in percent)

Gross Domestic Product:	
Δ GDP	34.4
Δ GDP/Population	13.3
Labor	
Δ Real Urban Minimum Wage	59.3
Δ Total State Employees	62.3
Sectoral Growth	
Δ Manufacturing Industry	37.8
Δ Agriculture	3.4
Δ Agriculture/Population	-15.2
Δ Construction	61.7
Δ Government Spending	78.4
Gross Investment	
Δ Total Investment	43.0
Δ Government Investment	63.6
Δ Private Investment	31.7
Foreign Sector*	
Δ Current Account Deficit/GDP	285.7
Δ Public Foreign Debt	366.7

* In *current* dollars, adjusted at the annual exchange rate

Sources: Banamex, *Mexico Statistical Data: 1970-1980* (México: Banamex, n.d.), pp. 6-10, 28-31, 39, 51, 55; Banco de México, *Información Económica, Producto Interno Bruto, Cuaderno 1970-1979* (México: Banco de México, 1980), p. 50.

Luis Echeverría's sexenio was marked by the process outlined above. Minimum wage increases were closely followed by general price increases. Between 1971 and 1976 real wages of industrial workers increased 41 percent, (Bortz, 1985, 93). Meanwhile, the average profit rate fell 20 percent, according to Leopoldo Solís (Solís, 1986, 302) The data supported the view that wage increases (at least in Mexico) came at the expense of profits. Table 4.1 demonstrates the profound unevenness of Echeverría's sexenio. Note the appreciable increases in minimum wages, government investment (and spending), construction, and components of the foreign sector along with the *decline* in per capita agricultural output and the relatively weak growth of private investment.

It was no simple task to break the death grip that bound the Mexican economy. Accustomed to an exceedingly and notoriously high profit margin—if not in industry, then certainly in trade and banking—the business elite was adamant and confident in its struggle to halt income redistribution. (Table 4.2 shows the extensive shift in the distribution

Table 4.2: Changes in the Share Distribution of Income: 1970-1976

	Income Share (Percent of Total)*		Percent Change
	(1)	(2)	(3)
	1970	1976	1970-1976
Labor's Share	35.67	40.26	+12.8
Public Sector	10.80	12.35	+14.4
Private Sector	24.69	27.31	+10.6
Capital's Share	50.46	44.89	-11.0
*State Income***	12.20	12.57	+3.0
Federal Government	9.45	10.96	+15.9
Parastate Sector (net income)	2.75	1.61	-41.5
Public Foreign Debt Payments	0.61	1.42	+132.5

* Does not sum to 100% due to exclusion of profits remitted abroad and interest on private sector debt.

** This includes *salary* payments to the top state functionaries and PRI officials, the importation of capital goods, the use of some parastate output, and state purchases of goods and services from the private sector. *Wage* payments are included under labor's share.

Source: Based on data presented in Julio Boltvinik and Fernando Torres, "Concentración del Ingreso y Satisfacción de Necesidades en la Crisis Actual," *El Economista Mexicano* 19, no. 2 (1986), p. 31.

of income against capital and to both labor and the state. Note that the decline in the parastate sector's share was due to increasing price subsidies to the private sector, that cut the parastate income.) The first difficulty to be encountered was that Luis Echeverría's economic cabinet failed to comprehend that wage increases could not be harmonized with the elite's profit expectations.[1] We might term this difficulty a *crisis of conceptualization*—something that has dogged economic policymakers from the early 1970s to the present.

A second difficulty was the absence of a project that would lead or pull the productive apparatus toward increasing cohesiveness. Presidents López Mateos and Díaz Ordaz had attempted to Mexicanize the mining sector and build an integrated national productive apparatus to produce autos, trucks, and tractors as well as a household electrical products industry. There was no such project under either Echeverría or López Portillo. (The latter's project to create an indigenous machine building sector was primarily developed on paper, with little implementation.) Had income redistribution been linked to the *expansion* of important sectors of the economy, the negative impact on profits from a pro-wage policy might have been short-circuited by the (profit-creating) positive sectoral growth effect of new state-led projects.

Finally, Echeverría never confronted the chief problem that any administration faces when a populist program is initiated—capital flight. There are ample examples of nations that have controlled capital flight, including Brazil in Latin America, to call into question the often-repeated assertion that Mexico has no recourse against it.

More than anything the failures of Echeverría's administration were failures of vision. Upon taking office, the new president combined his bold assertion that growth with redistribution was possible with assurances that he would maintain the free convertibility of the peso. That is, he would do nothing to stand in the way of capital flight. In other words, Echeverría was declaring his allegiance to the "monetarist" precepts of Antonio Ortiz Mena—the president would recreate the lost golden age of the stabilized growth period and not deviate from the established principles of protecting the peso and guaranteeing the "right" to capital flight. In this, Luis Echeverría revealed his institutionalized past. As a PRI politician of the stabilized growth period, he had internalized the monetarist principles of Ortiz Mena's model. Having been conditioned by his past to uncritically accept the monetarist precepts, Echeverría could no more than ruefully watch as the Banco de México imposed austerity programs whenever Echeverría's wage-boosting programs set the stage for a bout of structural inflation. The sexenio, then, was one cursed with the inconsistencies, if not chaos, of an economy alternately being expanded by boosts to aggregate demand and halted by restrictive monetary policies (and massive capital flight). It was, in short, a stop-and-go policy because the state apparatus was split. The monetarists in the Banco de Mexico were given free rein by Echeverría because he believed that theirs was the only way to achieve peso stability and free convertibility.

At a historical moment when the state needed to have an increasing degree of autonomy, the Mexican state exhibited an increasing degree of ambivalence and inconsistency. Echeverría, although seen as hostile to business, genuinely wanted to satisfy both the business elite and the underlying population. His policy inconsistencies were never understood by the state apparatus *as* inconsistencies. Rather, in one moment the state lurched toward a prolabor policy; in the next, it fell back on austerity policies engineered by the Banco de México when inflation ensued. Each was seen as essentially *separable* from the other. Somehow, it was imagined, this pattern could be broken—monetarism would set the basis for a *sound* expansion, that never came.

Stop and Go: 1971-1976

As a result of a nearly 100 percent increase in the deficit in the balance of payments in 1970 and the prospect of another serious deficit in 1971, President Echeverría opted for a tight money policy at the Central Bank (Guillén, 1984, 37; Tello, 1979, 54). Fearing that a devaluation of the peso could be imminent, the government slashed the state's investment program by 21.7 percent. This drop in investment largely explained the reduction in the GNP growth rate to 3.4 percent (with population increasing at roughly 3.3 percent) in 1971. Theoretically, a tight money policy plus the cut in government investment should have slowed down imports and improved the balance of payments. It did not. Imports went *up* slightly, while exports expanded by 8 percent. Thus, the balance-of-payments equations improved slightly, but not because of the policy moves of the government. The fact that on its own terms the austerity program of 1971 was a failure did not promote a rejection of that policy *per se*. Rather, the state (after a substantial debate) simply shifted direction with a 16 percent increase in total public outlays in 1972 (Tello, 1979, 54).

Fears of a falling peso were replaced by a desire to stimulate the economy. Echeverría's program of "adjustment" was over. As in so many other areas of policymaking, the state apparently found no compulsion to evaluate the adjustment program and learn from policymaking errors.

In 1972 and 1973 the state mounted a rapid push to expand the economy. Budgetary outlays rose 16 and 22 percent, respectively, with state investment leaping 42 and 33.8 percent—all in real terms (Tello, 1979, 54, 74). Unlike previous periods of expansion, however, the private sector failed to respond; private investment fell by 1 percent in 1972 and increased by only 4.7 percent in 1973. Meanwhile, by early 1973 inflation was rising at an annual rate of more than 10 percent; from midyear 1973 to midyear 1974 prices increased 25 percent (Tello, 1979, 101).

Responding in 1974 to inflationary pressures and fearing that the peso could fall given the more than 100 percent increase in the balance-of-trade (current account) deficit, the state again applied the brakes to the economy. State spending increased by only 9 percent while public investment fell by 1.6 percent (in real terms) in 1974 (Tello, 1979, 131, 136).

Compensating, to some degree, for this drop in public sector investment was the 13.8 percent increase in private investment. This paradox may be explained partly as a lag effect of the previous two boom years when the GDP grew by 7.3 and 7.7 percent, respectively. Also, with real wages falling by nearly 10 percent in 1974 and profits increasing by 55 percent (for the largest corporations), the jump in investment was not surprising (Tello, 1979, 103, 105). Very little was made of this short burst in private investment by those who carefully examined the period. E.V.K. Fitzgerald emphasized that this jump in investments was linked primarily to speculative activities such as real estate and inventory purchases (Fitzgerald, 1985, 237).

Growth slowed to 5.9 percent in 1974, and then virtual stagnation ensued (growth equal to or less than the increase in population). The GNP expanded by 4.1 percent in 1975 and only by 2.1 percent in 1976. Private investment declined in the prior year and barely increased in 1976.

Capital flight began in earnest in 1973 and grew chronically worse until in 1976 it reached the remarkable level of $2.4 billion (U.S.)—29 percent of the value of commodity exports (INEGI, 1985, vol. 2, 721–723). As the internal banking circuits were drained by capital flight, the government increasingly turned to the international credit markets for hard currency to fund imports, including the state's projects. Echeverría's government increased the foreign public debt by nearly 500 percent; most of this increase came in 1975 when the government expanded its total debt by 44.8 percent (Tello, 1979, 141).

After having slowed the economy in 1974 (in response to inflationary pressures), the state atttempted in 1975 to revive the economy—with foreign debt underwriting much of the 22.6 percent real increase in public spending. Unable to maintain its rate of foreign borrowing, unassisted by other components of the economy, and drained by unprecedented levels of capital flight, the government was forced to devalue the peso amidst the economic chaos of 1976.

The picture that emerged, then, was one of a brief contraction in 1971 brought on both by the Banco de México's and the private banks' refusal to fund Echeverría's new program of "shared growth." This was followed by a two-year boom funded primarily by very large jumps in public spending. Then in 1974 a slow, steady slide commenced that was crowned by the foreign exchange crisis of 1976. The latter then precipitated the acceptance of an IMF stabilization program of "recovery."

State Investments and the Macroeconomy

Given the very sizable bursts in state spending and state investments during various years of the sexenio, the question arises as to why these large, quantitative increases failed to ignite the economy or stimulate much collateral investment on the part of the private sector. The answer is partially that the programs were pursued in an exceedingly erratic manner. To this should be added the fact that many state projects were long term (such as investments in agricultural infrastructure), that would promote collateral investments only when completed. There was only one project pursued with any sense of consistent deliberation: Steelmaking steadily received a growing portion of state investments—from roughly 1.5 percent in 1971 and 1972 to 8 percent in 1975 and 1976 (SPP, 1978). But some of the major steel projects started during this period were only completed in the late 1980s. The steelmaking program was beset with a multiplicity of problems that undercut much of its ability to stimulate the economy.

From 1971 to 1973 school building absorbed an increasing share of state investments—from 5.5 to 14.6 percent—but by 1976 the program declined to roughly the same level as 1971. As a stimulant to the economy, school building had important but limited demand-side effects in terms of the use of labor and construction materials. Perhaps the program's most important single immediate impact was to employ some of the vast number of untrained workers (who were plentifully used as "peons") because of the extremely labor-intensive, backward construction techniques commonly utilized.

In 1973 the government began a crash program in telecommunications; this area of state investments jumped from 1.8 percent of outlays in 1972 to 6.2 percent in 1973, staying at roughly that level throughout the remainder of the sexenio (SPP, 1978). With telecommunications in need of much improvement, the state made a wise choice. Yet many components and parts had to be imported because industry was largely restricted in terms of its abilities to producing household electrical appliances. Had the state invested in the creation of a telecommunications *industry* in tandem with its investments in the *products* of this industry, an important stimulus to the economy could have been created.

Finally, from 1973 through 1975 Echeverría's administration stressed agricultural development, with outlays in this area rising from 14 percent of state investments to 18 percent but then dropping again to 14.7 percent in 1976 (SPP, 1978). Agriculture did not respond to this brief injection of funds. Productivity growth in this sector fell to zero between 1973 and 1978 (Huerta, 1986, 215).

Thus, inconsistency (holding aside the case of telecommunications) and pervasive discontinuities defined the state's investment program. Why were programs started? Why were they dropped? What was the development principle behind these efforts? It seems that aside from the theory of the "big push" in steelmaking and the consistent desire to create jobs through labor-intensive programs, there was no principle guiding state investments. This was improvisation with a vengeance. At the precise moment when the stabilized growth model had collapsed and when there was a paramount necessity to develop a new and careful strategy regarding state investments, the state pursued a profound eclecticism. The state, in short, was overwhelmed by the challenge it faced and very much daunted by the attack mounted by the business elite against statism.

An increasing portion of state investments was now being funded via debt financing, and an increasing portion of this government debt was attained through foreign borrowing. Thus, Mexico had to pay a current price for the inconsistencies of state investment in terms of resources largely lost (or very much underutilized) because programs were either not carried to their completion, or completed only after very long delays. A long-term price came in the form of paying down the foreign debt *without* the benefit of having sufficiently improved the stock of social capital. There was little expansion of the integrated, coherent productive base needed to generate a greater future level of output that would permit the repayment of the debt (without reducing future state investments).

Echeverría and Statism

During Echeverría's sexenio, the business elite decried the drift toward statism. To what degree was this charge justified? State spending increased from 26.1 percent of the GDP in 1970 to 38.5 percent in 1976. Measured against GDP, the *sales* of state companies increased from 13.6 to 17.6 percent in these same years. This was primarily a result of a sizable increase (in 1975) of the price of products produced by the state, such as electricity and petroleum. The largest increase in state income came from borrowing, that rose from 2.6 percent of the GDP in 1970 to 9.0 percent in 1976. Public investment increased from 5.4 percent of GNP in 1971 to 9.6 percent in 1975, after that it fell to 8.7 percent in 1976 (Looney, 1985, 154; Tello, 1979, 194). Thus, there was a *quantitative* increase in the role of the state.

But, statism, above all, is a qualitative distinction. There is no simple manner in which to address this issue. The largest business groups (the national industrial-banking conglomerates) were aided by the Echeverría administration, which passed legislation that controlled foreign investments and assisted in the building of bank holding companies. The charge that the administration was hostile *per se* to business—certainly an attribute of statism according to the ideology of the business associations—was not borne out in this regard (or in the administration's tenacious defense of the right to capital flight). Furthermore, the state had been the most important market for many business interests since the days of Cárdenas. Finally, the private sector had long enjoyed lavish favoritism from the state in terms of tax exemptions and ample subsidies.

Much of the increase in state spending during this sexenio went to increase the "social wage" (schooling, health care, recreation, social security). Because large businesses and the wealthy were all but exempt from taxes, the funds to support the increase in the social wage had to come from (1) taxes on the working class and the peasantry, (2) income taxes on the emerging middle class, and (3) borrowing. Nevertheless, there is no doubt that the administration sought to redress what it found to be an imbalance between capital and labor by using (as best it could) the weight of the state to protect and expand the wage share.

So on one level, the state was not hostile to business and continued to protect business interests. On another level, however, the charge of statism has some relevance in the sense that there was an increasing degree of *ineffectiveness* to the state's intervention *in terms of promoting private capital accumulation*.

In addition to the inconsistent and unsustained investment efforts undertaken by the state, there was a sizable increase in parastate firms— a trend that seemed to validate the statism charge. In 1970 the state owned 278 parastate firms (including "decentralized" firms such as PEMEX). Five years later there were 493 parastate firms—a 78 percent increase (Carrillo Castro and García Ramírez, 1983, 181). To this number should be added 107 new state entities created by *fideicomisos* (a type of state trust). Given these numbers, there is little wonder that the business elite, surprised and exasperated by the administration's insistence on supporting full-employment programs, attempted to apply the statist label.

Again, some caution is necessary. Aside from the giant new steel plant on the southern Pacific coast, the firms acquired were small; only a few intermediate and large firms were among the 216 new acquisitions. Thus (although a detailed breakdown of the value of the state's capital stock is not available), most of the value of the state's assets were to be found in PEMEX, CFE (the electric company), FERTIMEX (the fertilizer company), Telmex (the telephone company), and an array of sugar mills, steel mills, and firms producing autos, trucks, buses, tractors, and auto parts. Virtually all of these had been acquired prior to Echeverría's term. The *number* of acquisitions suggested a strong shift toward statism, but the *value* of the assets acquired in relation to those already accumulated was modest.

Benito Rey Romay, a former director of industrial development at Nafinsa, has recently published a study of 294 parastate industrial firms in *La Ofensiva Empresarial Contra la Intervención del Estado* (Rey Romay, 1984, 132–141). Using 1981 data, he showed that these parastates (the sample included all the major firms) had a book value of 1.053 trillion pesos. The sample registered 20 industrial firms acquired between January 1, 1971, and December 1, 1976, with a total book value of 32.97 billion pesos.

Echeverría's new acquisitions amounted to a mere 3.1 percent of the book value of the 294 industrial parastate firms sampled. Furthermore, 51.5 percent of the book value of the twenty industrial firms created and acquired in the Echeverría sexenio were accounted for by two steelmaking firms. Many, probably most, of the remaining 195 new state entities created between 1970 and 1975 were small nonindustrial organizations such as research institutes, financial agencies coordinating small funding programs for worker's housing, or small, rural wholesale food companies. There is no reason to believe that Benito Rey Romay's sample was biased. Echeverría made some sizable industrial acquisitions, but certainly these failed to warrant the statist charge, at least regarding the parastate sector. The acquisitions were well within the historical pattern established by previous presidents, including the most conservative.

Another important point regarding the growth of the number of parastate firms should be made: Many of the firms that were not government start-up entities (such as the steel complex, Siderúrgica Lázaro Cárdenas–Las Truchas) were acquired because private Mexican capitalists were able to sell their bankrupt firms to the government. The majority of the larger firms acquired in this sexenio (such as several household-appliance-producing companies) probably originated in private sector bankruptcies. Furthermore, it is universally assumed that the government acquired these bankrupt firms at well *above* the market price—providing yet a further subsidy to the private sector.

In viewing the twenty acquired industrial firms cited in Benito Rey Romay's sample, no pattern was found in terms of the existing structure of the state firms. There was no sector or group of sectors that the state attempted to rationalize with its acquisitions (aside from steelmaking). There was, however, some fit into previously emphasized programs. For example, the auto-truck-bus-tractor sector was strengthened by the acquisition of a tractor producer, Dina Komatsu; a truck axle producer, Dina Rockwell; a producer of metal machine lathes, AHMSA; and a maker of engine crankshafts. How well, if at all, these four new entities were integrated (horizontally and/or vertically) into the existing matrix of metal working firms is not known. Beyond these four acquisitions (and the two steelmaking companies), the remaining fourteen new parastates were a random collection of mismatched firms, linking neither to each other nor to the already existing parastates in most cases. An ethylene plant acquired may or may not have fit into PEMEX's petrochemical complex, depending on the new plant's location, production-capabilities, and level of technology. This is as close as one comes to finding any order or logic to the acquisitions. Thus, the Echeverría administration did not seem to focus on the *production* capabilities of the state, preferring instead redistributive programs designed to augment the social wage and poorly thought-out and inconsistently applied programs to benefit the peasantry.

Business-Government Relations
in President Echeverría's Sexenio

From 1973 to 1977 the burst in state investment in steelmaking resulted in new, installed, annual production capacity of nearly 4.5 million tons—up from only 5.5 million tons in 1973. A long-term program to expand petrochemical production (both by the private and public sector) resulted in increases in average annual output of 20 percent from 1970 to 1975. By 1975 petrochemical production was 500 percent greater than it had been in 1965 (Martínez del Campo, 1985, 105–108). Meanwhile, state employees had increased 62.3 percent between 1970 and 1976 (Cordera, 1980, Table II-C-1). However uneven these changes may have been, the state nonetheless was adding both to aggregate supply and to aggregate demand. Yet the private sector did not respond in proportion to the stimuli that the state offered. The question is why? E.V.K. Fitzgerald viewed the problem, in part, as one in which the increasing capital intensity of production pushed down the profit rate (Fitzgerald, 1985, 220–221). As was mentioned in Chapter 3, Leopoldo Solís and Miguel Ángel Rivera Rios emphasized the link between higher capital output ratios and lower profits—the overaccumulation (or overexpansion) of capital argument. A reading of the empirical data and the theoretical debates leads to the conclusion that the crisis of the 1970s was first *conditioned* by problems of overaccumulation, that were then *accentuated* by state redistributional efforts that further squeezed profits.

But this is only a partial explanation because there is no such thing as an "adequate" or an "inadequate" rate of profit. It is a subjective concept. A falling rate of profit does not immediately signal that investment must be foreclosed. Two other matters must be taken into consideration. First, the Mexican business elite was repelled by the direction that the Echeverría administration was taking with its shared growth concept. The business elite genuinely feared that the state, and a renewed popular movement, would seriously limit their powers and prerogatives.

According to Elvira Concheiro, the sense of betrayal carried over into the issue of Echeverría's financing of the government deficit through foreign borrowing. The business elite regarded this as an act of *autonomy* by the state against the historical control of the circuit of money capital by both the "financial oligarchy," that dominated Mexican banking, and the "northern faction" of (primarily) Monterrey-based industrialists and financiers. According to her research, the business elite (with the exception of what she termed the "moderates," who were grouped primarily into Canacintra) interpreted the state's pursuit of its shared growth feared program as a break in the implicit *pacto político* (political pact) between business and government. In response, argued Concheiro, the business elite sought ways to undermine the government, one of that was to reduce internal lending by the banks the elite controlled. In this formulation, then, the increase or decline in credit (that could be transformed into investment, capital formation, production, jobs, and increased demand) was determined not by the Banco de México as much as by these two interlocked factions of the business elite. In other words, a decision to engage in a "strike of capital" was taken for reasons that were not strictly *limited* to either the existing or anticipated rate of profit (Concheiro and Fragosa, 1979, 37–49). But when Echeverría was able to turn to the *international* circuit of capital by borrowing from the transnational banks, the financial oligarchy lost an important instrument that it had utilized to constrain the state—the veto control over credit.

Second, there was philosophical resistance among the business associations against shared growth. Comparmex, which was above all the voice of the banking elite and the northern faction, presented its own seven-point program for the new government to adopt in early 1971.[2] Because the accumulation model that they then advocated became central to policymaking in the 1980s, let us look at the specifics of the program: (1) reprivatization of the parastate industries; (2) an end to all state subsidies to parastate firms and increased efficiency in the public sector; (3) state promotion of exports; (4) an increase in direct foreign investment; (5) new emphasis on tourism as a growth pole, including the channeling of state-controlled credit and subsidies to this sector; (6) new state assistance to industry, especially to transnational corporations that were most capable of expanding export industries; and (7) an end to all land reform programs and a "reorganization" of the countryside (Labastida, 1972, 146–150). This plan, except for one element, was summarily brushed aside by the new administration. Worse, at least in the view of Coparmex, was the idea that the state would even begin to contemplate tax reform legislation without *first* consulting the business associations (Tello, 1979, 45). The *pacto político* had been broken.

It is one thing to feel betrayed and another to be able to do something about it. The business elite's sense of betrayal was inextricably linked to the private sector's organizational transformation, that had slowly welded a small number (less than three hundred) industrial firms, banks,

Table 4.3: Mexico, Sales of the 100 Largest Firms*

	1973	1975	1977	1979	1981
Sales of the 100 largest (as % GDP)	19.2	21.3	23.7	28.2	30.0
Sales of the top 23 "groups" of private national capital (as % of top 100)	32.8	34.2	41.1	43.2	48.0
Sales of the Transnational Firms (as % of top 100)	35.4	35.6	30.9	29.2	25.2
Sales of the Parastate Firms (as % of top 100)	15.5	14.9	15.2	15.4	16.8

*Excluding PEMEX: PEMEX is such a large entity that its exclusion is necessary in order to perceive underlying trends in the economy.

Sources: Based on data in "Las 500 Empresas Más Grandes de México," *Revista Expansión* (August, various years); Eduardo Jacobs, "La Evolución Reciente de los Grupos de Capital Privado Nacional," *Economía Mexicana* (1981), no. 3, p. 24.

and commercial capitalists into interlocked "national economic power groups." (For detailed research analyzing this transformation, see Cordero H., Santín, and Tirado, 1983; Jacobs, 1981). That these groups experienced a time of *ascendancy* in terms of their economic power throughout the stabilized growth period, particularly the 1970s, can be seen from Table 4.3. Note that the top groups were able not only to grow faster than the top parastate firms (excluding PEMEX); these groups were able to outstrip the top transnationals. (The groups tended to expand their sales in areas that were not directly competitive with the transnationals.) All of this occurred while concentration of sales among the top 100 firms increased by 58 percent—in less than a decade. The economic ascendancy of the groups quickly translated into political ascendancy (that is in terms of increasing power to realize the political objectives of large capital). Hence the sense of betrayal when the legitimacy of this process of national economic concentration and its results were fundamentally called into question by Echeverría's concept of shared growth.

As mentioned, Echeverría's inability to fully endorse the social results of the stabilized growth period (for example, the economic and political consolidation of the national economic groups) did not indicate unmitigated hostility toward the business elite. Indeed, the passage in 1973 of a law to regulate foreign investment and a law recognizing the legitimacy of holding companies both benefited the groups. The former created new opportunities to form joint ventures with foreign firms, which had to show 51 percent national ownership. In some rare cases foreign firms left Mexico, selling their corporations to the national groups of economic power. The latter allowed the banks in particular (and the groups in general), to "leverage" equity (and borrowed) capital from several companies, thereby creating new borrowing and lending opportunities designed to rapidly increase profits.

There are various interpretations as to why the level of hostility that the business elite expressed for the Echeverría regime increased so notably in 1973. Many link the timing to the administration's growing support for the Allende government in Chile. But there has been no discussion of the fact that by 1973 the business elite could no longer expect new large-scale benefits from the state. This is an additional hypothesis that does not preclude other points of discord, including the profound acrimony over the direction of foreign policy. Such a hypothesis might explain why Carlos Tello asserted that the business elite had *"paralyzed"* the government in 1973 (Tello did not offer any specific reason for the deepening of this struggle in late 1973.) (Tello, 1979, 81).

Eduardo González also argued that 1973 marked a crucial turning point in government business relations, although (again) his reason for the timing was decidedly vague. González claimed that once the business elite had defeated an attempt at tax reform in 1972 and the initiative for a forty-hour work week in 1973, it shifted from the *defensive* to the *offensive*. According to González, after 1973 the business elite "no longer attempted to preserve its prerogatives, it now attempted to eliminate one (social) project in order to open the way for another that went in the opposite direction" (González, 1981, 654). This interpretation of a shift from the defensive to the offensive was also emphasized by Salvador Cordero H., Rafael Satín, and Ricardo Tirado in their systematic study of the growth of the groups (although they did not focus on the year 1973) (Cordero H., Santín and Tirado, 1983, 185–186). A similar interpretation was offered by Juan Martínez Nava in his *Conflicto Estado Empresarios*:

> The confrontations of Echeverría's period indicate that the margin of the relative autonomy of the state has continued to be reduced given that the bourgeoisie has continued to grow and increase its strength, to the degree that it has become capable of exercising considerable power to shape the actions of the state.
>
> In contrast with the Cárdenas era, the bourgeoisie has demonstrated its capacity to successfully oppose almost any measure that it deems to be contrary to its interests (Martínez Nava, 1982, 170).

Among the numerous issues of confrontation between the business elite and the administration one is deserving of particular mention—

tax reform. There were failed attempts to change the taxation system in 1970, 1972, and 1975. It has been argued by Juan Martínez Nava, among others, that the question of tax reform went much deeper than the obvious need to increase (or in some cases *create*) taxes on high incomes. Rather, the fundamental issue of tax reform had to do with the degree of autonomy to be exercised by the state. If the state could increase its revenue base, it would be *structurally* more capable of exercising a degree of autonomy. If, however, the expansion of state spending could be achieved only by creating a deficit, then the *creditors* would have an implicit veto over new state spending. Thus, according to this interpretation, the Mexican business elite *preferred* a program based on domestic indebtedness to one that would institutionalize a greater degree of state autonomy via tax reform (Martínez Nava, 1982, 171). At the same time, as mentioned, the elite felt betrayed when the Echeverría administration was able to fund some of its social spending through foreign borrowing. A considerable victory for elite interests (such as the blockage of tax reform) was not sufficient.

Carlos Tello maintained that the business interests engaged in "economic terrorism" during Echeverría's administration (Tello, 1979, 80). Certainly the growing capital flight from 1973 onward fit into this category, as did the decline in private investment in 1975 and the virtual stagnation of private investment in 1976. Yet a question remains: If the business groups had switched to the offensive in late 1973, why did private investment grow by 13.8 percent in real terms in 1974 (Tello, 1979, 136)? A partial answer to this question has already been presented— the rise in investment was a response to the strong growth of the economy in 1973 and was made possible because profits rose while real wages fell throughout 1974. In addition, new laws limiting foreign investment and clearing the way for new profit-making opportunities via bank holding companies also helped explain what would first have appeared to be a paradox. To this list an additional factor should be added—speculation. Very little of the real growth in private investment in 1973–1974 went to create productive plant and equipment; most went into real estate, services, and speculation with inventories.

Given (1) that the state was incapable of directing large sums of invested capital into new leading sectors of the economy (that would have pulled private sector investors into the process of creating new productive capital), (2) that the national capitalists had largely exhausted the pool of high-profit projects made available to them during the stage of easy import substitution, and (3) that this business elite was both unwilling and incapable of seizing the initiative to orchestrate the creation of new leading sectors, the growing turn toward speculation (or rentier behavior) was an expected result. The speculative wave was stressed in most analyses of the period. It received particular explanatory emphasis in a study by E.V.K. Fitzgerald. As can be seen in Table 4.4, Fitzgerald employed a simple yet telling, division between "productive" and "other" forms of investment—the former being investments in agriculture, mining, and industry and the latter being investments in services and commerce, housing, finance, and tourism. In the 1940s the ratio of private *productive* investment to "other" (or largely unproductive) investment was roughly 4 to 1. In the 1950s the ratio fell to approximately 2 to 1. By the 1960s it was nearly 1 to 1 and in the 1970s close to 1 to 2. For every peso invested in plant and equipment two were now invested in elaborate bank buildings, luxury housing, and shopping centers (Fitzgerald, 1985, 237). Increasingly, as the Echeverría administration was unable to generate a viable new development model, the latent forces behind the rentier ethos came to the foreground.

The Consejo Coordinador Empresarial: *The New Voice of Economic Power*

One important manifestation of the shift toward the offensive on the part of the business associations, was the creation of the *Consejo Coordinador Empresarial* (CCE) in May 1975. The CCE grouped together the leadership of CONCAMIN (large industrial capital), CONCANACO (large commercial capital), Coparmex (the coordinating body of the northern faction), and the ABM. The first two associations were officially a part of the consultative apparatus of the Mexican corporatist model. They were to "dialogue" with the state in private and not attempt to engage in open policymaking. By contrast the CCE was created precisely to be an organization with a high public profile, working both within and against the state as the situation dictated. In other words, the CCE constituted both a way of presenting a united front of the business elite in their struggle with the state and a means for CONCAMIN and CONCANACO capitalists to simultaneously conform to and violate the corporatist model.

The timing of the creation of the CCE seemed to be linked to the selection of the new president to succeed Echeverría (although it was not known to what degree the business elite played a role in the successor's selection). Initially the response by researchers and social commentators to the CCE was that it was not a serious organization. The corporatist model of dividing and therefore presumably controlling or constraining large capital was not threatened with dissolution.

In the 1980s this view no longer prevailed. The CCE was seen to have major influence over policymaking. At the outset the CCE was controlled by the "radicals" in the business elite who rather amateurishly

Table 4.4: Productive and "Other" Forms of Investment (percent of GDP) and Public Investment Share (percent)

	1940-44	1945-49	1950-54	1955-59	1960-64	1965-69	1970-74	1975-78
*Productive Investment**								
Public	1.0	1.6	2.5	2.2	2.9	3.2	3.5	5.8
Private	2.7	4.8	6.4	7.1	5.6	6.3	4.5	4.2
Total	3.7	6.4	8.7	9.3	8.5	9.5	8.0	10.0
*"Other" Investment***								
Public	3.1	3.1	3.7	3.1	3.6	3.1	3.4	3.8
Private	0.5	1.5	3.2	4.3	4.3	6.1	8.3	7.8
Total	3.6	4.6	6.9	7.4	7.9	9.2	11.7	11.6
Total Investment								
Public	4.1	4.7	6.2	5.3	6.5	6.3	6.9	9.5
Private	3.3	6.3	9.4	11.4	9.9	12.0	12.8	12.0
Total	7.3	11.0	15.6	16.7	16.4	8.7	19.7	21.5
Public Share of Investment (percent)								
Productive	27	25	29	24	34	34	43	58
Total	56	41	40	32	40	34	35	44

*Agriculture, mining, and industry (including construction)

** Services, finance, tourism

Source: Based on Secretaría de Programación y Presupuesto data as cited in E.V.K. Fitzgerald, "The Financial Constraint on Relative Autonomy: The State and Capital Accumulation in Mexico, 1940-1982," in Christian Anglade and Carlos Fontin (eds.), *The State and Capital Accumulation in Mexico* (Pittsburgh: University of Pittsburgh, 1985), p. 237.

engaged in a blunt and shallow attack on Echeverría's policies—much of it descended to the level of a personal attack. But the CCE changed, even though at times it continued to act in an unsophisticated manner. It quickly learned the smoke-and-mirrors tactics perfected by the PRI's "alchemists" decades ago.

An organization subsidiary to CCE and of some importance also made its appearance—the Centro de Estudios Económicos del Sector Privado (Center for Economic Studies of the Private Sector, or CEESP). The CEESP became a major source of economic analysis that reflected a University of Chicago ultra-free-market orientation. The results of the CEESP's research were widely disseminated, especially in the daily newspapers of the capital. Given the growing similarities between CEESP's analyses/policymaking suggestions and actual policies implemented by the state in 1980s, the CEESP's influence within the state was probably very high (Huss, 1987).

The Peso Crisis of 1976 and the IMF

By late October 1976 the cumulative effects of capital flight and the slump in world trade had taken their toll on the Echeverría administration—the peso, stable since the late 1950s, had been devalued by more than 100 percent. The devaluation was seen by many as a real indication of Mexico's failing economic health. It was commonly argued that this was the final proof of the failure of Echeverría's (halfhearted) quest for a new model of accumulation. In the grip of a economic and social crisis not seen since the 1930s, Echeverría lashed back at his detractors in the northern faction calling them questionable Christians and "profound reactionaries who are the enemies of the progress of the people" (Tello, 1979, 164). This was the sort of acrimony that often dominated public discourse under Cárdenas, but it was unheard-of blasphemy in the 1970s.

The northern faction did not have long to wait for its revenge. The balance-of-payments crisis had forced the administration into accepting a three year IMF program that would essentially negate whatever modest progress had been made toward the goal of shared growth. As a matter of formality the new president López Portillo, would have to officially sign the "stabilization" program, but from September 1976 onward the Echeverría administration was increasingly altering its policies to facilitate the transition to the IMF's program. As is customary in such cases, the IMF maintained that Mexico's crisis was due to the fact that the public sector tended to use "resources" inefficiently. Consequently, the first point of the agreement was to cut the state's deficit—not by raising taxes or instituting the long-hoped-for tax reform but by cutting spending.

The first effect, of course, would be to create unemployment, that would lower the wage rate and, according to the IMF's theory, raise the profit rate. Thus, lower wages would be the incentive to recovery as the private sector renewed its investments, particularly (it was thought) for exports.

Then, because inflation had increasingly become a problem (before the devaluation in August inflation was nearly 30 percent on an annualized basis, compared to an average of less than 3 percent from 1958 to 1970), the IMF demanded as its second point that credit growth be restrained. This, of course, contradicted the first point of the agreement in that investment could hardly be expected to expand in the midst of a credit crunch. The third element of the agreement was to release government price controls and controls over imports. This was to be coupled with a "realistic" exchange rate—all under the heading of "getting prices right."

With a cheaper peso, exports were encouraged while imports became more expensive. But taking off internal price controls sped inflation; in spite of a slowdown in the rate of growth of government spending, inflation surged at a 21 percent rate in 1977 (CEPAL, 1981, 2). The balance of payments improved, but the economy did not recover; the growth rate was only slightly higher than the increase in population— 3.4 percent in 1977. Far from creating new investment opportunities, the economy faced one of its worst years, with public investment falling 7.2 percent and private investment declining by 10.5 percent (Huerta, 1986, 684).

José López Portillo and the Petro Boom

Above all, José López Portillo (1976–1982) wanted to achieve two things in his sexenio: first, regain the confidence of the business elite in the state and, second, pursue a policy of full employment and wage protection. The two, of course, were incompatible given Mexico's new era of economic instability. Only the oil boom momentarily allowed the administration (and the society) to believe that it had conjured away the specter of crisis. Consequently, neither the business elite nor the state was prepared when the petroleum bubble burst in midyear 1981. López Portillo then claimed that the government simply faced a "cash flow" problem. According to his administration, Mexico's fundamental problem was the *management of abundance.* Few were the voices of skepticism as López Portillo, aping his predecessor, borrowed amazingly large amounts from the private transnational banks in 1981 and 1982 to cope with his assumed "cash flow" problems. Dreams died hard. Most believed that the oil boom had brought back the economic miracle of the 1958–1970 period.

Although 1977 was basically a year of austerity, it was more for some than for others. The profit rate increased 72 percent from that of the previous year (Hernández Rodríquez, 1988, 120). Rogelio Hernández Rodríquez maintained that the private sector had made considerable gains in the course of the year in its campaign to reverse the populist emphasis of the Echeverría period: "By the end of the first year of the government the private sector had realized a series of invaluable victories. The new regime had openly condemned the former government and had accepted as the condition for economic recovery the return of business confidence as the indispensible prerequisite" (Hernández Rodríquez, 1988, 118).

Among the victories achieved was the passage of the Multiple Banking Law in 1977, which allowed for the rapid concentration of the banks. An additional victory was gained in 1978 when López Portillo eliminated price controls on 100 items. Yet for all his open generosity to business, the new president was poorly rewarded. Although the banks held adequate funds that might have been invested, credit was directed toward speculation. Capital flight continued to be a major problem with $1.3 billion (U.S.) leaving the country in 1977 and in 1978 (Ros, 1987, 108).

Whereas most researchers saw the López Portillo administration as largely moving to satisfy both the Mexican private sector and the IMF, Laurence Whitehead argued for another interpretation. Whitehead claimed that the weakness of the state *vis-à-vis* the business interests and the procapital "stabilization" program was more limited than it seemed. He argued that Mexico was able to manage considerable counterbargaining with the IMF. As a result, Mexico was able to insist on both *growth* and *protection* of employment. The austerity program was limited to modest wage declines (0.9 percent for most workers who received the minimum wage) and slight cuts in public sector subsidies (INEGI, 1985, vol. 1, 230). According to Whitehead, López Portillo quickly restored "confidence"—the IMF's austerity program was only important through 1977 (Whitehead, 1981, Part 1, 912–914). Regarding the ability of Mexico to resist and mold the IMF accord, Whitehead's argument was convincing.

The Oil Boom

In late 1977 the decision was made to hinge Mexico's development on the expansion of petroleum reserves under the control of PEMEX. Mexico began taking a renewed interest in its oil fields in 1971, when President Echeverría increased funding for exploration. By 1974 self-sufficiency in oil production had been achieved. By 1977 large amounts were exported. The oil boom was concentrated between 1978 and 1981—oil exports accounted for as much as 75 percent of all foreign earnings (Bonilla,

1984, 15). In the course of a few years Mexico had become a monoexporter, with all the vulnerability implied in the term.

The four-year boom was indeed spectacular. GDP increased by an annual average of 8.4 percent in real terms, while *total demand* increased even faster (10.4 percent) due to heavy foreign borrowing. This was a heady era when the government predicted 10 percent growth rates into the twenty-first century and claimed that Mexico's problem was no longer one of economic development but of "managing abundance." When this dream burst in 1982, the state was in no position to lead a restructuring of the economy. Both the state and the economy itself had been structurally weakened by the boom. This boom reinvigorated and further consolidated the rentier ethos within the state and the wider society.

In the first year of the oil boom the state followed PEMEX's lead without being capable of formulating a policy response to the newfound oil reserves. State spending increased 9.3 percent in real terms, primarily to increase petroleum output (Barker and Brailovsky, 1983, 312). In 1978, 32 percent of the nation's exports came from PEMEX's production, but PEMEX also accounted for 16 percent of the imports. The marginal increase in oil exports over 1977 (from 22 percent of exports to 32 percent) came at a high price in terms of the importation of exploratory drilling equipment.

When the boom began, PEMEX increased oil production from two new oil fields and one new gas field. Some new oil was very expensive to obtain (at least in the short term) because in one of the fields very deep wells (to 16,000 feet) were needed while the other field was offshore and thus demanded special technology in order to commence production. Mexico, then, was building its economic future on a questionable foundation—high-cost oil production. Oil revenues rose because of tremendous investments. In 1971 PEMEX's investment-to-production-costs ratio was .453; by 1979 it was .937 (Banamex, n.d., 43, 50—based on SPP data). In 1976 PEMEX received 25 percent of the public budget; in 1980 this portion was 45 percent. PEMEX's share of the public sector's long-term debt rose from 12 percent in 1975 to 21 percent in 1979 and then to 37.8 percent of total public debt in 1981 (Razónes, 1982, 17). In short-term accounting methods the oil revenues were a crucial benefit to state income—as a share of total public revenues they rose from 25 percent in 1976 to 50 percent in 1980 (Banamex, n.d., 46, 48—based on SPP data). Yet these increases in revenue masked the longer term costs of debt repayment. To make this type of financing of the oil boom pay in the long term, oil prices had to stay very high and real interest charges had to stay low. Because neither did, by 1982 Mexico's oil boom and the latest version of the Mexican miracle had evaporated.

Oil and Development

The preceding is only a small (and an adequately discussed) part of the oil boom. If we look deeper into the problems hidden behind Mexico's growth we can see two fundamental issues that were never addressed by state planners. Both indicated the increasing weakness and incoherence of the state sector and a rise in the rentier mentality. First, Mexico was engaging in the risky business of producing high-cost oil to sell as low value-added, unrefined petroleum products. The ratio of crude oil to refined petroleum products in 1979 was roughly 5 to 1. Clearly, further investments in petroleum refining would have been necessary in order to raise the output of gasoline, diesel fuel, lubricating oils, and feedstocks for the petrochemical industry. But some of this capital could have come from *reducing* outlays for exploration. Short-term considerations argued against this strategy because petrochemicals were then suffering world-wide overproduction. Nonetheless, price fluctuations were narrower for refined petroleum products than for crude, making the shift to high value-added forms of production worthwhile in a longer time frame (as Mexico, too late, recognized in the 1980s). The benefit of the shift would have been twofold. Mexico could have raised the value of its exports with a lower level of crude production (thus saving on imported drilling technology while maintaining greater longevity in the oil fields) *and* reduced imports of a range of petroleum-based products (plastics, paints, synthetic fibers, and so on) by vigorously stimulating import substitution in upstream production of petroleum-based products. This action might have been accompanied by a new aggressiveness in creating parastate firms in industrial branches using highly refined petroleum-based products.

Second, the existing parastate complex in steel production and metal manufacturing (and fabrication) could have been linked to the specific needs of the oil industry. Although many specialty products, such as drilling bits, were beyond the capabilities of the Mexican manufacturing sector, a considerable range of new products could have been produced by a carefully directed production plan that emphasized "downstream" products used in petroleum production. Drilling pipe, well casing, high pressure valves and gages, and hand tools were some of the relatively unsophisticated products that might have been produced by the parastate sector; instead, many such products were imported. The long-term benefit of such a program would have been to use the new state-owned manufacturing firms as a spearhead in an attempt to penetrate the global market in high value-added petroleum and petrochemical products. The oil industry alone might not have been sufficient to move Mexico into a sustained pattern of growth, but history will unlikely provide Mexico with a better opportunity.

Because Mexico was determinedly searching for a way to build a new capital goods sector, the fact that the possibility of producing such products for the oil industry was largely ignored was all the more curious. The machinists, lathes, and metalworking technologies needed to produce low-to-intermediate technology, materials-intensive products for the oil fields could have been easily reoriented from other pursuits, such as the auto-truck sector (unused capacity in Mexican industry, particularly heavy industry, had been a chronic condition). Even better, the capital goods industry had a *higher* labor ratio (labor/capital ratio) than did the production of either consumer or intermediate goods. Thus, the policy of industrial diffusion based upon oil production would have assisted in working down Mexico's growing supply of underemployed workers.

Given that the foregoing could have been quickly sketched by an economic planner with an industrial background who had sectoral knowledge of the oil industry, the question becomes one of why Mexico so determinedly passed up a historical opportunity of unprecedented magnitude? The matter was actually somewhat worse than one might conclude from the information thus far provided. The Secretaría de Patrimonio y Fomento Industrial's (Secretary of National Properties and Industrial Development, or SEPAFIN) 1979 *Plan Nacional de Desarrollo Industrial* had set a crude oil export target of 1.1 million barrels of oil per day, which was virtually achieved by 1980. The plan called for the export of only 200 thousand barrels a day of refined products. In 1988 Mexico still had not reached this second goal—exports were only 147 thousand barrels a day (Lomas and Alvárez, 1988, 26).

Only in 1988, with its Proyecto Petrolero del Pacífico, did Mexico begin to make modest steps to shift from a seller of high-cost, low value-added crude oil to higher value-added refined petroleum products and petrochemicals. One of the more interesting aspects of this new plan to develop a petroleum complex on the Pacific was the announced near completion of a new pipeline from the two major new oil fields. This would virtually double Mexico's capacity to export refined petroleum products and thus finally surpass the modest goal of 200 million barrels a day set in 1979. In 1981, PEMEX had purchased, imported, and *stored* the 267 kilometers of 48-inch pipe needed for the pipeline. This squandering of foreign exchange to uselessly buy and store steel products that might have been produced in Mexico was not a unique example of PEMEX's inefficiency.

In an unusual internal government document, PEMEX was described as suffering from "a lack of integral planning of the administrative system and of efficient organization that has led to poor management of the finances of the institution" (Ortega Pizarro, 1983, 6). According to the subdirector of planning of PEMEX (who authored this study), in addition to the preceding problems, the company suffered from a declining level of competitiveness, low productivity, managerial "extravagance," and corruption. Given (1) that 50 percent of government revenues were coming from PEMEX in 1980 and (2) that this sum translated into an amount equal to 25.3 percent of the entire gross national product of Mexico, such a dismal *internal* assessment of PEMEX tended to support the almost universally held opinion in Mexico that PEMEX simply dissipated the greater portion of the oil boom through sheer ineptitude (and less than honorable behavior). Given the potential political importance of solid data that would allow one to make a scientific assessment of the role PEMEX actually played in the use of the surplus arising from the oil boom, it is doubtful that we shall ever know the behind-the-scenes reality of this period.

In 1979 PEMEX announced that it would soon build seventy new petrochemical plants, which, according to *Business Week*'s assessment at that time, "could put Mexico into the big leagues in petrochemicals" (Business Week, 1979, 74). The stated goal was to achieve annual output of 22 million tons of primary petrochemicals by 1982. In 1982 only 71 percent of this goal had been reached; by 1988 Mexico was still nearly 20 percent behind an output goal set in 1979 (Lomas and Alvárez, 1988, 26). After reaching its production objective of 1.1 million barrels per day of crude exports in 1980–1981, PEMEX pushed crude exports up to 1.54 million barrels per day in 1983. Yet even in 1988 PEMEX could not meet basic output goals set for refined petroleum products and petrochemicals set in 1979. Why?

PEMEX was an exploration and crude oil production company with little interest in or talent for the high value-added aspects of the petroleum industry. Relative to the oil giants such as the "seven sisters," PEMEX spent next to nothing on basic research and development of petroleum products when José López Portillo turned over the directorship of PEMEX to his longtime friend, Jorge Díaz Serrano. Díaz Serrano knew the oil business. This was a most unusual accomplishment for a director of a major parastate firm, where loyalty to the PRI and personal ties (amiguismo) usually outweighed such technocratic concerns. Díaz Serrano had spent a lifetime in the oil industry in Texas and Mexico and had been a drilling contractor for decades with PEMEX. López Portillo could have done no better than to pick a man who knew where the oil was and how to arrange for the coordination of the U.S. technicians who for the most part handled the management functions of drilling, transportation, storage, and shipping at the outset of the boom (Goodman and Reasons, 1979, 15). Díaz Serrano also knew how to perpetuate the myth that only Mexican technicians were managing the boom, thus protecting the nationalist image of PEMEX. But Díaz Serrano knew very little about the refining and "upstream" aspects of the oil business; he was not a chemist with years of experience in petrochemical laboratory research. He knew what had to be done to get the oil and gas from the ground and to a shipping point, but he did not seem interested in the high value-added aspects of the oil business.

The Power of Ideas

In the López Portillo administration there were four key policymakers: López Portillo, Díaz Serrano, David Ibarra Muñoz as the secretary of the Treasury (after November 1977), and José Andrés de Oteyza as the secretary of SEPAFIN. Ibarra Muñoz was a university economics professor prior to his elevation to the Treasury. From his writing he appeared to be a Keynesian in orientation. He was sufficiently conservative, however, to have been one of the two individuals that the business associations deemed adequate to succeed López Portillo—the other being Miguel de la Madrid Hurtado. Ibarra Muñoz had an interest in planning and saw the necessity for it. But there was no indication that he approached planning from the *sphere of production*—that is from the standpoint of the labor process, the production process, the relation between inputs and outputs within and between industries, and so on. As a Keynesian, his orientation was toward *circulation* (savings, investment, consumption, GDP growth, foreign trade balance, fiscal and monetary policy) and only secondarily toward *production*.

His approach to policymaking in the petroboom period was to award sizable tax exemptions, known as Certificaciónes de Promoción Fiscal (Certificates of Fiscal Promotion, or CEPROFI) to firms that would (1) expand their capital equipment, (2) move to (or start firms in) prioritized regional zones, and (3) hire more workers (SHCP, 1979). The CEPROFI program showed the normal Keynesian bias toward fiscal policy (over monetary policy), the emphasis on the creation of demand, the wariness of permitting parastate firms to produce the output the Keynesians hoped to promote, and a trust in indicative methods of planning (such as tax subsidies) to promote production in prioritized areas.

Given the spectacular growth in demand and given that Mexican businesses already could avail themselves of plentiful subsidies, it is doubtful that the CEPROFI program had more than a marginal impact. Balanced against the loss of tax revenue and against the fact that the petroboom would have been an ideal time to impose the major tax reform that economists such as Ibarra Muñoz had urged for decades, it is difficult to maintain that the CEPROFI had a significant, positive impact upon the economy. This conclusion is reinforced by the fact that, as the *Plan Nacional* emphasized, the state had a rare opportunity to exercise a degree of autonomy that had previously been missing (SEPAFIN, 1979, 22). As "never before" the plan argued, the state could play a role because it could draw on its "own resources." The degree of state autonomy seemingly could rise but only through a new emphasis on petroleum-related parastate firms producing both downstream from oil exploration and upstream for a national integrated petrochemical industry. In tandem with such a project to build an integrated parastate sector based in petroleum extraction, SEPAFIN'S major objective of creating an indigenous capital goods and machine building sector could have become a likely possibility.

It was the secretary of National Properties and Industrial Development, José Andrés de Oteyza, much more than Ibarra Muñoz, who urged massive debt financing to boost Mexico's growth rate up to 10 percent per year for ten years. Only thirty-four when he assumed one of the four most powerful positions in the state apparatus in 1977, de Oteyza was a major source of the Cambridge influence in López Portillo's administration. (The theory of this group maintained that spectacularly large sustained deficits would call forth, with lags, equal increases in aggregate supply.) De Oteyza urged breakneck growth rates, while he and his cohorts claimed that Mexico need not face supply bottleneck problems. The *Plan Nacional* would identify priority areas, channel credit to these areas, and largely exempt such industries from taxation. Nowhere, however, in the SEPAFIN's *Plan Nacional* was there an attempt to show how this form of indicative planning would promote a long-term balance between leaps in demand financed by oil exports and concomitant increases in supply.

The plan was nothing but a vague shopping list of prioritized areas—for example, agriculture and some downstream industries linked to petroleum production, such as drilling equipment, pipe and tubing, and valves (SEPAFIN, 1979, 148). Most emphasis was placed upon the fabrication of machinery and equipment (and related pursuits) linked to the creation of a capital goods industry. Oil, then, was a means to create a machine-building sector that in itself was *not* oriented toward the oil industry and petrochemicals. There was no awareness of the possibilities of constructing a viable new leading sector based in oil extraction. It is difficult to overlook the persistent resistance to analyzing the possibilities of diversifying the economy by seizing the opportunity that the oil boom presented to develop downstream and upstream oil-related industrialization and linking the development of the machine building sector and agriculture to this new base. The *circulationist* emphasis was even stronger in the policymaking views of de Oteyza's SEPAFIN than in Ibarra Muñoz's Treasury. In spite of brave words about a new era of autonomy of the state, reinvigorating the parastate industries remained a taboo subject. López Portillo sought, above all, to placate the business elite and assure it that the state would not overstep the new bounds to which it had been limited as a result of the clash of government and business under Echeverría.

Distributing the Benefits

Giving free reign to the oligopolists and monopolists who controlled the productive and distributive apparatus of the private sector meant that the state would forfeit control over prices. As a consequence, inflation averaged 37.3 percent in López Portillo's sexenio—a figure that was 200 percent greater than that under President Echeverría (Ramírez, 1988, 54). Because inflation was, above all, a *redistributive* device, it came as no surprise that real wages declined steadily from 1976 onward (with the exception of 1981). Wages for average workers (minimum wages) fell 10 percent in the sexenio of the oil boom (INEGI, 1985, vol. 1, 230–231).

In spite of the decidedly procapital stance of the administration, capital flight never halted. By 1979 it had increased to $2.1 billion (U.S.), the next year it rose to $4.8 billion, and in 1981 (according to some) it stood at $15 billion. In that year international borrowing reached $20 billion. This meant that after paying interest and principle on the previously accumulated debt, Mexico's *net* income via international capital flows was either close to zero or was negative (Ros, 1987, 108; Guillén, 1986, 210).

The state's generosity to business knew few limits in the petroboom period. According to the *Plan Nacional,* Mexico should use its newfound oil wealth for the benefit of national producers. A conscious policy of selling petroleum products to national business interests at between two to seven times *less* than world market prices was to be pursued. Again, the hyper-Keynesian assumptions behind this policy were that low costs for energy and materials would translate into high profits, that would translate further into new investment and therefore into continued growth. Following this policy the state expanded its subsidies, tax exemptions, and tariff benefits to the private sector. One econometric study of the subsidies showed that overall benefits extended to the private sector were very large. Gerardo Davila Jimenez convincingly demonstrated that state transfers and benefits to the business elite grew from 3.6 percent of GNP in 1970 to 13.4 percent of GNP in 1981 (Davila Jimenez, 1982, 243).

Were the rising profits reinvested in productive assets? From 1977 through 1981 public investment increased in real terms 94.2 percent,

Table 4.5: Private Nonresidential Investment (% Share)

	1970-77	1978	1979	1980	1981
Agriculture	10.2	1.2	11.7	10.7	n.a.*
Mining	3.0	2.3	4.4	4.6	n.a.
Oil	0.0	0.0	0.0	0.0	n.a.
Manufacturing	50.8	30.3	32.8	36.1	33.0
Electricity	0.0	0.0	0.0	0.0	n.a.
Commerce and Services	36.0	53.0	51.1	48.6	50.9
Total	100.0	100.0	100.0	100.0	100.0

* n.a. = not available

Source: Based on Jaime Ros, "Mexico from the Oil Boom to the Debt Crisis," in Rosemary Thorp and Laurence Whitehead (eds.), *Latin American Debt and the Adjustment Crisis* (Pittsburgh: University of Pittsburgh Press, 1987), p. 72.

while private investment increased 55.9 percent. National *production* of machinery and equipment increased 67.8 percent in these years, while the *importation* of machinery and equipment rose 124.7 percent. In absolute terms the increase in the importation of machinery and equipment was slightly *larger* than the domestic production of such products (INEGI, 1985, vol. 2, 611).

In the 1970–1977 period 50.8 percent of private investment (excluding residential construction) found its way into manufacturing industry. As can be seen from Table 4.5, during the oil boom years of 1978–1980 the share of private investment devoted to manufacturing declined to 33 percent, while investments in commerce and services, which had stood at 36 percent in the 1970–1977 period, rose to 50.9 percent (Ros, 1987, 72). The burgeoning of machinery and equipment imports and the increased emphasis on investments channeled toward services and commerce would suggest that the profits taken by the Mexican business elite were increasingly reinvested (when reinvested at all) in sectors of the economy in which returns would be quick, technological demands would be minimal, and risks would be small. The increasing role played by capital flight indicated that the private sector's reaction to the very sizable subsidies proffered by the government (coupled with the stimulus provided by large increases in government outlays) did not serve to proportionately increase real productive capacity. In short, the data suggested an increasing role for the rentier ethos.

When SEPAFIN claimed that it would be possible to achieve 10 percent real growth for ten years, it assumed that import controls would be strengthened. SEPAFIN's model demanded that the importation of consumer goods be restrained so that a portion of the oil revenues would be used to build domestic industrial capacity to expand future consumer goods production. The president, however, opted to maintain the free importation of products in line with the IMF agreement signed early in 1977. He also wanted to maintain the stability of the peso in spite of the fact that Mexico's inflation rate was well above that of the hard currency nations. Overruling SEPAFIN, López Portillo insisted on a policy mix that drew in imports of consumer goods at a rapid pace. René Villarreal termed this process the "desubstitution of imports" because national manufacturing was quickly being displaced by imports even as the manufacturing base grew (but by less than that of final demand) and profits remained high (Villarreal, 1982, 28–56). (See, for details, Table 3.3, Chapter 3.)

With oil revenues rising 300 percent (in U.S. dollars) in 1980 over those of 1979, little attention was paid to the distorting affects that the oil boom was having on the internal productive apparatus. With predictions that oil might soon rise to $100 a barrel, little attention was devoted to the question of a "proper" exchange rate. For a short period of time ground rents from oil served to mask the fundamental damage done to the Mexican productive apparatus during the heady days of the oil boom.

The Economic Breakdown of 1981–1982

The growing disequilibria brought on by the cumulative mismanagement of the oil boom reached an acute stage in mid-1981. Oil prices fell roughly 11 percent. Capital flight accelerated. (The flight rose from $4.5 billion in 1980 to $15 billion in 1981.) The balance-of-payments deficit increased. (There were no controls whatsoever on convertibility. Exchanging pesos for dollars was viewed as an "economic freedom" to be protected by the state.) The peso was allowed to devalue about 20 percent in the course of the year. In July the government announced a 4 percent cut in budgetary outlays for the remainder of the year. In December 1981 the government announced that the budget would not grow in real terms throughout 1982. Unexpectedly, in February of 1982, the peso was devalued 78 percent, with an additional 20 percent devaluation scheduled through the course of the year. In April 1982 the government announced (1) further spending cuts, (2) a tightening of the domestic supply of credit, (3) a sizable increase in controlled prices (especially products produce by the parastate firms), and (4) the negotiation of a new loan of $1 billion to cover short-term state spending. De Oteyza's scheme for 10 percent growth and Díaz Serrano's predictions of Mexico's quick end to debt financed growth were now to confront a reality that CEPAL had stressed from its outset—commodity booms were ephemeral, as five hundred years of Latin American history had proved.

Once Miguel de la Madrid Hurtado (1982–1988) had been elected in July 1982, the government announced further price increases—some as much as 100 percent. Secretly, negotiations began with the IMF. In August another devaluation sent the financial system into a complete state of chaos.

Throughout 1981 and 1982 the government borrowed massive amounts of short-term capital from the private international banks; public debt increased 102 percent from 1980 through 1982. According to research into the state's financial procedures, much of this money was never used by the state. Instead it was placed in the private banking system to protect the exchange rate. A study by Eduardo Jacobs and Wilson Peres noted that during 1981 the state generated 64.4 percent of the foreign exchange but utilized only 35.1 percent. Meanwhile, the private sector generated 35.6 percent of the foreign exchange but utilized 64.9 percent (Jacobs and Peres, 1983, 110). This then allowed the private sector (and above all the national groups of economic power that owned the private banks) to convert their liquid assets into U.S. dollars and take them out of the country (Fitzgerald, 1985, 223). As a result of speculation during the devaluations in 1981 and 1982, entire fortunes were accumulated, literally overnight. Dollars were bought before the devaluation, shipped out of the country, and then shipped back in to be converted into pesos at the more favorable exchange rate.

By 1981 relations between José López Portillo and the business elite had become particularly strained. This appeared to be a paradox because it would have been difficult to find an administration more solicitous of the needs of business. According to Mexican researchers, the explanation was as follows: A new and self-confident generation of businessmen (whose fathers' companies in many cases had grown and prospered under the helpful ministering of the state) were gaining influence within the business elite during the 1970s. These individuals ("juniors" in some accounts and "radicals" in others) were much more closely wedded to the most conservative (University of Chicago–Austrian School) views of the necessity and infallibility of the market than were the preceding generation of business magnates. According to their philosophical position, carefully summarized and presented by Salvador Cordero H. and his colleagues in *El Poder Empresarial en México*, the state had to be transformed into a mere provider of infrastructure and a keeper of the rules of the marketplace (Cordero H., Santín, and Tirado, 1983, 149–200). Given such a point of view, José López Portillo could only satisfy the business groups by destroying the Mexican state—something that he, as a devotee of Hegelian philosophy, was never capable of contemplating. As the business elite read the *Plan Nacional's* candid statement about the new autonomy that the state had gained by virtue of the oil boom, and observed the strange combination of Keynesian and hyper-Keynesian (Cambridge) economists operating the levers of state policymaking power, the elite undoubtedly realized that the concessions it had wrung from the López Portillo administration could quickly be canceled by a new turn toward statism. By 1978, noted Rogelio Hernández Rodríquez in his carefully researched book on government-business relations in the López Portillo sexenio, "the private sector believed that the years of stabilized growth had returned with the addition that now they could condition the action of the government. In this sense, it should be emphasized that while the old model of enrichment seemed to have been reconstructed the attitude of the private sector was now distinct in regard to the state" (Hernández Rodríquez, 1988, 150). This new attitude was "not to negotiate but to impose; the objective was to realize a radical victory that would eliminate even the remotest possibility that the state could affect the interests of this sector" (Hernández Rodríquez, 1988, 163).

José López Portillo, having entered office with an older and much more pragmatic generation of business leaders controlling the business associations, was at first nonplussed by this new attitude. By early 1982 the major business associations had become more strident, demanding prior consultation on all economic policymaking by the state and the power to condition de la Madrid Hurtado's presidential mandate. At this point President López Portillo began to strongly resist what he saw as a break in the decades-old corporatist *pacto* between the state and the private sector. As the crisis deepened in the spring of 1982, President López Portillo was unable to understand the magnitude of the disaster that had overtaken Mexico. As a Hegelian he resorted to moralizing—appealing to nationalism and national unity—while maintaining his *idée fixe* that there should be no controls on free convertibility of the peso (and that the peso should remain "strong"). According to Hernández Rodríquez's reconstruction of this fateful period, the top functionaries in the Treasury and at the Banco de México were *hiding* the magnitude of capital flight from the president (Hernández Rodríquez, 1988, 220). Hernández Rodríquez also noted that Díaz Serrano was operating with increasing autonomy at PEMEX during the same period. In the face of the crisis the state fell into disarray.

With speculation in retail commodities rampant in late February (after the 78 percent devaluation of the peso mentioned above) the Secretary of Commerce placed price controls on 47 groups of commodities. (This, had it been strictly enforced, would have given the state price-setting powers over 5,000 specific commodities.) He fined some of the biggest retailers (and most prominent representatives of the commercial oligarchy) for their violation of price controls. This, predictably, was viewed as confirmation of López Portillo's latent statism. The large retail and commercial interests united with the business elite's radicals in their open confrontation with the administration. (Commerce and trade capital accounted for more than 30 percent of the value of output of the entire economy. Including banking, transportation, and other services, the "service" sector accounted for 56 percent of GNP in 1975—a situation that did not changed in the 1980s [Solís, 1986, 170, 220].) The radicals could henceforth rely on powerful Mexican commercial and trade capital as allies in their assault on the state. This signaled a major shift in business-state relations.

As late as March 1982 the president was still pleading for national unity and loyalty to the nation, which indicated the degree to which he failed to comprehend the depth of the economic crisis. Hernández Rodríquez captured the president's inappropriate response—a demand that business behave responsibly—in the following statement:

> In March of 1982, when the Banco de México was virtually empty (of foreign exchange), with speculation and capital flight at an unprecedented level, and with evidence that the business elite had played the dominant role in all this, the President still was requesting that they should be bound by an obligation that they had not honored since 1977, when they had commenced taking advantage of the weakness of the government making a mockery of their [corporatist] obligations and going so far as to boldly challenge them (Hernández Rodríquez, 1988, 230–231).

Betrayed and isolated from the very interests that he had protected and nourished throughout the oil boom, President Lopéz Portillo was forced at this crucial juncture to alter his established pattern of behavior in business-government relations. Secretly he and a small group of advisers began to plot a new course that would culminate in the surprising bank nationalization of September 1982.

The Bank Nationalization

As Carlos Tello related in his account of the bank nationalization, José López Portillo placed Tello in charge of generating a plan to nationalize the banks in March of 1982 (Tello, 1984). At that time it was not certain that any drastic steps would be taken to control the private circuit of financial capital. The nationalization scheme was only one of several plans—including controls over capital flight (none existed)—that were under consideration. Meanwhile the business elite continued to chafe at the new controls over prices, while capital flight remained at its already high rate. By June, according to Tello, an "organized campaign" by the business elite to attribute to the government full responsibility for the chaotic economic situation had achieved complete success (Tello, 1984, 99). José López Portillo's crisis of legitimation extended to his own cabinet, where the head of the Banco de México refused to inform the secretary of the Treasury and other members of the government of the true status of the hard currencies reserves of the country. On August 1 Mexico announced to a stunned international financial community that it simply could not continue to pay interest and principal payments on its international government debt. In a word, the country was bankrupt. Officially, the debt crisis of the Third World had begun. On August 7 the peso was devalued again—this time by 60 percent.

August of 1982 would live on in the memory of all Mexicans old enough to experience the wild financial turbulence of those days. The peso commenced to float on a daily, and even hourly, basis. Few would quarrel with the notion that for thirty days Mexico endured a sustained financial panic. The size of the external debt was known only in the vaguest sense, with the government underestimating it by a third or more. The amount of capital flight was unknown, but rumors of quick riches abounded. The government seemingly was willing to do no more than permit the chaos and commence (in July) serious negotiations with the IMF for a rescue plan.

Still reeling from the 40 percent price increase in a number of government-controlled commodities (such as gasoline and electricity) in July, the middle class had to accept another bitter lesson in powerlessness: Currency exchange was suspended for a week on August 12, while dollar-deposit bank accounts (that the middle class had extensively utilized as a hedge against devaluations, particularly in 1981 and 1982) were frozen. When, weeks later, some withdrawals were allowed, only pesos were paid and at an exchange rate 30 percent below the rate on August 12. In the last two weeks of August, with the peso fluctuating wildly (by more than 30 percent), those with dollar deposits lost as much as 54 percent of their savings by drawing out funds (if they could manage this) at the market rate of exchange. In a nation where currency stability and free convertibility had been bedrock tenets of economic policymaking for decades, the harsh treatment that the middle class received profoundly contributed to a new and deep sense of political illegitimacy and breakdown.

On September 1 López Portillo delivered his last annual presidential *informe*—a speech that is often several hours in duration and takes place during a national holiday. In a country where secrecy is the *modus vivendi* of rule, and where political rumor is the natural counterpart, it is normally possible to penetrate the veil of secrecy by carefully weighing the rumors. Yet there was no rumor of a bank nationalization. José López Portillo was being watched on television by millions of Mexicans because they were angry, anxious, and frightened—not because they thought that he had anything constructive or new planned for the remaining three months of his rule. They wanted to see him humbled and shamed. Instead, in one stroke, he changed the political and economic climate in the country, gaining renewed legitimacy among the poor, organized labor, sections of the middle class, and particularly the Mexican Left. His actions demonstrated, once again, that the state had formidable institutional powers to draw upon in a crisis situation. But this came at a price in terms of changing the rules of the game between the state and the business elite.

How large a blow to the business elite was delivered by the bank nationalization? According to a study conducted by the journal *Estratégia*, the banks and the holding companies that they owned/controlled accounted for roughly 8-10 percent of the total value of the assets of the 500 largest private companies in Mexico (Estratégia, 1982, 14). The 54 private banks that were nationalized either controlled or participated in the management of nearly 1,000 firms, including some of the largest and most dynamic (Morera and Basave, 1981). Moreover, the assets held by the banks constituted funds that could be highly leveraged (they could be utilized to control very large amounts of capital that were lent by, or through, the banks). Because of the unusual profit-making capabilities of these funds, it is not analytically correct to minimize the significance of the nationalization on the grounds that "only" roughly 10 percent of the assets of the private sector were expropriated by the state. The nationalization was a real economic blow to the business elite.

The impact went beyond the interests of the financial oligarchy because what had happened in finance could be easily extended to virtually every other sector of the economy. This was not lost on the business elite, which immediately began to change tactics in its ongoing war of position and movement against the state. As we shall see in the Chapter 6, the business elite was able almost immediately to bring about the partial denationalization of the banks under Miguel de la Madrid Hurtado. (His successor, Carlos Salinas de Gortari, subsequently became the target of the financial oligarchy's pressure to completely reverse the nationalization.)

As Carlos Tello (architect of the nationalization) maintained, there were more than conjunctural reasons for the steps taken on September 1, 1982. The banks had undergone a rapid process of concentration. In 1950, 75 percent of total bank assets were spread among forty-two banking companies. By 1981 only six banks remained to control the same share (75 percent) of the assets (Tello, 1984, 29). The top four banks controlled 60 percent of all bank assets. As the power of the handful that remained increased, these banks were able to wrest a growing share of the economic surplus from other sectors of the economy. For example, Tello's data showed that bank profits, adjusted for inflation, increased 140 percent in the four-year period 1978–1981 (Tello, 1984, 56). By way of contrast, what is known in Mexican national incomes accounts as the "surplus of exploitation"—roughly the profit share in national income—*declined* slightly even as the national income rose nearly 40 percent in real terms in this period (Huerta, 1986, 229). Thus, with the profit *share* on the decline, a 140 percent increase in the profits of the banks had to translate into a reduction in the share of total profits going to the nonfinancial sector of the economy. As such, the financial sector of the economy, an essentially nonproductive component, was appropriating profits from the productive elements of the economy and thus reducing their capacity for real expansion.

Furthermore, the banks were playing an important role in policymaking circles because the major banks were well represented on the board of directors of the Banco de México. In addition, due to their interlocks and/or associations and affiliations with the transnational banks, the banks were important participants in the process of granting the Mexican government international loans from the private transnational banks. For these reasons Carlos Tello viewed Mexican "finance capital" as "the dominant faction of capital in the 1970s" (Tello, 1984, 45). To this list of activities, that suggests the complex and powerful role that the private banks played in the economy, should be added another—the banks were crucial to the government in funding and refunding Mexico's *internal* debt. Given the debt-driven model of Ortiz Mena, the banks had long ago been catapulted into a unique position of power. It would be naive to believe that they had not learned to exploit their role as necessary intermediaries in refinancing the government's debt during the course of a quarter century of systematic debt-driven growth.

If, in fact, the reaction at the time to the bank nationalization was a bit overblown, it is nonetheless an exaggeration in the other direction to minimize the significance of the nationalization on the grounds either that "only" 10 percent of the capital of the "financial oligarchy" had been expropriated or that the government banks already controlled the majority of bank assets. Nafinsa, Somex, and several other government-owned banks did indeed control the majority of bank assets in a strict accounting approach. But Nafinsa and Somex had their assets sunk in vast industrial projects, whereas the private banks were turning over their banking capital at a rapid rate and taking "promoters' profits" in arranging loans, floating bond issues, and carrying on similar tasks.

Thus, it is a distortion of the structure of the Mexican banking sector to maintain or imply that the nationalization was not of great significance merely because the banking sector was "mostly" owned by the state.

Having listed several reasons for arguing that the bank nationalization constituted a *fundamental rupture* with the past pattern of business-government relations, it is nonetheless necessary to caution against overstating the importance of the act. There were numerous academic studies that emphasized the power of finance capital in Mexico in the 1970s—often to the point of suggesting that finance capital dominated other forms of national capital *and* exerted determinant pressure over policymaking within the state. For example, in an otherwise illuminating study of various factions of the business elite, Concheiro and Fragosa greatly overstated the autonomous power of finance capital. They claimed that the ABM was "the owner of the country" (Conchiero and Fragoza, 1979, 245). In a similar study emphasizing the asserted *instrumental* relationship between the state and finance capital, María Elena Cardero and José M. Quijano claimed that

> the monetary and financial policies that the state applied between 1978 and 1981 . . . very probably reflected the desires of the private banks. This leads one to think that, apparently, the banking sector has a weight relatively superior to that of industrial capital at the moment when certain aspects of economic policymaking are decided, and furthermore, in their interaction with industrial and commercial firms the banks continue to be dominant (Cardero and Quijano, 1982, 196).

In a *conjunctural* sense it seems clear that the private banks did gain power during the 1970s *vis-à-vis* national industrial and commercial capital, transnational capital, and the state. But in the structural sense of there having been a long-term or lasting transformation toward bank dominance *over* the state, the very act of nationalization would argue against the weight that Tello, Concheiro, *et al*, and Cardero and Quijano attributed to Mexican finance capital.

By 1982 the capitalist-rentier state was clearly in danger of becoming simply a rentier state and the logic of capitalism had to be imposed upon the banking sector. Thus, there was a *systemic* need for a redefinition of the relationship between bank and nonbank capital. This took the dramatic form of the bank nationalization. With hindsight it is apparent that those who opted for a finance capital interpretation of Mexico's economy greatly understated or fundamentally misunderstood the structural role that the state had to play in an economic system that was *fundamentally*, but certainly not entirely, capitalist. This was the interpretation advanced by Jorge Basave in a study co-authored by Julio

Mogel, Miguel Rivera, and Alejandro Toledo. They pointed out that many scholars were guilty of "expressing erroneous conceptions of the character of the Mexican state in that they locate that state in terms of its being the *exclusive* representative of the interests of only one faction of the bourgeoisie—the financial" (Basave, Mogel, Rivera, and Toledo, 1982, 56).

Basave and his associates proceeded to offer one of the more acute observations to be found in the vast literature that touched on the nationalization: "The consequences of the particular development of finance capital in Mexico and of the economic policymaking of the state have obscured the fundamental character of the latter as well as the degree of latitude consistent with the central role that it occupies in the process of capital accumulation in Mexico" (Basave, Mogel, Rivera, and Toledo, 1982, 5). These writers correctly concluded that the bank nationalization "is a measure that alters the power relationship within the interior of the power bloc and reveals the high degree of autonomy that the state still can put into play in critical moments against the distinct factions of the bourgeoisie" (Basave, Mogel, Rivera, and Toledo, 1982, 58).

It was interesting to note that the younger "radicals" of the business elite, particularly of the financial oligarchy, greatly overestimated their own power over the state and society. They neglected the institutionalized power of the state and the historic ties of much of the business elite to the state. Immediately upon announcement of the nationalization, the radicals sought an open confrontation with the state. Decrying the act as representing a distinct shift toward socialism (a view echoed by most of the Left whose misinterpretation of the event was notable), the ex-bankers and the CCE called for a general strike of business to bring the economy to its knees. But, as Cristina Puga noted, these and similar efforts by the radicals failed miserably (Puga, 1984a). The younger radicals of the financial elite and their counterparts in industry and commerce overestimated their own power, misunderstood the historic structural role of the state in the economy, and underestimated or failed to understand the nature of the profound divisions of interest between financial capital and industrial and commercial capital. The state was able to gain outright support for the nationalization from some Mexican industrial capitalists who had been rather shabbily treated by the banks. Other business elements found their ties to the state to be of more importance than their allegiance to the interests of bank capital. Thus, the majority of the business groups simply did not lend their support to the efforts of the radicals to engage in an open confrontation with the state in late 1982. In part, some of the lack of cohesiveness exhibited by the business elite in the face of the nationalization undoubtedly arose from the view that a quieter effort to undo the nationalization would succeed (as it did) once the probusiness, conservative de la Madrid Hurtado was in power.

Yet on a deeper level, as Celso Garrido, Edmundo Jacobo, and Enrique Quintana maintained, the implicit *pacto político* between the business elite and the state had been violated (Garrido, Jacobo, and Quintana, 1987, 532). If in the short term the radicals were left to appear shrill and foolish, in the longer term the business elite would move to ensure that the degree of state autonomy that the nationalization exhibited would become a thing of the past. In the short term the business elite lacked the organization and the commitment to confront the state as a united entity. Many were willing to accept the short-term benefits of a restructured banking system that would channel credit in a more orderly fashion toward productive activities. But the long-term need to restructure the state in such a manner as to *constrain* and *redefine* the limits of state autonomy were made ever more apparent and pressing with the nationalization. During the next sexenio the Mexican state would in fact be fundamentally and perhaps irreversibly restructured. Many radicals would merge into the mainstream (at that stream turned Right), and Mexico would construct a brave new neoliberal state.

Notes

1. The source that best demonstrated the inability of the economic cabinet to comprehend the key problem that it confronted was Carlos Tello, *La Política Económica en México*. Tello, subdirector for credit of the Secretary of the Treasury, offered a detailed account of Luis Echeverría's sexenio, yet he could not explain why the economic cabinet failed to put together a viable program for growth (Tello, 1979).

2. Coparmex had 15,000 affiliated members in 1986. The businesses controlled by members employed 2 million workers—that is, 24 percent of the full-time private sector jobs in Mexico (Bravo, 1987, 92).

5

The Structure of the State Sector: The Parastate Firms

The parastate sector has been the vanguard of national development.
—Miguel de la Madrid (1981)

Total public sector income in Mexico, standing at 30.3 percent of national income in 1987, was not high in relation to that of the advanced capitalist nations. What was notable about the Mexican public sector was the size of the parastate firms. In 1987, 41.2 percent of the income of the state came from these firms, according to the government's method of compiling the data (CIEN, 1988a, 10). In fact, such data greatly understated the role played by the parastates—in particular that of the petroleum parastate PEMEX. Under a separate heading the government compiled its tax income from petroleum—domestic and export. If these taxes, which logically derived from PEMEX's products, are attributed to the parastate sector, then 57.8 percent of the income of the state came from that sector. Table 5.1 presents data on the relationship between parastate sector income and income of the entire state sector in 1983—when the state's income reached its peak as a share of GDP—and in 1987 and 1988 (the two most recent years available). Note that in spite of the large reduction in state sector income since 1983 (expressed as a share of GDP in column 1), parastate income has remained of vital importance (column 2). Note further that the decline in oil export revenues explained only 42 percent of the decline in the share of state sector income (column 4 and 1).

To put the matter in perspective, the 1987 income of the parastate sector (strictly defined) was 3.3 times larger than that taken from the income tax—the next largest revenue source. Although overwhelming in its size, PEMEX is far from being the only major source of revenue for the state. In total, the other parastate firms had a net income 1.8 times greater than that of PEMEX in 1987 (CIEN, 1988b, 136). Following behind PEMEX are a number of quite sizable state-owned firms, the largest being the CFE, which produces and sells all the electric power

Table 5.1: State Sector Income

Year	(1) State Income as a Share of GNP	(2) Parastate Income as a Share of State Income	(3) Parastate Plus Oil Export Income as a Share of State Income	(4) Oil Export Income as a Share of GNP
1970	19.5%	n.a.	58.5%	n.a.*
1978	27.4%	n.a.	62.2%	n.a.
1983	34.6%	42.7%	62.2%	6.8%
1987	30.3%	41.2%	57.8%	5.0%
1988**	27.4%	39.8%	53.4%	3.7%

*n.a. = not available

** estimated

Sources: CIEN, "Las Finanzas Públicas: 1982-1988," *CIEN 100*, 9, no. 2 (September 1988), p. 10; Robert Looney, *Economic Policymaking in Mexico* (Durham, N.C.: Duke University Press, 1985), p. 154.

in the nation. Other major parts of the state sector include TELMEX, the telephone company; FERTIMEX, the fertilizer monopoly; Sidermex, the state-owned steel complex; and CONASUPO, a state-owned food buying and retailing company with a presence throughout the nation. The state has also been very active in the sizable mining sector of the nation—producing 75.5 percent of the value of total mining output in 1985 (Tamayo, 1987, 261).

An approximate idea of the importance of the parastate sector can also be derived via national income accounting. The national income accounts in Mexico draw a distinction between the value-added by the public sector and by the parastate sector. Included in the former but excluded from the latter are governmental services of an administrative and managerial nature at the level of the municipalities, states, and the federal government. Examples would include public works, outlays for the military, police, courts and prisons, the office of the president and its many secretariats, and most educational programs. The public sector accounted for 24.4 percent of total national income in 1984—a figure that included value-added produced in the parastate sector. The parastate sector *alone* accounted for 17.0 percent of the national income in 1984 and included such diverse elements as government-operated mines, the petroleum industry, 328 manufacturing firms, 1 telephone company, several research institutions, the banks, 2 social security agencies, the major airlines, the railroads, toll roads and bridges, and CONASUPO (Tamayo, 1987, 260; Ruiz Dueñas, 1982, 30–31).

Although it is necessary to resort to indirect methods of accounting and estimation, it can be readily demonstrated that the bulk of the value-added by the parastate sector derived from a relatively narrow range of state activities. Thus, in 1984 PEMEX produced 11.1 percent of the total national income, the state's numerous manufacturing enterprises created 3.7 percent of the national income, the two nationalized electric corporations produced 1.0 percent of the national income, and the mining firms owned by the state produced 0.66 percent of the national income (Huerta, 1986, 201; INEGI, 1985, vol. 1, 314; Machado, Peres, and Delgado, 1985, 123). Adding these figures, we find that the preceding activities accounted for 16.46 percent of the national income. The residual of 0.54 percent derived from the state's activities in communications and transportation.

Given the abnormally large service sector of the economy—which accounted for 50.5 percent of total national income in 1984—it might be more appropriate to compare the value of nonservice sector production against that of the parastate sector in order to situate the role of the parastates in the national economy. Given the pervasiveness of monopolistic practices in the service sector, coupled with the grossly inefficient practices that prevail in the financial institutions and throughout the small business retailing sector, it is more accurate to compare the role of the parastate sector to the primary and secondary sectors rather than to that of the economy at large. Nonservice parastate production came to 16.46 percent of total national income, as mentioned, but it accounted for 33.3 percent of the value-added of the *total nonservice production of the economy* in 1984.

Assigning significance to the relatively high level of state participation in the combined primary and secondary sectors would depend upon how one viewed a very old debate in economic theory over productive versus unproductive activities. To the classical economists such as Adam Smith and David Ricardo, making such a distinction was a matter of some importance in analyzing the issue of economic development. In contemporary neoclassical formulations of the matter, the distinction is not considered to be viable. To the classical economists, it seemed that primary and secondary activities (such as agriculture, fishing, timber harvesting, mining and extractive industries, the production of power, construction and manufacturing) took logical precedent over transportation, communications, banking, and insurance (the service sector). The primary and secondary sectors *produced* things of value, while the service sector (at best) merely distributed them and kept account of their value. The first function (production) logically preceded the second. To the degree that one is persuaded by the classical distinction between productive versus unproductive activities one is more likely to assign significance to the sizable representation of the parastate firms in the primary and secondary sectors. Clearly, the matter cannot be discussed at length here. Yet its potential significance is such that it can scarcely be ignored in any final assessment of the significance of the parastate sector.

Concentration in the Parastate Sector

From the aforementioned material it is clear that the majority of the approximately one thousand parastate firms held by the state in 1984 did not contribute significantly to the state's level of production. This can be seen more clearly with the data presented in Table 5.2. Here use is made of a study of a sample of the parastate firms that was conducted by Benito Rey Romay using data from 1981 (Rey Romay, 1984, 132–141). In this sample, 294 of the largest parastate firms were analyzed—the sample accounts for more than 90 percent of the economic activity of all the parastate firms. The top 10 state-owned firms accounted for 90 percent of the total capital of the sampled state firms (column 2) and 77 percent of the total sales (column 3). In most discussions of the *size* of the parastate sector the issue is discussed in terms of the *number* of firms controlled by the state. Data such as those in Table 5.2 demonstrate that this commonly used numerical method is deceptive. It is also important to understand the extreme degree of concentration in the state sector.

Growth and Structure of the Parastate Sector

Tables 5.3, 5.4, and 5.5 provide summary descriptions of the growth and structure of the parastate sector. Table 5.3 conveys an impression of the dynamics of the growth of this sector from the 1930s onward. It includes both a depiction of the rate of expansion of the key parastate firms and the total of all state sector firms and financial trust funds *fideicomisos* and other financial entities in 1984 and 1988. The data from 1934 through January 1985 depict the creation of core state entities such as manufacturing, mining, agricultural, and service-related firms. It excludes purely financial entities and trust funds as well as public firms involved in health and education. Although insufficiently detailed, it, along with the accompanying tables, helps to form a composite picture of the parastate sector.

As has been discussed in the preceding chapter, the noticeable increase in core state firms between 1970 and 1982 was somewhat deceiving because many of the new firms were quite small in relative terms.

Table 5.2: Concentration in the Parastate Sector

(1) Parastate Firm	(2) % of Total Capital	(3) % of Total Sales	(4) Products
PEMEX	.52	.55	Oil, petroleum products, petrochemicals
Comisión Federal de Electricidad	.24	.07	Electricity
Fundidora Monterrey*	.01	.01	Steel
Siderúrgica Las Truchas	.014	.009	Steel
Ingenios Azucareros Estatales (52 firms)**	.015	.028	Sugar
FERTIMEX	.016	.022	Fertilizer, pesticides
Altos Hornos de México	.045	.031	Steel
Industrias Peñoles (21 Firms)***	.013	.021	Mining: lead, zinc, copper, iron ore, silver
Mexicana de Cobre***	.015	.006	Copper
Grupo Condumex (19 firms)****	.007	.012	Cables, conductors, auto parts
Top 10 parastate firms as % of total sample of 294 parastate firms	89.5%	76.9%	

* Liquidated in 1986
** Privatization sale began in 1988.
*** The mining sector commenced privatization in 1988.
**** As of 1988 the state declared it would sell all auto-related industries.
Sources: Based on data and information provided by numerous Mexico City newspaper accounts of liquidations and privatizations (1986-1988) and calculated from from material in Benito Rey Romay, *La Ofensiva Empresarial Contra la Intervención del Estado* (México: Siglo Veintiuno Editores, 1984), pp. 132-141.

Table 5.3: Core* Parastate Firms (Date of Creation) and Total Parastate Firms

Period	Number of Core Parastates	Number of All Parastates
Before 1934	2	
1934-1940	11	
1940-1946	6	
1946-1952	14	
1952-1958	17	
1958-1964	31	
1964-1970	55	
1970-1976	160	
1976-1982	98	
1982-1985	2	
Date of creation not specified	102	
Total 1985	498	n.a.**
Total 1984	n.a.	1212
Total 1988	n.a.	448

* Excludes financial entities, bank holding companies, and health and education entities

** not available

Sources: María Amparo Casar and Wilson Peres, *El Estado Empresario en México: Agotamiento o Renovación?* (México: Siglo Veintiuno Editores, 1988), p. 34; José Antonio Zuñiga, "Concluirá la Desincorporación de 702 Paraestatales Este Sexenio, Dice la SHCP," *Uno Más Uno*, June 13, 1988, p. 13; José Antonio Zuñiga, "El Sector Paraestatal Quedará Integrado por Solo 448 Empresas y Organismos al Terminar Este Sexenio," *Uno Más Uno*, July 15, 1988, p. 14.

Nonetheless, the reach of the state steadily increased through 1982, albeit at a pace somewhat slower than the cumulative numbers cited in Table 5.3 would suggest. By 1984 the state participated in 1,212 firms and entities, some quite small. By December 1988 the privatization drive had eliminated an estimated 764 of these entities, leaving a total of 448. As can be seen from Table 5.4, the privatization drive had a particular impact upon the parastate firms in the industrial sector. Here the "core parastate firms" are divided in terms of commerce, services, and industry for the years 1984 and 1988. It is notable that 283 of the 375 *industrial* parastate firms were privatized, merged, or liquidated. (The privatization program will be examined later in this chapter.)

Most research regarding the parastate sector has concentrated on the state's manufacturing firms because researchers have presumed a very direct causal link between the industrialization of the nation and the participation of the parastate firms within the industrial sector. Consequently, data has been compiled from the industrial census that describe

Table 5.4: Core Parastate Firms, 1984 and 1988

Sector	Number of Firms (1984)	Number of Firms (1988)
Commerce	43	d.u.*
Services	80	d.u.
Industry	375	92
Mining	(47)	d.u.
Manufacturing	(328)	d.u.
Total	498	d.u.

* d.u.= data unavailable

Sources: María Amparo Casar and Wilson Peres, *El Estado Empresario en México: Agotamiento o Renovación?* (México: Siglo Veintiuno Editores, 1988), p. 34; Theresa García and Noe Cruz, "El Estado Optar Solo por Regular la Economía: SEMIP," *El Financiero*, December 1, 1988, p. 33.

the weight of the parastate firms according to types of industrial products. Table 5.5 indicates the degree of state influence in consumer, intermediate, and capital goods, when state ownership reached its highest point. Although Table 5.5 presents merely a static depiction of the distribution of the state's industries in terms of goods produced, it should also be noted that from 1970 to 1981 the annual rate of growth of the state's industrial sector was 9.4 percent—far in excess of that of the industrial sector at large, that had annual growth of 6.6 percent (Machado, Peres, and Delgado, 1985, 126). Thus, the industrial sector grew much faster than did that of the total economy from 1970 to 1981 (the industrial share of national income rose from 34.4 percent in 1970 to 38.2 percent in 1982). But the state's industrial firms grew even faster (Huerta, 1986, 201). Such a pattern suggested that the state's industrial firms were the *leading* component within the leading sector of the economy.

The data presented in Table 5.5 do give some support to the state monopoly capitalism theory of the Mexican state. As discussed in Chapter 2, the theory of state monopoly capitalism maintains that the state's role in the industrial process is largely limited to that of providing intermediate goods to the largest private sector corporations at low prices, this policy represents a subsidy to the private sector firms. In 1983, 78.5 percent of the state's industrial output was concentrated in intermediate goods (Machado, Peres, and Delgado, 1985, 126). At minimum, the theory of state monopoly capitalism provides a framework for predicting the product mix of the state's industrial sector, which is confirmed by the available

Table 5.5: State Share of Industrial Production
(in percent)

Type of Product	Year	
	1981	1983
Consumer nondurables	4.7	5.5
Consumer durables*	11.4	4.4
Intermediate goods		
Nonpetroleum	14.7	15.2
Petroleum derivatives and petrochemicals	94. 1	95.8
Capital goods	6.7	8.3
Share of total industrial production	12.7	16.2

* The drop in consumer durables production was due to the privatization of the State's holdings in autos, trucks, buses, and parts for this sector.

Sources: Based on data from Secretaría de Programación y Presupuesto, *Cuentas de Producción del Sector Público, 1975-1983* (México: Insitituto Nacional de Estadística, Geografía e Informática [INEGI] and SPP, 1984), and Jorge Machado, Wilson Peres, and Orlando Delgado "La Estructura de la Industria Estatal, 1970-85," *Economía Mexicana*, no. 7 (1985), p. 124.

data. Based on his study of 294 industrial parastate firms, Benito Rey Romay (a retired high-level career official at Nafinsa) vigorously supported this interpretation of the state's industrial corporations:

> In broad terms it can be concluded that the state firms, notwithstanding their monopolistic structure and capitalist social relations, never engage in profit making for their own purposes; rather they transfer such profits to the private sector, allowing them to have levels of profitability in the last decade that are without precedent and that strengthen their growth and expansion (Rey Romay, 1984, 88).

He did, however, maintain that since 1983 (with the adoption of the "real prices" policy that pushed up virtually all parastate prices), the program of massive subsidies to the private sector via underpriced intermediate products (such as oil and natural gas) has been seriously curtailed.

Issues of the State Sector

Having now discussed several empirical aspects of the economic apparatus of the Mexican state, it is necessary to turn to a decidedly subjective and ideologically charged issue—the impact the state has had on the economy. Critics of state intervention point to what they believe are the weaknesses of state intervention, particularly the state's fiscal deficit. This they see as a manifestation of the essential incapacity of state institutions to operate efficiently when unconstrained by market competition. Pragmatic defenders of Mexico's state intervention maintain that the conditions of undevelopment demand extraordinary measures, many of which can be best undertaken by the state. Populists have argued that only through the state can the radical goals of the Mexican Revolution be realized.

The discussion has not taken place in a historical vacuum, nor has it been an idle one. Deep passions are involved on both sides. It would not be overstating the matter to argue that the debate over the state has been *the* public policy issue since the breakup of the stabilizing growth model in 1970. What Carlos Tello and Rolando Cordera aptly called "the dispute for the nation" in their widely read 1981 book of that title has continued—at least through the presidential election of 1988 (Reding, 1988; Cordera and Tello, 1981). Eighteen intensive years of dispute over the role of the state had passed without any clear social resolution to the matter—a point underscored by the presidential electoral challenge in 1988 to the PRI's political monopoly by the populist Cuauhtémoc Cárdenas (Cypher, 1988b, 9–11, 21).

The critiques and attacks on statism have come from the political Right (both in the business sector and the Catholic church) and more recently among sectors of the middle class (Loaeza, 1985; González Gary, 1985; Vargas, 1985). The business sector has raised two issues: (1) the *size* of the state and the nature of its functions and (2) the *growth* of the state.

The Business Sector's Critique of the State

Two ideological strains are to be found in the business elite's attack on what it defines as statism. Rolando Cordera and Carlos Tello defined the first as "the Neoliberal project," which advances the essential ideas of neoclassical economic theory (Cordera and Tello, 1981, 78–106). In this view, the role of the state is limited to that of the "watchman" who sets the rules of the market, enforces them, but does little else. The key assumption of the neoclassicals is that with the free play of market forces there will *automatically* be set into motion economic agents that will interact to achieve growth and full employment. State intervention diverts these economic agents from achieving such ends and assures that resources (land, labor, and capital) are utilized either suboptimally or in an unproductive manner. Without considering whether the backwardness of the economy might warrant special consideration, particularly in terms of the role of the state, many Mexican businessmen subscribe to a carbon copy of the position taken in England by the nineteenth-century Manchester liberals.

A second, more visceral, free-market stance is also to be found. Its intellectual debt is not to Manchester but to the Austrian School's libertarian thinkers, such as Ludwig von Mises and Fredrick von Hayek (Huss, 1987; Cordero H., Santín, and Tirado, 1984, 99–136). In this view, the emphasis shifts from the logic of the free market to the fragility and importance of *individual incentives* and the inviolability of private property. In this philosophical variant—particularly championed by Coparmex and the CCE (among others)—the state has virtually no role to play in the economy aside from preserving individual prerogatives over the free exercise of private property (Puga, 1984b, 187–201).

An apocalyptic orientation is, at best, scarcely disguised. That is, virtually any move toward state intervention is seen as nurturing the quick-sprouting seeds of socialism. Of the two approaches to the question of the state, the Austrian approach appears to most deeply entrenched. Indeed, one well-known Mexican economist, Hector Guillén, has maintained that the Austrian principles in fact guided the restructuring of the Mexican state under Miguel de la Madrid Hurtado (Guillén, 1988).

In contrast to the neoliberal and Austrian positions that dominate the terrain of ideological discourse over the role of the state, it should not be forgotten that in the 1940s, 1950s, and 1960s an indigenous strain of Keynesianism was to be found among sectors of the business elite. As discussed in Chapters 3 and 4, this Keynesian position, most strongly associated with the new group of industrialists, was discredited by the failures of hyper-Keynesian forms of policymaking in the 1970s. Nevertheless, through the 1980s, Canacintra adopted a position that was broadly Keynesian. That is, Canacintra opposed the "austerity" programs of the de la Madrid Hurtado administration (and those of the IMF) on the grounds that the internal market was being disrupted, if not destroyed, by deep cuts in the standard of living. Moreover, Canacintra opted for tariff protection in opposition to the neoliberal and Austrian position that argued that Mexico should end all state intervention in international trade. Canacintra sought a strong, growing internal market, which in Mexico has long been associated with the growth of the public sector and a reliance on that sector to create opportunities for expansion. By the early 1980s Canacintra's position had become an isolated one within the policymaking apparatus. The hegemonic ideological position drew from and combined elements of the neoliberal and Austrian approaches to political economy.

The Failures of the State?

The neoliberal and Austrian critique of the state centers, in part, on the fact that the parastate sector has not been able to cover its costs of production and expansion. This has been taken as *prima facie* evidence of the innate inefficiency of public sector enterprise. In the period 1970–1982 the parastate firms were the source of 60 percent of the total deficit of the public sector (Tamayo, 1987, 276). In the late 1970s the share of the deficit attributable to the parastate sector as a whole was roughly 3.7 percent of the GDP (Ros, 1987, 78). By 1987 the parastate sector's deficit had been trimmed to 1.6 percent of GDP and amounted to only 10 percent of the total public sector deficit (CIEN, 1988b, 121, 129). Thus, the deficit of the state firms *was* significant in terms of the macroeconomy prior to the neoliberal enforcement of "real prices." The real prices approach cut the parastate firms' deficit (expressed as a share of GDP) by 57 percent from the late 1970s to 1987. (With large increases in the price of petroleum products and, particularly, of electricity, the deficit declined again in 1988.)

In 1982, the peak year for the public sector deficit—which stood at 17.9 percent of GDP—the parastate sector's deficit was attributable to PEMEX, CFE, and FERTIMEX. Ninety-four percent of the parastate deficit was due to PEMEX and the CFE, with the latter accounting for 63.8 percent of the total (Tamayo, 1987, 278). Thus, on balance, the other roughly 1,000 parastate firms were paying their way in 1982. Sizable, hidden subsidies to industry, business, and consumers in the form of below-cost pricing accounted for the deficits at PEMEX and the CFE.

Given these data, the blanket charge of innate inefficiency would seem to be without basis if such inefficiency is to be measured in terms of the crude yardstick of covering total costs. The parastates no longer are an important source of the public sector deficit. Yet that deficit in 1987 came to 16.9 percent of the GDP. (See Chapter 6, Table 6.4, for these data.) That the public sector deficit remained at near record levels even after the restructuring of prices in the parastate sector was due primarily to the steady increase in the size of the public sector's debt and the increasing costs of servicing that debt. Interest outlays absorbed more than *two-thirds* of the public sector's revenue income in 1987. According to the neoliberal argument, most of the 1987 deficit was nonetheless attributable to the parastate sector because this sector contracted more than three-quarters of the public sector's debt in the 1950s, 1960s, and 1970s (Ayala, 1979, 417).

Although there is a considerable degree of truth in the neoliberal's insistence that the public sector's deficit in the late 1980s should be linked to the past financing methods of the parastate firms, defenders of the public sector have pointed to a number of factors that must be considered in any final assessment of the matter. First, it is argued that the state has been forced to undertake several projects that are by nature extremely capital intensive. In this view, borrowing is a structural necessity determined by the development pattern of the nation (Tamayo, 1987, 275–280). Accordingly, the large investments of the parastate firms should be viewed in terms of their long-term impact on the development of the nation rather than in narrow annual profit/loss accounting methods.

Second, although the parastates contracted most of the debt, much of the international credits received were deposited in the national banking system and then utilized as foreign exchange for capital flight purposes by the economic and bureaucratic elite (Fitzgerald, 1985). Conservative estimates of Mexico's total capital flight suggest it amounted to two-thirds of the value of the total external debt (Ros, 1987, 108). Much research needs to be conducted to determine what portion of the parastate sector's external debt arose because of actual investment needs and what was in fact accumulated because the parastates were being utilized as a rentier mechanism to channel foreign currency to the economic and bureaucratic elite. Until this matter can be categorically settled, it is not possible to determine the role the parastates have played in the growth of the debt. What *does* seem beyond debate is that the neoliberal attribution of the public sector's deficit to past errors committed by the parastate sector (ignoring as it does the process of capital flight in that the private sector strongly participated) is greatly exaggerated.

Third, an undetermined yet certainly not inconsiderable portion of the debt arose because the state had long played the role of buying out the private sector's worst economic miscalculations. Indeed, María Amparo Casar and Wilson Peres demonstrated that fully 53 percent of the parastate firms originated from private sector bankruptcies (Casar and Peres, 1988, 31–32). When these firms were acquired, the state also assumed the burden of their internal and external debts.

Fourth, in the aftermath of the debt crisis of 1982, the state assumed the risk of foreign currency revaluations of the private sector's foreign debt. (Between 1983 and 1985 the state borrowed, and used its reserves, in order to spend $10–$11 billion to subsidize the foreign debts of a handful of firms owned by the groups [Garrido and Quintana, 1988, 54].) Exactly how much of the current public sector debt is due to (1) assumption of the debts of bankrupt firms, (2) debts from firms acquired during the bank nationalization in 1982, and (3) schemes that enabled the private sector to shift the burden of debt revaluation onto the public sector has not been carefully enumerated. It is, however, clear that a significant portion of what is normally understood as the public sector's debt is in fact *the socialized debt of the private sector*. A great deal of caution must be exercised in interpreting the relationship between the size of the public sector's debt (external and internal) and debt that in fact arose because of the contraction of debt by the parastate agencies. The two, clearly, are quite far from being synonymous.

Fifth, Nafinsa, as *the* state development bank, had the authority to contract most of the public sector's foreign debt. Yet Mexico's private banks participated heavily in the debt accumulation—partly because they owned shares in many of the parastate firms (which were in fact jointly owned by the private sector and/or transnational corporations). When Nafinsa negotiated with the transnational banks for public sector credits, the Mexican banks were involved in attempting to steer Nafinsa toward *their* international affiliate banks. In other words, the private sector banks were actively engaged in seeking "promoter's profits" from the public sector's expanding indebtedness. Furthermore, they were often seeking to expand debt in firms in that they were partial owners. Finally, the major banks, through joint private-public sector advisory roles and through the ABM were active participants in the public sector's debt buildup. The neoliberal critique, which draws a hard-and-fast distinction between the public and private sector, ignores these institutional factors within the structure of the Mexican economy.

In summary, some of the state's debt arose from a pricing structure that subsidized users of petroleum products and electricity—much as state monopoly capitalism theory would predict. A significant portion of the state's debt arose from the state's assumption of private sector debt when either bankrupt firms were acquired or the state assumed the risks of foreign exchange revaluations. Much of the public sector's debt was channeled via the private banks into private capital flight rather than into capital formation. Finally, the private banks (through 1982) were active participants in the growing public sector debt and profited from it in many ways.

The State as a Source of Inefficiency?

It has been maintained, particularly by the neoliberals, that state sector industries are inefficient and that this inefficiency underlies the public sector's deficit. In reviewing this debate, researchers María Amparo Casar and Wilson Peres found little support for the argument. Excluding PEMEX (that otherwise would skew the results), industrial productivity (output revenue per worker) in the parastate sector was 35 percent *greater* than that of all Mexican private sector industrial firms in 1965—falling to 5 percent greater in 1981 (Casar and Peres, 1988, 84). In 1983 public sector manufacturing firms were 7 percent *less* productive than were private sector firms. But Casar and Peres argued that this was due to the combined effect of the deep depression of that year (which shrunk revenues) and the state's reluctance to dismiss workers (that artificially increased the number of workers compared to those that would be necessary to run the state's industries). Even though less than 25 percent of the public sector's employees work in the parastate firms (including PEMEX), it seems clear that in this sector at least the state is not a source of inefficiency if the yardstick of labor productivity is utilized.

There is another aspect of the inefficiency argument that is more deserving of attention. The size of the parastate sector creates possibilities for rentier-type behavior to flourish. Benito Rey Romay, with thirty years of management experience in the parastate sector (some derived from being on the boards of directors of thirty-five parastate firms between 1972 and 1982), maintained that the parastate sector could be much more efficient if managers were selected on the basis of objective criteria. Instead, argued Rey Romay, they are selected for their loyalty and usefulness to the PRI or simply because they have the "right" names (Rey Romay, 1984, 93). In Rey Romay's view, top management in the parastate sector fails not simply because of personal corruption but also because of the timidity of managers who believe that it is sufficient to merely *enforce* the rules of the firm's organization. In Rey Romay's view, such managers should exercise an entrepreneurial function— something totally foreign to the dutiful PRI functionary who, at best, seeks not to break the rules (written and unwritten) of bureaucratic management. To exercise entrepreneurial powers is to risk mistakes. A riskless "yes man" approach is more likely to move one upward. At worst, a riskless strategy will never cause demotion or censure. Benito Rey Romay found that a principal source of inefficiency in the state sector arises from timidity:

> The extensiveness of this conduct is such that it is no exaggeration to say that the procedures by that the directors, managers, presidents and members of the boards of directors of the parastate firms are selected are the cause of almost all their existing undesirable characteristics; from the waste of resources to the excessive indebtedness to the low level of productive efficiency to many labor conflicts, etc. (Rey Romay, 1984, 98–99).

Often, maintained Rey Romay, technically competent managers are placed at the head of parastate firms but without regard to fitting the particular competence of the manager to the firm. Thus, for example, by the time an electrical engineer masters the fundamentals of a copper mine, he is shifted to an irrigation project and then moved again in successive presidential sexenios. In summary, although the parastate sector may be no less efficient than Mexican industry at large, experienced and frank observers such as Benito Rey Romay argue that the parastate firms fall well below their *potential* due to a variety of institutional and cultural factors.

In Defense of the State

The foregoing discussion of the public sector has concentrated on the neoliberal critique of state intervention (and its Austrian variant) because a fundamental reordering of the state has been launched through the application of ideas arising from this ideological perspective. Before reviewing in some detail the magnitude of the shift toward privatization it would be well to discuss arguments advanced by proponents of state intervention.

In a vigorous 1977 statement entitled "The Public Enterprises," René Villarreal and Norma Rocío R. Villarreal maintained that the public firms served a fourfold function: (1) they created necessary, previously nonexistent institutions, (2) they maintained national sovereignty over resources, (3) they served to expand sectors that were inadequately developed by private initiative, and (4) they existed to fulfill necessary social welfare needs (Villarreal and Villarreal, 1977, 83–85). Specialists in Mexican public administration, such as Jorge Barenstein and Jorge Ruiz Dueñas, emphasized a fifth function—to help maintain an adequate employment level (Barenstein, 1982; Ruiz Dueñas, 1982). Casar and Peres added a sixth—given the capital intensity of many of the state industries and projects, the state catalyzed private investments and served as a motor force driving ahead the entire macroeconomy and pulling a weak private sector along with it (Casar and Peres, 1988, 91–93). Finally, Benito Rey Romay added a seventh—the state acted as a key agent in introducing important and fundamental new products and industrial processes into the industrial sector and the economy at large (Rey Romay, 1984, 51–54). If, then, the state has done so much for the economy at large, and if the neoliberal critique of the state is less than compelling (based upon the discussion up to this point), why has there been such a considered and determined effort to relegate the state to a minimalist role? Is this debate merely ideological?

Clashing with the Private Sector

Although ideology should be given its due—and in Mexico ideological positions have clearly been important in determining the course of real events—there are also important *objective* matters to consider in the debate over state intervention. In spite of the economic importance of the subsidies that the state has extended to it, the private sector has nurtured sustained fears of the state's limited autonomy. In part, this fear arose from the general growth of the state. For example, the public sector share of economic activity (in value-added terms) grew from 14.6 percent of gross domestic product in 1975 to 25.6 percent in 1983—a 75 percent increase in less than a decade (Tamayo, 1987, 260). Alternatively, total state expenditures (state income plus borrowing) rose from 9.2 percent of GDP in 1950 to 12.5 percent in 1960, 21.1 percent in 1970, and 48.7 percent in 1982 (Looney, 1985, 154; and Table 6.4, Chapter 6). By commanding such a growing economic share of the economy, however defined, the state presumably would have a greater capacity to exercise its autonomy should it choose to do so. As has been mentioned, this deep concern with the *potential* degree of autonomy was more than justified from the perspective of the private sector by the astonishing bank nationalization of 1982.

More focused was the fear that the growth of public firms would result in undesired competition for private sector oligopolists. Briefly, an important clash between the state and the private sector will be analyzed in order to illustrate a point that is central to the discussion. In the early 1970s the Monterrey Group undertook two major investment projects in the petrochemical industry. One project, to build a plant to produce polyester near Tampico, was described by this group as the largest single private sector investment project in Mexico. When, however, the plant was at the point of completion, it was learned that the state (through Somex) had commenced plans to build an *identical* plant that was large enough to fulfill the entire demand of the domestic market, leaving one-third of its capacity for exports (Concheiro and Fragosa, 1979, 96–97). This, predictably, outraged the most powerful banking-industrial capitalists in Mexico. The Monterrey-based industrialist and bankers were unremitting in their criticism of what they regarded as a treacherous transgression of the unwritten (but very formalized) rules of the game between the public and the private sectors. These industrialists were facing the failure of their largest single industrial investment.

They also bitterly complained that the secretary of Industry and Commerce had denied them a permit to directly import a chemical that they needed for their new plant. Instead, the secretary allowed PEMEX to be the sole importer of the chemical. This enabled PEMEX to double the price of the material before it was finally sold to the Monterrey Group's Tampico chemical plant (Conchiero and Fragosa, 1979, 96–97).

At approximately the same time another dispute surfaced that involved the chemical group CYDSA—also a Monterrey-based industrial conglomerate that operated some twenty-five large firms. CYDSA commenced a major expansion of a plant producing chlorine in 1974. In 1976, however, CYDSA learned that the government was also constructing an identical plant, in the same area as the private sector plant. CYDSA noted that it had some eighteen years of experience in producing this particular chemical and unequivocally denounced the government for allocating investment funds in the chemical industry when vital infrastructural needs were not being funded by the public sector (Conchiero and Fragosa, 1979, 74).

Objectively, very large amounts of investment funds were involved in these two projects. Thus, these disputes with the state were of considerable importance. *Subjectively*, the matter went much further. It seemed to the major industrialists that strong objective evidence of a *trend* was to be found in these cases. The state was encroaching on the private sector's domain. Worse, perhaps, was the perception that the state could use its vast resources to engage in "disloyal" competition; for example, the state need not cover its costs in any *particular* enterprise, thereby ensuring that the private sector could not survive against such competition. Finally, an image of the state as a blustering giant undertaking projects without regard to any developmental plan or guidelines, heedlessly duplicating industrial efforts in technically complex sectors of the economy, was readily exploited by the business elite in its increasingly confrontational attempt to undercut the Echeverría administration's populist stance.

The Shift Toward Privatization

Precisely situating the new policy of privatization in terms of its origin, purpose, and scope is no simple matter because the Mexican government has issued only the most general statements (Poder Ejectivo, 1983, 1984). Nor, unfortunately, have recent book-length treatments of the subject by either María Amparo Casar and Wilson Peres or René Villarreal developed a serious analysis of this issue (Casar and Peres, 1988; Villarreal, 1988).

According to official government documents and statements by high-level policymakers, the purpose of the privatization program was not merely to reduce the size of the parastate sector but to make it more *powerful* (Hernández Cervantes, 1988a; de la Madrid, 1987). Thus, according to official rhetoric, the state would be more capable of performing its "rector" role over the economy because it would have at its disposal a more efficient, integrated apparatus that would only incidentally be smaller. The official discussion of the "restructuring" of the parastate sector commenced with President de la Madrid Hurtado's *Plan Nacional de Desarrollo 1983–88* (Poder Ejectivo, 1983). The document was decidedly vague concerning the precise meaning and extent of the state's restructuring. Nonetheless, the plan was interpreted at the time as an indication of a fundamental turning point in state—private sector relationships. Analyzing the plan in the weekly magazine *Proceso*, Oscar Hinojosa concluded that

> the business interests are content because in the *Plan* the government has conceded to private firms a role of primary importance in the national development project and because the public sector has given its guarantee that it will not expand its economic activity—both principles that have been emphasized by the private sector during intense anti-government campaigns (Hinojosa, 1983, 10).

More specific was the announcement by the secretaría de Energía, Minas, e Industria Paraestatal (secretary of Energy, Mines, and State Industries, or SEMIP) on May 6, 1983, that the state planned to sell or liquidate 255 industrial parastate firms in the course of de la Madrid Hurtado's term of office (Ortega Pizarro, 1983b, 10). At this time the journalist who analyzed the significance of these declarations, Fernando Ortega Pizarro, noted that "the mistrust of the private sector in the increasing expansion of the state will be overcome by a new public law that will limit the economic activities ofthe state" (Ortega Pizarro, 1983b, 11). This, indeed, turned out to be the case when in the course of 1983 the de la Madrid Hurtado administration made three major changes in the Constitution of Mexico known as Articles 25, 26, and 28.

Of particular importance was Article 28, which confined the scope of the state's possible industrial activity to petroleum and basic petrochemicals, railroads, nuclear energy, electricity, and satellite communications. These would be defined as *strategic* areas of economic activity reserved only for the state. In addition, the state could engage in *priority* activities, although these were left vaguely defined at the time and subsequently (Secretaría de Gobernación, 1988, 52). According to the government's official interpretation, *priority* activities could be undertaken either by the state or through joint ventures with the private sector. Priority areas "are not fundamental for economic development or for maintaining national sovereignty but areas that at a given moment must be given preferential attention" (Secretaría de Gobernación, 1988, 52).

One important question that has yet to receive a definitive answer concerned the origin of the 1983 program for structural change and privatization. Journalists and economists were quick to link the new direction taken by the public sector to the IMF's stabilization program, which the government had accepted early in 1983. Writing in *Proceso*,

Juan Antonio Zuñiga maintained that it was the rectorship of the IMF that was being exercised in the new *Plan de Desarrollo,,* although the government had predictably demurred from mentioning the source of inspiration for its new project (Zuñiga, 1983, 9). Economists such as Sarahí Ángeles Cornejo asserted that behind SEMIP's new privatization plan was the policy of the IMF (Ortega Pizarro, 1983, 11). In 1987 Miguel de la Madrid Hurtado, Carlos Salinas, and several high-level government economists analyzed the nature of the new program for structural change in *Cambio Estructural en México y en el Mundo* (Structural Change in Mexico and in the World) (de la Madrid, 1987). In this work, the most ample statement to date of the structural change program provided by the de la Madrid Hurtado administration, the program for structural change in Mexico appeared to be initiated by the Mexican state. A much different interpretation was provided by *New York Times* journalist William Stockton, who noted, "in reality 'structural changes' are code words for a new economic direction that President Miguel de la Madrid is attempting, which would bring to Mexico the sort of free-market economy long advocated by President Reagan as the best engine of economic growth" (Stockton, 1986, 4F).

Ultimately it would not be surprising if researchers concluded that the IMF, the Mexican state, *and* the Reagan administration all played significant roles in redirecting the Mexican state—as did, of course, the Mexican private sector. Missing from this discussion, surprisingly, was the formative role that the World Bank played in constructing a new policy devoted to structural adjustment/structural change. (The role of the World Bank is discussed in greater detail in Chapter 6.) The World Bank became deeply involved in forcefully urging upon borrowing nations programs of structural adjustment prior to the onset of the deep Mexican economic crisis in the summer of 1982. Indeed, by 1983 this program was quite advanced. Only later did the IMF become involved in structural adjustment programs similar if not identical to those of the World Bank (Cypher, 1988c; Cypher, 1989).

Uppermost in the World Bank's discussion of structural adjustment programs was the role of the state. Parastate firms should, argued the World Bank, be privatized because they contributed to the public sector's deficit in many cases. In any case, they were important sources of "distortion" in developing economies. Although the IMF's programs in Mexico have received adequate attention, the role of the World Bank and the interaction between the Fund and the Bank on the issue of the role of the public sector have received very little attention. The Bank has been deeply involved in Mexico, particularly since 1982. By 1986 Mexico was the largest single recipient of World Bank funding. To have achieved this status without conforming to the new policy initiatives of the Bank was inconceivable. Yet the Mexican government scrupulously avoided any mention of the role of the World Bank in reducing the state. Instead, the government claimed that structural change merely *strengthened* the state's capacity to guide the economy. Because such a strengthening was precisely what the World Bank sought to deny as a *sine qua non* of its lending, it is difficult to accept the Mexican government's assertion.

It is interesting, therefore, to note that researchers in Mexico whose earlier work on the state is well known seem to *agree* with the government's claim that the rectorship of the state *was* strengthened by the privatization program. This is the position taken in two major studies published in 1988. Both María Amparo Casar and Wilson Peres in the *El Estado Empresario en México: Agotamiento o Renovación?* (The Entrepreneurial State in Mexico: Termination or Renewal?) and René Villarreal in *Mitos y Realidades de la Empresa Pública: Racionalización o Privatización?* (Myths and Realities of Public Firms: Rationalization or Privatization?) arrived at similar conclusions by way of quite dissimilar arguments. Yet they did agree on one central issue: Many state firms were acquired indiscriminately, particularly in the 1970s, and divestiture of these millstones would enable the state to avoid the waste of resources and deficits involved in maintaining such firms.

Researchers Casar and Peres claimed that SEMIP, once it was divested of more than 70 percent of the entities that were under its power in 1983, would be able to exercise control in a more efficient manner. They assumed the tight coordination of a block of state firms whose activities would be more closely integrated into the structure of the economy (Casar and Peres, 1988, 172–173). Although this might be the case, two points are here deserving of examination. First, such an argument was in fact an assertion because no evidence was provided to support the statement. Second, this was a stock-in-trade assertion of the government, that also provided no evidence to support its contention (Hernández Cervantes, 1988a).

Casar and Peres claimed that "reconversion" also meant that the state, unburdened of hundreds of unproductive or unnecessary state entities, would engage in new investment projects to strengthen the few remaining firms that fitted into the categories of either strategic or priority areas. Through 1988, however, such a statement amounted to no more than an assertion because almost no sizable new investment projects commenced during de la Madrid Hurtado's administration (Casar and Peres, 1988, 196).

Finally, their central argument regarding the privatization program was made in the following terms:

The program of disincorporation seems to have held a key message and destiny. The privatization program sought to produce the effect of recuperating confidence and to demonstrate the commitment of the government in the sense of finding a way to make operative criterion that would describe distinct areas between the principle economic agents—a demand that has been widely upheld by the business sector—and strengthen the proposition that the motor of economic development ought to be the national businessmen (Casar and Peres, 1988, 172).

Two points can be made regarding this statement. First, if the privatization program was the realization of a long-standing demand of the business elite (and it does seem that there can be little debate on this point), how could such a demand to cut the size and power of the state possibly be construed as an opportunity to *strengthen* the state? Here Casar and Peres appeared to undercut their own argument as well as that of the de la Madrid Hurtado administration. Second, given that the privatization program constituted the realization of a long-standing objective of the most powerful elements within the business elite, it does not follow that this elite will act to *promote* economic development.

Turning to René Villarreal's study, we are presented with the argument that the state was being strengthened within the process of privatization because the state would utilize "indirect" means to guide the economy— tariff policies, exchange rate manipulations, and monetary and fiscal policy would all be used more astutely (Villarreal, 1988, 15). This, of course, was another argument by assertion. Given that Mexico's record of controlling the macroeconomy via these instruments has been considerably less than successful, Villareal's assertion could not be read as more than an offhand remark. The state, claimed Villarreal, would be stronger because without its superfluous entities it would better serve as a lever to promote development: "The importance of the parastate sector has never resided in the number of public firms nor either in the size of its capital or the value of its production. . . . The importance of the sector has always been in its role as a strategic lever for the economy of the country" (Villarreal, 1988, 107).

Villarreal conceived of a new way of achieving this role that essentially prescribed to the state a role complementary to that of market forces. In this view, the state would be active in the economy only in terms of reaching specific goals and primarily through indirect state policies to support development. If new firms had to be created, the state would first pursue joint venture projects. Only as a last resort would it create state-owned firms. Once such state-owned firms had achieved their objectives, they could be privatized (Villarreal, 1988, 83). For Villarreal, privatization was not a goal in and of itself but rather part of a broader strategy to shift Mexico from an economy whose industrialization has been based on the growth of the internal market to one based in the expansion of the export market. The state's project was now to facilitate a new "regime of accumulation," a new definition of the "mixed economy," whereby Mexico would become an intermediate industrial power by the year 2010. The state should facilitate the modernization needed to achieve such a great transformation (Villarreal, 1988, 99–107). All of this, then, was what Villarreal intended to convey through his interpretation of what constituted a *strengthened* public sector.

By assuming, as he did, that market forces would essentially guide the Mexican economy into a new regime of accumulation based in industrial exports, the role of the state could be reduced to that of a complementary agent. This, however, was a heroic assumption that Villarreal failed to support with either data or sound argumentation. There was scarce evidence in Mexico's recent economic history to suggest that the private sector would be capable of playing such a catalytic role in the 1990s.

In arguing that Mexico's state was passing through a period of rationalization, Villarreal attempted to minimize the scope of the privatization project. In this he followed an argument strongly advanced by the Secretaría de Gobernación (Secretary of Internal Relations). According to the government's data, only 2.9 percent of the share of the national income produced by the state was shifted to the private sector under the privatization program (Secretariat de Gobernación, 1988, 90). Unfortunately, the government data were presented in such a manner as to make it impossible to determine how these calculations were made or at what date they were completed. According to Villarreal's data, which drew on the national income accounts, between 1982 and 1986 the state's share in national income fell by 27 percent due to privatization (Villarreal, 1988, 147). Given that in 1986 the privatization project was very far from being completed, it is difficult to understand how a 27 percent drop in the state's share of national income could not to be construed as significant. Since 1986 a number of areas then considered to be priority, such as steel, sugar, pharmaceuticals, and petrochemicals, have been privatized (or are under serious consideration for such changes). Even roads, bridges, public transportation, and other forms of infrastructure are considered to be likely candidates for privatization or coinvestment under President Salinas de Gortari (1988–1994). Thus, until sufficient time has elapsed, any argument based upon the limited size of the shift toward privatization cannot bear much weight, particularly given that major mining companies were privatized in late 1988 (some with assets in the $1 billion range). It then appeared that the pace of the privatization effort might be increasing.

Unlike Casar and Peres, and Villarreal, the prominent economist Alonso Aguilar viewed the selling off of the parastate firms as much more important in terms of both the quantity and the quality of the firms involved. Aguilar stressed the fact that the concept of priority sectors was arbitrary and essentially left undefined. What was defined as strategic was done so only by decree. (No political discussion had preceded the mandated distinction.) He reserved his strongest criticism for the decision to withdraw the state from the general promotion of the capital goods sector (Aguilar, 1988, 22). In Aguilar's view, the privatizations in the parastate sector would fundamentally weaken the country, both because progress toward the creation of a capital goods industry had been reversed and because certain interlocking links of industrial clusters (or chains) had been broken by the sell-off of the state firms. This was particularly true in parastate industries that were heavily dependent upon other state firms for their inputs or markets (Aguilar, 1988, 23).

Alonso Aguilar conceded that it was difficult to systematically analyze the overall impact of the privatization effort because the government had released very little data regarding (1) what had been sold, (2) the figures involved in these sales, and (3) the new owners. He viewed the privatization project as a short-term tactic encouraged (if not conceived) by the business elite to acquire the assets of state corporations at below market prices. This would temporarily maintain the profit level of the private sector firms that made such acquisitions. Yet this was costly for the economy at large. As the development banks such as Nafinsa and Somex suffered massive declines in the firms and the resources that they controlled, the country would become starved for long-term investment funds because the private sector would not amass such funds (Aguilar, 1988, 24). Nor would the deficit of the state sector decline much (as had been commonly claimed) because the firms most responsible for the deficit in the public sector would remain public firms. Most, if not all, of the large parastate firms had long-term debts (often contracted abroad). Thus even if current prices of the products sold by these firms covered their current operating costs, their large capital debts would ensure that the public sector deficit would remain.

Nonetheless Aguilar, Latin America's foremost exponent of the theory of state monopoly capitalism, did not believe that the various changes in the size and nature of the state were *fundamental*. The state, he asserted, would continue to play a basic role in the accumulation process—we were witnessing a change of *form* but not of *substance* (Aguilar, 1988, 29).

There were, then, certain broad parallels between the analysis of Alonso Aguilar and that of orthodox analysts such as Casar and Peres and Villarreal—in particular, the state is not about to wither away. Yet, Aguilar's argument was undercut to some degree by the fact that two important components of the state firms that he believed would escape the privatization drive (the state-owned sugar mills and Aeroméxico, the state's largest airline) were privatized. Meanwhile, persistent attempts to sell off part of the state's steel complex and privatize the national telephone company suggested that the period of massive privatizations were far from complete.

According to political scientist John Saxe-Fernández, far from strengthening the rectorship of the state over the economy, the purpose of the privatization program was to deliver the state's economic components to the private sector—both national and transnational (Saxe-Fernández, 1988a, 7, 11). Holding forth in his weekly column in the preeminent daily newspaper *Excelsior*, Saxe-Fernández maintained a steady barrage of criticism over the sizable privatization programs engineered in petrochemicals, mining, sugar mills, and other sectors that had previously been defined as either *strategic* or *priority*. Saxe-Fernández viewed the rise of the neoliberal stance within the state apparatus as, in effect, a *coup d'état* that had effectively delivered a great part of the national sovereignty of Mexico to the private sector and to transnational corporations (Saxe-Fernández, 1988b, 7, 8). In Saxe-Fernández's view, there were no objective limits to the privatization process because those who occupied the pinnacle of political power within the state philosophically agreed with the most Austrian elements of the private sector (which urged the virtual elimination of state intervention). By June 1988 Saxe-Fernández had taken this position regarding the state-business relationship: "The link between the government and the most exclusive business and financial circles is so tight that it is very difficult to determine the difference between the official pronouncements of the government and those of the business elite. Today government is a business and the business interests are the government" (Saxe-Fernández, 1988c, 7).

If Saxe-Fernández's interpretation was essentially correct (or even largely correct), Alonso Aguilar's interpretation, along with those of Casar and Peres and Villarreal, would of necessity be negated. Not only would the state be fundamentally weakened, thus denying arguments suggesting the reorganizing and strengthening the state, but the theory of state monopoly capitalism would cease to have explanatory power. Clearly the transition of the Mexican state remains incomplete. It is too soon for categorical positions such as those adopted by Saxe-Fernández.

Nonetheless, it would be well to keep in mind how profound were the philosophical shifts within the PRI during the de la Madrid Hurtado administration. Consider, for example, the views of Ángel Acerves Saucedo, who in 1986 occupied the position of director of the PRI's

Institute of Political, Social, and Economic Studies—a position considered key in the expression of the dominant ideological position of the PRI. At the elite and conservative private Universidad de las Americas (University of the Americas) on April 3, 1986, Acerves commenced his speech at a conference entitled Reflections on State Intervention by acknowledging his intellectual allegiance to Milton Friedman and the direct influence of Fredrick von Hayek and Ludwig von Mises (Chavez, 1986, 22). He then continued by claiming:

> State intervention has entered into a situation of diminishing returns.
> . . . The crisis of the eighties has resulted in the rethinking of state intervention, particularly because of the predominance of neoliberal ideas among the decision making agents who design and make economic policy. At the most general level we can affirm that there exists a tendency to reexamine the role of the State not only in developed nations but also in those least developed. . . .
> That which remains central to this discussion is the thesis of privatization of the parastate sector as the instrument to achieve improvement in the functioning of the market (Chavez, 1988, 22–23).

Was Acerves Saucedo's frankly stated position representative of the new philosophical orientation of the dominant elements of the PRI? Given that high-level PRI politicians such as the president and his key secretaries must appeal to a broad constituency, it is unlikely that they will ever make such clear-cut statements or publicly proclaim their allegiance to key ultraconservative ideologues such as Milton Friedman or Fredrick von Hayek. Nonetheless, when the president and the future president of Mexico sponsored a world conference on structural change in 1987, they chose as the keynote speaker the U.S. economist Martin Feldstein, an outspoken acolyte of Milton Friedman, and invited prominent British advocates of Thatcherism. The five presentations by the highest level members of Mexico's economic cabinet, including those of the president and the forthcoming president, contained nothing that would antagonize Acerves Saucedo. Rather they advocated his objectives in an opaque language filled with optimistic predictions of the national benefits of a new *laissez-faire* philosophy (de la Madrid, 1987).

The "Logic" of Privatization

Privatizion of state firms is a piecemeal method of undercutting any future turn toward populism in Mexico. Privatization is not an irreversible process. Yet a populist government, *if* it had sufficient political power to do so, would be forced to rebuild the economic power of the state very slowly and only with the greatest of difficulty. The short-run consequences of such a step would likely be to make a poor economic situation worse by fanning the flames of ideological debate and hastening the hair-trigger response of the business elite toward massive capital flight, given the smallest of pretexts. Thus, privatization of the state sector is in itself a very powerful political tool and objective. Without the framework of a large parastate sector, the state must rely on the cumbersome mechanisms of monetary and fiscal policy to promote its socioeconomic goals and development plans.

Privatization has important economywide implications for labor-capital relations. Should a populist government take power, wage increases and general improvement of conditions of employment within the state sector would be anticipated. Such improvement for the working class and professionals within the public sector creates an atmosphere in which workers in the private sector seek to match the gains achieved by their cohorts in the parastate sector. Doing away with public sector firms reduces the possibility that the state can have a fundamental impact in strengthening labor's power.

Finally, privatization has important short-run consequences in terms of artificially raising the profit level of private sector firms. This can be achieved in five ways. First, public sector firms can be sold at a price that undervalues their assets. Second, private sector buyers can in some cases buy Mexico's foreign debt in the secondary market by paying roughly one-half the price of the face value of these debt instruments. These firms in turn can present Mexico's foreign debt instruments to the government and "swap" the debts for the physical assets of a state firm. The buyers receive the face value of the debt instruments when purchasing the assets of the state firms, while the government can trumpet the retirement of its foreign debt as a policy victory. Third, the state can sell vast tracts of land that hold valuable mineral rights at well below their true asset values (given proper exploitation of these minerals). Fourth, in the process of selling off public firms labor contracts can be abrogated. As in the widely publicized sell off of Aeroméxico in the summer of 1988, the private sector buyers can attain control of a state firm and achieve a restructuring of labor relations without openly challenging existing labor laws or contracts. (Such activities have economy wide implications in terms of capital-labor relations.) Fifth, private firms, even if they pay the full market value for the assets they obtain, can in certain cases raise their profit rate through the acquisition of firms that are *complementary* to the existing conglomerate structure. This tends to lower costs of production within important sectors of giant conglomerates controlled by Mexico's largest private business groups. As a related matter, by eliminating the yardstick of public sector firms that compete with or overlap with private sector producers, it will be much easier to raise prices and thereby increase profits. Thus, there are important long-term and short-term, political and economic, economywide and specific, reasons for the neoliberal project of destructuring the state that go well beyond simplistic platitudes regarding the assumed virtues of a market-driven society.

Some researchers have attempted to demarcate stages of progression in the privatization project. Jorge Machado, Wilson Peres, and Orlando Delgado, writing in early 1986, maintained that there were three stages. First, in 1983 and 1984, limited, sector-specific privatization occurred when the government reduced its holdings in autos, auto parts, bicycles, and related firms. Second, in 1985, the economic cabinet decided upon a general restructuring that removed the state from the production of consumer goods. Third, in May 1986, with the forced bankruptcy of the state's steel company in Monterrey, a period of *massive destructuring* of the state commenced (Machado, Peres, and Delgado, 1985, 129–132). Returning to this theme in a book co-authored with María Amparo Casar, Peres marked off a *fourth* stage beginning in 1988 in which formerly *priority* areas, such as capital goods, tractors, and trucks were privatized (Casar and Peres, 1988, 176). By late 1988 evidence had accumulated that a *fifth* stage was either imminent or in process—the selling off of various parts of the state apparatus that had only recently been defined as *strategic* (Guadarrama and Cruz, 1988, 24).

With the state passing through as many as five stages in less than five years, the value of a stage model would appear to be limited. By late 1988 the only identifiable pattern that had emerged from the privatization program revealed two underlying characteristics. First, the categories "priority" and "strategic" had become virtually meaningless in terms of defining an inviolate area wherein the state had free rein. Second, the state continued to own production processes that produced intermediate products such as electricity, oil and gas, and steel. If these state firms continued to sell their products at subsidized prices to the largest private sector firms, a major tenet of the theory of state monopoly capitalism would continue to hold. If, however, the neoliberal project to "get prices right" should result in an end to such subsidies, much of what remained of the explanatory value of this theory of the state would be undercut. By mid-1989, with President Salinas de Gortari firmly committed to major new privatizations (such as TELMEX), it remained an open question as to how far down the *hyper-laissez-faire* road the PRI would march. Every turn in this twisted road seemed to be to the Right.

6

President de la Madrid Hurtado's Sexenio: The Crisis and the Neoliberal Ascendancy

This chapter analyzes the underlying causes of the crisis of the 1980s. First examined is the "drain-centered" conjunctural theory of the crisis, which stressed the effects of debt repayments. Next, three theories of the crisis are discussed; (1) the overinvestment/underinvestment theory, (2) the falling-rate-of-profit theory, and (3) the monetarist theory. The changing nature of state–private sector relations under President de la Madrid Hurtado, which led to the abandonment of the decades-old import-substitution model of development is then reviewed. The final sections of this chapter analyze the new development model of export promotion—how it came to be, what it is, and why it has failed—as a *growth* model. The chapter closes with a short summary of the 1987 Solidarity Pact.

Crisis, What Crisis?

For those at the top in government and in the private sector the 1980s were not necessarily bad years. In fact, for many they were the best of years. The top 10 percent of Mexico's income recipients had placed abroad through capital flight from $64 to $80 billion (or more) by 1988 (Ros, 1987, 108—data based on my estimates since 1984). Most of these funds were earning assets (stocks, bonds, and so on). Thus, the economic elite could utilize income from these assets to advantage by transferring funds back into pesos whenever frequent devaluations allowed the elite to maximize its buying power. Moreover, with wages down, profits were up in many but not all cases. Furthermore, the hyperinflation and changes in the financial structure of the economy created new, and often massive, openings for speculators who, following well-nurtured rentier propensities, were able to exercise economic alchemy in the financial sphere. (Of note was Mexico's spectacular stock exchange boom and bust. The market stood at 46,000 points on January 1, 1987; it rose to 373,000 points by October and rested at 106,000 points on December 30, 1987.)

Provisional data bore out what was obvious to any observer—the post-tax distribution of income was polarizing at a rapid pace in the 1980s. In 1983, for example, the official data on income distribution attributed 33.5 percent of Mexico's annual income to the top 10 percent of the population (Lustig, 1988). By 1987, according to the Secretary of Programming and Budgeting this stratum received 36.6 percent of the income—an increase in its share of total income of 9.3 percent (El Financiero, 1988, 19). It is difficult to imagine how a much greater shift in income could have been engineered during an economic crisis.

An Overview of the Macroeconomic Fluctuations

To the extent that one can rely on official data to describe the movements of the macroeconomy, the de la Madrid Hurtado sexenio was defined by extreme stagnation coupled with two serious downturns.[1] This movement stood in sharp contrast to the 40.6 percent real cumulative growth of José López Portillo's preceding sexenio. De la Madrid Hurtado's first year in power was the worst (economically) since the days of the revolution, with GDP declining 4.2 percent.

Yet by mid-1983 optimism returned among high-level economists both within and outside of the government. They saw the 1982–1983 crisis as a "conjunctural crisis" brought on by the collapse of oil prices and high real interest rates.[2] By July 1983 prominent economists were proclaiming that Mexico had "touched bottom" and that recovery was imminent.

Each subsequent downturn was seen as "temporary" and "conjunctural." When the economy expanded at a sluggish 3.5 percent rate in 1984, this was viewed by many commentators as an encouraging sign of transition—1985 was sure to be a very good year. It was not. But the 2.5 percent growth of 1985 and the 3.9 percent decline of 1986 were attributed to the drop in oil prices and difficulties with the foreign debt. Optimism surged again at the beginning of 1987. Mexico successfully renegotiated much of its foreign debt in late 1986 and early 1987. By March 1987 it appeared that Mexico would have access to $12 to $13 billion of new capital lent by the IMF, the World Bank, the U.S. government and the private banks.[3] Furthermore, in 1985 roughly $2 billion of flight capital *returned* to Mexico, while outflows in 1986 were surprisingly moderate. The consensus view seemed to be that the long awaited recovery was now under way. But the ill-founded euphoria of early 1987 melted away with the crack in the stock market in October 1987. The mood now swung toward deep, but realistic, pessimism. To no one's surprise, 1988 was bleak—with the economy expanding by an estimated 1 percent.

The Conjunctural Theory of the Crisis:
The Drain-centered Theory

The government was far from alone in viewing Mexico as being in the grip of a profound, yet short-lived, series of crises. With few exceptions, observers across the spectrum maintained that the crisis arose from *exogenous* forces and factors. First on the list, of course, was the drain incurred from interest and principal payments on the foreign debt. Books and articles centering on the issue of the debt and the repayment drain poured forth in such a steady stream as to make specific citations impossible and irrelevant.

Table 6.1 isolates the two main components of the drain on the Mexican economy in the 1980s—debt repayment and capital flight. How well can the drain elements, particularly payments on the debt, explain the fluctuations in the GDP in the 1980s? In answering this question, we must first isolate the net debt drain (column 4). This is derived by deducting net new borrowing (column 3) from total debt service payments (column 2).

Note that beginning in 1982, the net debt drain came to 0.8 percent of GNP (column 5). Was that a significant figure? Significant enough, that is, to precipitate the crisis of 1982 or set the stage for the stronger downturn in 1983 (column 1)? It is difficult to see how this could be the case given the modest size of the net debt drain. Casting back to the discussion of the events of 1982 (Chapter 4), we can note that the problem of the debt drain played little or no role in the discussion of pivotal events of that period. Key to the crisis of 1982 was President López Portillo's growing frustration over his impotence in controlling the profitable, but destabilizing, financial manipulations then undertaken by the financial elite. Indeed, as can be seen from column 6, the role of capital flight is of a totally different magnitude than that of the net debt drain.

Was the massive capital flight of 1982 a principal precipitator of the economic crisis? This seems most likely, much more likely than an explanation that hinges on the question of the debt drain. Such an interpretation immediately raises a deeper question, however: Why did the massive capital flight occur in 1981–1982 and not, say, in 1980? Any answer to this question forces one to locate a deeper and more fundamental cause of the crisis. In the process the role of capital flight must be

Table 6.1: The Debt Drain

Year	(1) ΔGDP (percentage)	(2) Debt Service $Billions (U.S)	(3) Net New Borrowing	(4) Net Debt Drain (column 2-3)	(5) Drain as % of GNP	(6) Capital Flight $Billions (U.S.)	(7) Total Drain Column (4+6)	(8) Total Drain as % GDP
1982	-0.5	9.42	7.7	1.72	0.8	9.50	11.20	5.6
1983	-4.2	11.45	6.8	4.64	2.4	4.50	9.14	4.8
1984	+3.5	11.29	3.5	7.80	3.9	2.70	10.50	5.2
1985	+2.5	10.98	0.4	10.58	5.1	(2.10)*	8.48	4.1
1986	-3.9	8.75	4.7	4.05	2.4	0.44	4.49	2.3
1987	+1.4	11.37	8.3	3.07	1.5	0.86	3.93	2.0
1988**	+1.0	---	---	---	---	---	---	---

* denotes inflow

** estimated

Sources: IDB, *Economic and Social Progress Report* (Washington, D.C.: Inter-American Development Bank, various years); Banco de México, *The Mexican Economy, 1988* (Mexico: Banco de México, 1988), pp. 128-129; Jaime Ros, "Mexico from the Oil Boom to the Debt Crisis," in Rosemary Thorp and Laurence Whitehead (eds.), *Latin American Debt and the Adjustment Crisis* (Pittsburgh: University of Pittsburgh Press, 1987), p. 108.

reduced, in part, to that of *effect* rather than cause. As will be discussed, a synthesis of the overinvestment/underinvestment and falling-rate-of-profit theories of the crisis better serves to explain the underlying forces that gave rise to the crisis from 1982 onward.

Yet a nation that is hemorrhaging more than 5 percent of its GDP due to the net debt drain and capital flight (column 8) is unlikely to achieve a very high rate of growth. Nevertheless, some care must be taken even with this statement. For the economy *did* grow in 1984 at a 3.5 percent rate even though the total drain (column 8) *increased*. This is precisely the opposite of what a drain-centered theory of the crisis would predict. Note also that the size of the total drain did not differ significantly from the annual average of the drain for the years 1982 and 1983. Thus, the drain-centered theory alone cannot explain much when the economy moves in opposite direction (at different times, of course) even as the total drain remains nearly constant. To empower such a hypothesis, other factors must be brought into the analysis.

There are two further anomalies worth mentioning. First, the yearly drain declined by 21 percent from 1984 to 1985. This, according to a drain-centered theory, should have caused the economic situation to improve. But the growth rate of GDP (column 1) declined by 28.6 percent. Second, the change in the size of the drain should have been inversely related to the growth in the GDP—for example, a decline in the drain should have served to stimulate the economy and *vice versa*. The evidence from 1986 stands in stark contrast to this notion—the total drain was cut nearly in half, yet the GDP *declined* at a rate that was roughly equal to that of 1983.

None of the preceding analysis should be taken as a statement that the total drain was of little or no significance. Rather, the point to be made here (a fairly obvious but neglected one) is that the question of the drain has to be placed within a particular historical context. It forms part of a deeper analysis of the crisis that incorporates the total drain (and the fluctuations in oil prices) into a comprehensive structural framework of both accumulation and ruptures in the accumulation process.

In such a framework the data expressed in Table 6.1 take on a different form and meaning. For example, had there not been a fundamental weakening of the autonomy of the state, and had there not been an ideological shift toward neoliberalism within the highest circles of the Mexican political elite during the early years of the de la Madrid Hurtado administration, the Mexican state could have altered its passive stance in regard to capital flight. Had that flight been greatly reduced, if not stemmed, Mexico's situation *vis-à-vis* the debt drain could have been fundamentally altered. Had the state cajoled and pressured those who held billions abroad (from episodes of flight prior to 1982) to repatriate a goodly portion of such funds, a new situation would have emerged.

It has never been demonstrated that the administration did everything in its power to reduce the burden of debt service. The debt service payments were the result of a series of political and economic decisions and choices. They were particularly conditioned by the fact that the Mexican state under de la Madrid Hurtado became a more instrumentalist, neoliberal state as the sexenio progressed. The total drain was significant because it demonstrated that the state had failed to become as active a participant in debt payment renegotiations as it might have been. To understand why it acted as it did, one needs not only a theory of economic crisis but a theory of the state and an understanding of the evolution of the state form. A drain-centered theory of the crisis begins with the assumption that other things being equal the debt drain had principal explanatory power. Yet "things" did not remain equal.

Investment: Qualitative and Quantitative Changes

What, then, explains the crisis? Table 6.2 presents data that must be taken into consideration in any interpretation of the crisis. Taken together they describe a *threefold movement* in the relationships between investment and gross domestic product. First, from 1980 through 1987 there was a fundamental shift in the relationship between private and public sector investment. The relative importance of private sector investment rose by 18 percent (columns 4 and 5). Second, this shift took place within the context of a significant decline in the role of investment in the economy (columns 3 and 6). The level of annual investment *fell* by $19 billion from 1980 to 1987—an amount equivalent to 9.5 percent of the *total* GDP in 1987.

Third, construction rose from roughly one-half of total investment to two-thirds of the total during the 1980s (column 8). Note that construction rose while the share of public investment in GDP fell (column 7). Did the government devote relatively more of its declining investments to construction, such as infrastructure? There was no evidence whatsoever that such was the case. For example, in 1982, 59 percent of public investment went to fund infrastructure—roughly equivalent to construction—while in 1988 the projected figure was 40 percent (Benitez and Cruz, 1988, 25). Alternatively, in 1986, when private investments in construction fell 7.3 percent, public investment in construction fell 13.3 percent. In 1987, while private investment in construction rose 6.4 percent, public investment in construction fell 4.9 percent (Zepeda, 1988, 5).

Table 6.2: Gross Domestic Product and Investment (in percent or constant, 1986, U.S. dollars)

Year	(1) ΔGDP	(2) GDP 1986 ($Billion)	(3) Gross Investment ($Billion)	Shares (4) Private	(5) Public	(6) I/GDP	(7) I(Pu)/GDP	(8) Constr./I
1980	8.3	$187,689	$50,973	57.0	43.0	27.2	11.6	53
1981	8.1	$202,141	$58,887	56.6	43.4	29.1	12.6	51
1982	-0.5	$201,513	$41,986	55.7	44.3	20.8	9.3	58
1983	-4.2	$190,840	$32,329	58.5	41.3	16.9	7.2	65
1984	+3.5	$201,376	$34,301	60.5	39.5	17.0	6.1	63
1985	+2.5	$206,577	$38,407	64.5	35.9	18.6	6.8	63
1986	-3.9	$198,405	$30,567	66.9	33.1	15.4	5.0	65
1987	+1.4	$201,244	$31,970	68.6	31.4	15.9	5.2	64
1988*	-----	-----	-----	67.1	32.9	-----	-----	-----

* estimated
GDP = Gross Domestic Product
I = Investment (Gross)
I(Pu) = Public Sector Investment
Constr. = Construction
ΔGDP = Annual Growth GDP

Sources: IDB, *Economic and Social Progress Report* (Washington, D.C.: Inter-American Development Bank, various years); Torben Huss, "Proyectos Empresariales y Reestructuración del Capitalismo Mexicano," *Economía Informa* 159 (December 1987), p. 28.

This threefold movement in investment illuminates many of the underlying forces that undermined the economy in the 1980s. First, with gross public investment cut approximately in half, the private sector could no longer rely on the state to open up new areas of investment. Major new public investment projects all but ceased in the 1980s. There was a *causal* relationship to be noted: As public investment declined in relation to GDP, private investment declined as a result (column 6). (In 1980 private investment—in 1986 U.S. dollars—stood at $29 billion. In 1987 it had dropped to only $21.4 billion.) Second, with output declining much less than investment (column 2 versus column 3), it must follow that the existing capital stock was being exhausted—normal replacement rates were not maintained. A further result can be hypothesized but not demonstrated with existing data: With machinery and equipment wearing out, production was being maintained through a speedup in the labor process. The work force had to increasingly devote time to repairs *and* had to maintain production norms. (As a counterpart to this process injury rates for workers rose as breakdowns of increasingly dangerous machinery became more prevalent.) Because technical change was most often "embodied" in new machinery and equipment purchased for production, and because such embodied new technology normally constituted a most important element of increases in labor productivity, a long-term drop in investment such as described in Table 6.2 would imply slow, to no, growth in labor productivity. This, in turn, would suggest little or no growth in total product—precisely the result described in column 1.

Of equal, if not greater, importance was the implication to be drawn from the rise in construction investments amid the profound drop in total investment. Clearly the impetus for construction investment was coming from the private sector. Such investments were made in seven areas. First, the 1980s witnessed a boom in the construction of luxury housing from 1984 onward. Second, the government began to emphasize tourism as a quick foreign exchange earner. De la Madrid Hurtado's largest single new investment project, for example, was the Bahías de Huatulco. This widely criticized program developed the southern Pacific coast of Mexico for tourism. The Huatulco project, however, was never conceived of as state dominated. The luxury hotels were owned by major transnational corporations and Mexican real estate developers. The government built the infrastructure—airport facilities, roads, utilities, marinas, and so on.

But tourism, although it gained quick foreign exchange, did next to nothing to develop the skills of the labor force. Unlike industry, where investments tended to be linked with changes in technology and thereby yielded increases in productivity, tourism was an essentially static, and perhaps transitory, way to gain quick foreign exchange.

Third, apartment complexes absorbed some of the construction funds as speculator-landlords sought profitable transactions in an inflationary environment. Fourth, due to the shift in income toward the rich, U.S.-style shopping-centers catering to luxury goods consumers became increasingly commonplace throughout Mexico. Fifth, luxurious new restaurants serving the Mexican elite mushroomed, even as the index of malnutrition climbed higher. Sixth, an office building boom occurred in some cities, particularly Guadalajara. Seventh, crowning all other forms of unproductive and parasitic "investments" stood the Mexican stock exchange—a barometer of the growing rentier ethos sweeping Mexico in the 1980s. This symbol of "casino capitalism" was, beyond doubt, the fastest growing form of parasitic investment until the spectacular stock market crash of 1987.[4]

The Parallel Financial System

As many observers have stressed, the rise of the stock exchange was part of the development of the "parallel financial system." This system emerged in the 1980s as the old financial oligarchy sought to recoup losses suffered from the bank nationalization. Although he could not undo the bank nationalization, de la Madrid Hurtado did whatever possible to ensure that the state ministered to the needs and caprices of the old financial barons.

The process of restoring the financial elite was complex. But, in essence, it was reducible to the following: First, compensation was paid for all nationalized property; second, the ex-bankers could own up to 34 percent of the stock of the nationalized banks and could function as managers on the boards of directorship of the public banks; and third, the ex-bankers could buy back from the government all nationalized property, except the *deposit* banks. In effect the *investment* banks (known as "nonbank financial intermediaries") were again taken over by the financiers of Mexico. Finally, and most importantly, the stock exchange became the vehicle by which the government sought funding for the internal debt. With payments on the internal debt (annual interest) amounting to as much as *double* that paid on the external debt, the operators of the stock exchange were able to capture an extremely lucrative underwriting business. In short, the largess that the de la Madrid Hurtado administration exhibited in dealing with the ex-bankers had no equivalent during his term (Rivera Rios, 1986, 116–120; Alvarez, 1987, 112–115).

In the wake of the bank nationalization, it would be surprising if the ex-bankers had not at least equaled, if not exceeded, their previous privileged position within the economic system. Indeed, along with the new role played by the stock exchange, the ex-bankers were given the privilege of operating the *casas de cambio* (exchange houses) that handled the bulk of foreign-exchange transactions. With the peso dropping more than 2,000 percent against the dollar in the course of the sexenio, the *casas de cambio* had adequate opportunities to speculate against the peso in anticipation of the recurring devaluations.

The Decline in Real (Nonspeculative) Investment

Saddled with the burden of pressing interest payments to be made on its previously accumulated foreign debt, the government attempted to maintain the peso at an "undervalued" exchange rate in order to stimulate the export of Mexican industrial products. Mexican industry, however, remained dependent on the importation of machinery and equipment. Given the difficulty of obtaining foreign exchange and the exceedingly high price of capital goods because of the undervalued peso, Mexican industrialists (and foreign-owned subsidiaries) drastically cut back on their plans for capital expansion. Thus, the "gimmick" of twisting the exchange rate had a quite real, long-lasting, and deleterious effect on Mexico's economy, even to the point of undercutting its production potential and thereby reducing its export capacity as the capital stock became increasingly worn and in many cases obsolete.

The little real investment that did occur was sometimes linked to other gimmicks. For example, the recovery of 1984–1985 was led by a 26.6 percent rate of growth in auto industry output for 1984. While the economy expanded by a modest 3.5 percent, investment in machinery and equipment grew by 8.9 percent. A first glance at the data, then, suggested that Mexico's recovery might well be off on a sound footing. A second glance, however, revealed that what appeared to be an investment-led recovery was merely a bizarre short-term episode. It turned out that the Mexican Congress had decided to allow businesses a 75 percent accelerated depreciation allowance on all new cars bought in 1984—with the figure dropping to a still substantial write-off of 50 percent in 1985 and 25 percent in 1986. (Relatively low-grade technicians and salesmen as well as all levels of management normally receive a company car for business and personal use as part of their wage payment.)

The expected result was realized—investments in vehicles soared to a 33.4 annual rate. Meanwhile, if we remove vehicle purchases from the investment data, the recovery collapsed—investment expanded at an anemic 3.2 percent annual rate (Ros, 1987, 100). Indeed, the investment that *did* occur (aside from placing thousands of new, and presumably unneeded, luxury autos on Mexico's precarious road system) arose from tax advantages that made it possible to import foreign-made machinery and equipment. What, at first, seemed to be an investment-led recovery turned out to be little more than a rentier boom—primarily an increase in new luxury goods that deceptively appeared in the macroeconomic data as "investment in machinery and equipment." In terms of macroeconomic performance, 1984 was the best year in de la Madrid Hurtado's sexenio. Yet a closer look at that "recovery" revealed its essentially chimerical nature.

"Businessmen Earn What They Spend"

If the case can be made that the stagnation of the 1980s was primarily determined by a deep decline in investment, and if the modest amount of investment that was undertaken in the 1980s was qualitatively inferior to that of earlier periods (because of its essentially rentier nature), the question remained as to why all this has occurred. If we set aside for the moment the more obvious, but limited, explanations such as (1) the draining effects of foreign debt payments, (2) the collapse of new transnational bank lending in the 1980s to large debtor nations, and (3) the decline in oil and other key commodity prices that heavily impacted on Mexico's foreign exchange earnings, two hypotheses tend to be confirmed by the available data. The first could be termed Keynesian or post-Keynesian in that it centers on the destabilizing effects of investment during an intermediate time period. The second, discussed in the following section, arises from classical Marxism.

According to Keynesian analysis, particularly that of the Left Keynesians such as Joan Robinson and Michael Kalecki, the balance between investment and growth is at best precarious (Robinson, 1956; Kalecki, 1969).[5] Given rising profits and/or the expectation of future increases in the profit rate, capitalists will likely increase their investments at a very rapid pace. If the growth in future markets matches the plans made by the business elite, the system continues to expand. If it does not, and the Keynesians doubted that it would, problems—including the possibility of deep depressions—arise. One difficulty in moving through time is that the market signals offered (to those who participate in fundamental expansions of industrial capacity within sectors) are not of much use. Thus, Joan Robinson and others emphasized that the investment decision comes down to little more than shooting in the dark. A certain "pack mentality" seems to exist. That is, when one capitalist believes that the time is ripe for fundamental expansion, so (often) do others. This has the unintended effect of flooding a given sector with excess capacity after a certain period of time has elapsed (sufficient to construct the new capacity) because the *collective* response to the presumed strong future market conditions constitutes an over response. Each capitalist alone presumes that he or she can gain market share by making well-timed new investments. Collectively they provide too much capacity—the market is flooded and investment is then halted. Slowly the excess capacity is whittled away through scrappage, use, merger, and bankruptcy.

How well does the boom of the late 1970s and early 1980s (and then the stagnation of the de la Madrid Hurtado sexenio) fit the *overinvestment/ underinvestment* model? From 1963 to 1975 private investment grew at an average annual rate of 8.9 percent. Meanwhile, public investment played an even stronger role—it grew by an average rate of 11.7 percent. During the petroboom period, 1978–1981, nonresidential private sector investment expanded at an annual rate of 23.3 percent—a 160 percent faster rate of growth than in 1963–1975. The response in the private sector was even stronger than in the public sector. Public sector investment grew at an annual rate of 20.4 percent in the petroboom period (Ros, 1987, 70–71). Could the private and public stock of capital increase by more than 80 percent in a mere four years without generating problems of excess capacity (and/or inflationary pressures on production costs) that would force down the rate of profit? In the abstract, it is difficult to conceive of an economy that could expand its capital stock at this pace without creating fundamental problems. In reality, as we shall see in the next section, the rate of profit did fall.

What accounted for the spate of overinvestment in the 1977–1982 period that set the stage for declining investments for virtually all of the remainder of the decade? Frenzied attempts to capture the profits and possibilities of the boom period certainly explained a great deal. A very strong peso relative to the dollar underwrote capital goods imports, while tax credits for investments amplified the boom mentality. The transnational banks, flush with cash and searching for markets, lent on a grandiose scale—often at interest rates that were well below the rate of inflation. This combination proved irresistible to most of Mexico's industrial and banking groups.

The Falling Rate of Profit

Marx and classical Marxist economists have maintained that the accumulation process slows down and enters into crisis when the rate of profit declines. The relationship is not mechanical because a decline in the rate of profit may not bring on a crisis or a business cycle. The response to a falling profit rate is conditioned by the counteracting forces at play, that may later reverse the decline, *and* on how the capitalists subjectively react to the decline. Although Marx sketched a compelling approach to the measurement of the rate of profit, controversy has raged both over how to best interpret this model and how to make it operational within the context of currently used methods of national income accounting.

At least two Mexican economists have recently employed a falling-rate-of-profit argument to explain the crisis of the 1980s. (Neither, however, presented a full-fledged defense of the statistical categories used.) The most detailed discussion of the profit rate within the tradition of classical Marxism unfortunately ended with data from 1976 (Rivera Rios, 1986, 177–179). Commenting on the post-1976 situation, Miguel Rivera Rios argued that the petroboom was essentially an epiphenomenon momentarily disguising a fundamental rupture in the accumulation process that commenced in 1968. In other words, the period from 1968 to 1988 was one of a "long crisis." But this "long wave" model tended to diminish the significance of the considerable accumulation that was achieved from 1969 through 1982.

Based upon five selected years between 1950 and 1960, Rivera Rios showed an average rate of profit on invested capital in the *industrial* sector of 13.8 percent. He then found a slight drop in the profit rate, to 13.0 percent, in the period 1963–1967. Then, taking the period 1970–1976, he showed a 25 percent drop in the profit rate to 9.7 percent per year (Rivera Rios, 1986, 177). Updating the Rivera Rios date but using what appeared to be a different methodology, José Rangel found a further drop in the average profit rate of 19 percent for the years 1980–1982 from that attained in the 1970–1975 period. Then, however, the average profit rate *increased* by 48 percent in 1983–1984 over that of the 1980–1982 period (Rangel, 1988, 5).

If the Rangel data are correct, why was there a boom in investment in the late 1970s through 1981 even as the rate of profit continued to fall? Marxian theory would predict the opposite results—particularly when the onset of the falling-rate-of-profit seemed to have come in the late 1960s. According to falling-rate-of-profit theorists, counteracting forces such as a strengthening of capital's bargaining power might lead to a boom in investment, even if the existing profit rate were low. Table 6.3 allows one to understand, to a greater degree, the relationship between capital and labor during the petroboom period.[6] Note that income to capital (column 9) shows a share *decline* of 4.8 percent from 1977 to 1981. The wage share received by private sector workers *fell faster*, however; labor's relative income share fell by 9 percent in the same years. Consequently, the *profit share* (capital income/private sector wage income) in the *private* sector rose slightly from 63 percent to 64.5

Table 6.3: The Functional Distribution of Income in Mexico (percentage share of GDP)

| | Income Going Abroad | | | (4) | Labor's Income (net of direct taxes) | | | |
| | (1) | (2) | (3) | Income | (5) | (6) | (7) | (8) |
Year	Total	Interest on Public Debt	Profits Remitted (+) Interest on Private Debt	Received by Mexicans	Total	Private Sector	Public Sector	Labor Abroad
1970	1.67	0.61	1.06	98.33	35.67	24.69	10.80	0.18
1971	1.59	0.61	0.98	98.41	35.48	24.57	10.75	0.16
1972	1.58	0.58	0.99	98.42	36.94	25.59	11.19	0.16
1973	1.64	0.68	0.96	98.36	35.88	24.85	10.87	0.16
1974	1.69	0.81	0.88	98.31	36.74	25.47	11.12	0.14
1975	1.68	0.96	0.72	98.32	38.08	26.62	11.34	0.13
1976	2.27	1.42	0.85	97.73	40.26	27.31	12.35	0.61
1977	2.65	1.88	0.77	97.35	38.87	25.87	12.25	0.75
1978	2.74	1.97	0.77	97.26	37.89	24.93	12.08	0.88
1979	3.05	2.15	0.90	96.95	37.72	24.65	12.11	0.96
1980	3.18	2.12	1.05	96.82	36.06	23.41	12.11	0.55
1981	3.73	2.28	1.44	96.27	37.35	23.52	13.26	0.58
1982	8.53	6.12	2.42	91.47	35.81	21.41	13.46	0.93
1983	7.58	5.68	1.89	92.42	28.77	16.37	11.39	1.02
1984	7.31	5.66	1.65	92.69	27.72	15.78	10.58	1.35
1985	6.11	4.89	1.21	93.89	28.29	16.50	10.66	1.13

B.

Year	(9) Capital's Share (Net of Direct Taxes)	Income of the State			
		(10) Total	(11) Federal Gov't (Revenue Minus Wages)	(12) Parastate Sector (Revenue Minus Wages)	(13) (Col 10-2)
1970	50.46	12.20	9.45	2.75	11.6
1971	50.89	12.04	9.28	2.75	11.4
1972	49.05	12.43	9.74	2.69	11.9
1973	49.84	12.65	10.00	2.65	12.0
1974	49.78	11.79	9.29	2.50	11.0
1975	47.05	13.18	10.93	2.25	12.2
1976	44.89	12.57	10.96	1.61	11.2
1977	44.93	13.56	11.58	1.97	11.7
1978	45.53	13.83	12.28	1.55	11.9
1979	45.01	14.21	12.86	1.35	12.1
1980	44.31	16.45	14.93	1.52	14.3
1981	42.74	16.18	14.84	1.34	13.9
1982	40.48	15.18	16.06	-0.88	9.1
1983	43.72	19.93	15.64	4.29	14.3
1984	45.46	19.51	14.96	4.55	13.9
1985	46.47	19.13	13.64	5.49	14.2

Source: Julio Boltvinik and Fernando Torres, "Concentración del Ingreso y Satisfacción de Necesidades en la Crisis Actual," *El Economista Mexicano* 19, no. 2 (1986), p. 31.

percent. These data demonstrate that in the distributional sphere capital was able to slightly expand its power over labor. This shift in power relationships between capital and labor (in the private sector) would help explain why a surge in investment was realized in this period in spite of a modest profit rate.

Note that much of the decline in capital's share (column 9) appeared to arise along with the strong increase in that of public sector employees' share (column 7) until 1982. Likewise, the growth in the state sector (column 10) seemed to come at the expense of capital's share. Once we net out interest payments abroad made by the state sector (column 10 minus column 2), the real role of the state sector and its relative growth are much less dramatic (column 13). From 1970 through 1981 the increase in the total income share received by workers in the public sector was 2.46 percent. Meanwhile, in the same years, if we adjust for interest payments flowing abroad, the public sector's relative income share rose from 11.6 to 13.9 (column 13)—a net increase in income share of 2.3 percent. Given data such as these, the contradictory situation of the private sector is illuminated. Within the private sphere of the economy, the private sector's power rose during the petroboom, but in its struggle against the state, its role diminished.

Finally, it should be noted that in relative terms the rate of increase in *industrial* investment was not strong. Table 4.5, Chapter 4, demonstrates that the surge in private sector investment during the petroboom period was inordinately devoted to commerce and services in relation to the pattern of investment in the 1970–1977 period. (Recall that manufacturing accounted for 51 percent of all private sector [nonresidential] investment in the 1970–1977 period but only 33.1 percent of such investment in the 1978–1981 period. Meanwhile, investments in commerce and services soared from 36 percent of private investment in 1970–1977 to 50.9 percent in 1978–1981.) This suggests two conclusions. First, the rate of profit in industry was not sufficient to justify an explosion in manufacturing investments. Second, by way of contrast, the rapid growth in imports created opportunities for highly profitable investments in services and commerce. Yet there is no question that the strength of the commerce and service sectors was also a measure of the ephemeral nature of much investment during the petroboom era. Mexico's capital stock did not grow in step with the overall growth of the economy—manufacturing became a lagging sector for the first time since 1940. Thus, it does appear that the falling-rate-of-profit theorist can employ a powerful argument to partially explain the movement of the economy in the 1970s and 1980s.

The overinvestment/underinvestment and the falling-rate-of-profit theories of crisis are to some extent complementary, although their methodological bases are quite diverse. The first focuses on the question of the rate of growth of demand and the difficulty of maintaining a balance among the components of total demand in a dynamic economy. The second focuses on the cost side (or supply side) of the economy, emphasizing the difficulties of maintaining a high rate of profit as the economy expands. The Keynesian models virtually ignore the cost side of the economy, while the classical Marxist formulations downplay the role of demand.

The difficulty with the later omission is that as the growth of the share of income received by capital expanded rapidly in the 1982–1985 period (see Table 6.3); the stagnation of aggregate demand best explained why investment remained below the level attained in 1982 and well below that of 1981 (see Table 6.2). With real wages falling by roughly one-third from 1981 to 1985, and with the "rate of exploitation" for the entire economy soaring—Boltvinik and Torres computed the increase from the petroboom years (1977–1981) to the 1982–1985 period at 42 percent—why did investment fail to recover (Boltvinik and Torres, 1986, 23–24)?[7]

The answer, in part, was that *some* recovery in private sector investment was realized, presumably because of a favorable capital-labor relationship (for capital). From its low point in 1983, private investment grew 31 percent by 1985. Nevertheless, even then private investment was barely above that achieved in 1982 and 24 percent below that achieved in 1981. A steep drop in total demand, particularly demand generated by public sector spending and investment, took its toll on the private sector profit rate, even as the labor situation (from capital's perspective) improved. Fixed costs for capital, inventories, land, and borrowed funds had to be met even as the volume of sales declined. This raised the per-unit cost of fixed capital and cut into the profit rate. The cuts in public sector wage rates particularly diminished the potential for the private sector to raise its rate of profit in the 1982–1985 period—due to the weak internal market.[8]

The Monetarist Explanation of the Crisis

As incomplete as they may be, taken separately or in combination, the Keynesian and classical Marxist theories of crisis at least have the virtue of insisting that their formulations should fit the empirical record. The monetarists make no such demands upon themselves. Their analysis of crisis begins and ends with certain assumptions regarding the functioning of a capitalist system. It is claimed that if these assumptions hold, the monetarist theory will explain how and why the accumulation process has been derailed. The monetarists *know* that their assumptions hold, so they are not interested in checking their theory against the facts (Cypher, 1988c; Toye, 1987, 1–94).

The monetarists at the IMF reason from what is known as a "general equilibrium" model of an economy (Brett, 1983, 7–85). The core assumption of this model must never be forgotten: Without any "distortions"—such as government intervention into the labor market (such as minimum wage or full-employment policies) or monetary disequilibria such as inflation—all resources (land, labor, and capital) *will be fully employed at their best (most productive) use.* The "invisible hand" will see to this. This model abstracts from historical context and from the very nature of a disarticulated peripheral-capitalist social formation such as Mexico's.

According to the monetarists the economic crisis has its origins in the imbalance between public sector expenditures and revenues. A public sector deficit can occur because developing nations attempt to intervene too readily into the market economy (Brett, 1983, 7–85; Toye, 1987, 1–94). Thus, by supporting minimum wages, retirement programs, health and safety regulations, union rights, and social security legislation, the government tends to "misallocate resources." The attempt to boost government spending on behalf of labor is matched by overambitious capital-intensive development projects financed by the state—particularly by borrowing. In other words, a developing country has a structural propensity to raise government spending beyond its "appropriate" level.

The deficit can be papered over in two ways. First, a nation can borrow abroad. But this essentially alleviates a short-term problem at the expense of creating an even greater one later when the debt must be paid. Second, the government can discretely attempt to put more money into circulation. But this, according to the monetarists, creates a problem because inflation will interfere with rational economic calculations, especially regarding investment. As the inflation continues, funds for investment will dry up. Speculation will displace fundamental capital formation. Once inflation has taken hold, the economy will slide down the slippery slope into exchange-rate instability, which will add to the tendency toward crisis.

Notice that at the center of the monetarist analysis we find not money but the state. Nor are the monetarists concerned with the state *per se* so much as they are concerned with the possibility that the state can become a medium through which economic *power* may be redistributed. Note that the monetarists do not suggest that a fiscal deficit be eliminated through tax increases. Although they decry the public sector deficit, the monetarists ignore research that would reveal the ridiculously low level of taxes placed upon capital—especially in Mexico—and the tendency for such taxes on capital to decline over time. Furthermore, the monetarists, in Mexico and elsewhere, have overlooked the fact that much of the public sector deficit can be traced to subsidized prices on petroleum products, electricity, and other goods that primarily reduced the cost of production of private sector producers.

The monetarist "solution" to the crisis requires a presumed short-run period of austerity in which the level of public sector spending is reduced and unemployment is allowed to rise. Inflation is wrung out of the economy through a steep drop in demand and a chain of bankruptcies. Real interest rates are increased on the premise that this will induce savings. As savings rise, argues the theory, investment will rise (another key and heroic assumption). As investment rises, capital formation will rise, productivity will rise, demand will rise, wages will rise (but not by "too" much), and total demand will rise. The state will be reduced to that of a "watchman," and all resources will find there proper use—the economy will be fully employed.

Moving from this mechanistic monetarist schema into the complex dynamic of the Mexican economy in the 1980s cannot be a smooth transition. Only with difficulty can one discover the threads of monetarist analysis and influence in the twists and turns taken by economic policymakers from 1982 onward. At the outset attention was riveted on the deficit of the public sector, which stood at the very high level of 17.9 percent of the GDP in 1982. De la Madrid Hurtado entered office with an IMF agreement to reduce this deficit to 8.5 percent of GDP. This was essentially achieved through (1) renegotiation of more than $20 billion of the public sector's foreign debt payment, (2) a 28 percent cut in public sector investments, (3) a cut in average wages paid to public sector workers of 16.4 percent, (4) a sizable increase in the prices charged by parastate firms, and (5) an increase in indirect (regressive) taxes (Ros, 1987, 84–85).

President de la Madrid Hurtado certainly achieved the monetarist objective of trimming the role of the state. As can be seen from Table 6.4 public sector expenditures (column 2) fell from 48.7 percent of GDP in 1982 to 44.8 percent in 1983 and then again to 40.5 percent of GDP in 1984. With taxes and prices charged by the parastate firms rising and expenditures dropping, the public sector deficit fell from 17.9 percent of GDP in 1982 to "only" 8.7 percent in 1984. Note also that a larger proportional drop was experienced in state expenditures after interest payments had been netted out (column 6). Total interest payments (external and internal) rose from 9.1 percent of GDP in 1982 to 10.8 percent in 1984 (column 4 and 5).

Table 6.4: The Public Sector (% GNP)

Year	(1) Income	(2) Expenditures Total	(3) Deficit	(4) External Interest	(5) Internal Interest	(6) Noninterest Expenditures
1970	19.5	21.1	1.8	0.61	---	---
1975	26.3	33.3	7.5	0.96	---	---
1976	25.1	32.0	7.2	1.42	---	---
1977	26.0	31.5	5.1	1.88	---	---
1978	27.4	32.8	5.3	1.97	---	---
1979	28.6	34.8	5.4	2.15	---	---
1980	33.3	39.5	6.5	2.12	1.9	35.48
1981	27.7	42.2	14.5	2.28	3.3	36.62
1982	30.7	48.7	17.9	3.50	5.6	39.60
1983	34.6	44.8	9.0	4.50	8.1	32.20
1984	34.1	40.5	8.7	5.00	5.8	30.00
1985	31.8	43.1	10.0	5.20	7.4	30.50
1986	30.1	46.2	16.3	5.50	12.2	28.50
1987	31.3	48.1	16.9	4.80	16.2	27.50

Sources: Table 6.3, text, and Arturo Huerta, *Economía Mexicana: Más alla del Milagro* (México: Ediciónes de Cultura Popular, 1986) p. 219; CIEN, *La Economía Mexicana 1988* (México: CIEN, 1988), pp. 135-141; Jaime Ros, "Mexico from the Oil Boom to the Debt Crisis," in Rosemary Thorp and Laurence Whitehead (eds.), *Latin American Debt and the Adjustment Crisis* (Pittsburgh: University of Pittsburgh Press, 1987), p. 83.

From Theory to Reality: A Long, Hard Road

What followed next, however, widely diverged from the monetarist prescription. Public sector expenditures soared upward after 1984, once again reaching approximately the peak level of 1982 in 1987 (column 2). Moreover, the public sector deficit nearly equaled the record level set in 1982 in both 1986 and 1987. What had gone wrong?

On the revenue, or income, side of the ledger, the state commenced in 1984 to offer new tax deductions for investments, particularly those that would increase exports. Increasing evasion of taxes (difficult to document) was another important factor in the declining revenue situation. Then, too, with a deep recession in effect the mass of taxable activities declined. The opening to foreign trade meant the gradual elimination of taxes on exports and most imports, that caused a modest, but in this situation important, decline in revenues. Most important from mid-1985 onward was the slow, and then precipitous, drop in oil prices. (Oil taxes on internal consumption and exports had accounted for 40.6 percent of total revenues in 1984.) Through 1988 Mexico was forced to pay a high price for its dependence upon a monoexporter strategy. The consequences of strategic blunders taken in the mid-1970s were still reverberating in 1988.

The de la Madrid Hurtado administration reached a crucial turning point in 1985. For the first two years of the sexenio, the watchword had been austerity. Now, however, the government moved to reflate the economy—hoping to engineer a state-led boom in manufacturing exports. As had been commonplace since the days when Ortiz Mena formalized Mexico's model of debt-led stabilizing growth in the 1950s, the administration sought to expand the real economy through government deficits. Yet foreign credits were not available for such a strategy. Under a three-year stabilization program from the IMF, Mexico could not look to foreign creditors for much new funding. (Indeed, the IMF, frustrated over the new reflation policy, withheld scheduled stabilization credits in 1985.)

There was one remaining option: to run a deficit by way of printing money and borrowing from the economic elite. Here it is necessary to pause and take note of an important institutional change that commenced in 1983: As part of the process of creating the "parallel financial system," two important changes were made regarding public debt instruments. Until 1983 the Banco de México had funded 75.5 percent of all internal public debts. Whatever the size of the internal debt, three-fourths of the interest paid simply went from one part of the state apparatus to another. Furthermore, the government traded its own bonds. After 1983 roughly 57 percent of the debt was funded in the private sector, while the trading of the bonds was left to the stock exchange (CIEN, 1988b, 132–134).

This had important consequences—particularly for the distribution of income. The elite became the most important source of borrowed funds. With only roughly 10 percent of total tax revenues arising from the income tax, the economic elite was favored by an internal deficit. When its money was returned (with interest), most of the interest paid would be raised from indirect (sales) taxes that would fall on the middle class, the working class, and the poor.

Thus, growth of the internal deficit opened up a new avenue for income redistribution. The economic elite could also gain "promoters' profits" by underwriting and selling the debt via the stock exchange and by trading in the debt instruments. Note how surprisingly large these interest payments became by 1987—16.2 percent of total GDP (column 5 of Table 6.4). The benefits accruing to the economic elite explain why the administration could raise the state's deficit back to record levels only achieved in 1982 without unleashing a barrage of criticism from the business associations.

Yet the reflation policy did *not* work to buoy the economy, even as it *did* work to massively redistribute income to the economic elite. (Note that this second effect, redistributing income upward, is consistent with monetarist, and particularly Austrian School, economic theory. At the same time it is inconsistent with the first effect [continued economic stagnation] because according to these theories, the market will find productive uses for the newfound wealth accruing to the economic elite.) According to monetarist theory, Mexico needed high real interest rates in order to encourage savings. Yet by setting rates quite high (at least in nominal terms), the government was forced to annually pay back in interest most of what it had annually borrowed (in interest payments alone). Consequently, with the reflation efforts leading to price increases by the companies owned by the economic elite, and with the government determined to set interest payments on the internal debt quite high, the state created a vicious circle. Ironically, after deducting for total interest paid (column 6 of Table 6.4), the state actually had *less* of a share of total expenditures in 1987 than it had in 1984 before the reflation strategy commenced. The soaring internal debt and the rocketing stock market had become the two pillars of Mexico's new casino capitalism model.

Applying the Doctrine of "Real Prices"?

Does the monetarist doctrine of "real prices" signal the death knell for the theory of state monopoly capitalism? Parastate prices did rise; indeed, they were one of the major reasons for the increased rhythm of inflation in the 1980s. Yet a study of the pricing policies of PEMEX concluded that the subsidies granted to the private sector by this parastate *increased* by 36 percent in the 1982–1985 period over those of the petroboom period (1978–1981) (Manzo, 1988, 66). Nor were these subsidies small; converting to the U.S. dollar, José Luis Manzo showed that subsidies came to approximately $1 billion during the period. Manzo noted a shift in the beneficiaries of the subsidies under de la Madrid Hurtado. Formerly, such subsidies were enjoyed by consumers, businesses and trucking companies, and companies that bought natural gas, petrochemicals, and other petroleum products. In the 1982–1985 period, however, the subsidies were much more directed toward large corporations, including transnationals. They were allowed to purchase petrochemicals, petroleum derivatives, and natural gas at very low prices relative to the international market *if* these companies were linked (directly or indirectly) to endeavors that would result in an increase in manufacturing exports.

The results of changes in state policymaking were not quite what they appeared to be. The real prices doctrine, so avidly pursued by the monetarists, was simultaneously honored and breached. Most importantly, the beneficiaries changed. Whereas during the petroboom period the economic elite was forced to share a considerable portion of the subsidies it received from PEMEX with the middle class (and even the more "privileged" members of the working class), now virtually all of the subsidy remained within the confines of the 100 largest groups and their partners/rivals—the transnational corporations.

The Misery of Monetarism

What had the monetarists *cum* Austrians wrought? They had presided over an era of increasing monetary instability that had brought record rates of inflation along with unprecedented rounds of devaluations. They had failed to revive industrial investment while opening the way to a new era of speculation in real estate and finance. They had managed to raise the public sector deficit to all but record levels while continuing the now time-honored tradition of borrowing heedlessly to fuel the growth of public sector spending. Their crowning achievement, and presumably their *raison d'être*, unquestionably was to be found in the rapid shift in the distribution of income. Nonetheless, their ruthless pursuit of this goal failed to restore "confidence" because capital flight continued to be a latent, and sometimes manifest, problem. Their greatest failure was to be found in the growth statistics. It was an open question whether Mexico was any closer to real prices throughout the economy than it had been, even if the state subsidies now went to different sectors of the population. Looking back over this debacle, the questionably elected president, Carlos Salinas de Gortari, promised in November 1988 to *borrow* Mexico's way out of the crisis in the 1989–1994 period.

Business-Government Relations
Under de la Madrid Hurtado

For almost all of his term, President de la Madrid Hurtado struggled to exorcise the trauma that the business elite experienced as a result of the bank nationalization. Creation of a parallel banking system through which the old financial oligarchy could restore its lost economic power and exercise renewed political influence was not enough. This did not obliterate the awareness that *potentially* the state had the power to do something similar and on little or no notice. Only by destroying the demon within—the state—could de la Madrid Hurtado satisfy his critics among the business elite.

President de la Madrid Hurtado, however, had risen to his office by way of a lifetime of loyal service to the PRI. He clearly believed that the state had an important role to play in the economy and in the society. Many of his writings and speeches prior to the 1982 election showed this quite clearly. His views underwent a process of change in the course of his term in office. In his first years his *Plan Nacional* and related economic plans suggested to the business elite that the struggle against statism had simply entered a new phase.

His unilateral move to change the meaning of Articles 25, 26, and 28 of the Constitution were met with universal dismay by the business elite (Casar, Gaspar, and Jacobo, 1988, 216). Article 25 was changed to affirm that the state had the official power to be the "rector" of national development. Article 26 gave the state the power and obligation to "organize a system of democratic planning of national development." Article 28 reserved to the state certain "strategic" and "priority" areas of the economy. It was possible to view these changes in the Constitution as evidence of a determination to maintain a statist posture.

Lost in the discussion were several subtle changes that went far to meet long-standing demands of the business elite. A shift in emphasis could be found in relation to Article 27. This article declared that the rights of the state could take precedence over the rights of the private sector and/or over the social sector. The total effect of revised Articles 25, 26, and 28, however, was to *raise* the role of the private sector while lowering that of the state. Henceforth, there were to be *three equal categories of rights*—the rights of the state, private property, and civil society (Blanco, 1985, 411).

This did not assuage the business elite, of course, because at that time it sought formal (or at least informal) guarantees that civil society would play virtually no role in the determination of national policy. Rather, public policymaking would become a matter and province of business-government interaction with the former having a determinant role (Casar, Gaspar, and Jacobo, 1988, 215–219). Traumatized as it was by the bank nationalization, the business elite badly misinterpreted the posture assumed by the administration in its first three years.

As a follow-up to the *Plan Nacional*, the government published a key document, the *Programa Nacional de Fondo y Comercio Exterior* (the National Program for Foreign Trade and Industry, or PRONAFICE) in 1984. The presentation of this program unleashed what has been termed "one of the largest reactions against any government plan ever mounted by the businessmen" (Alcocer and Cisneros, 1985, 220). Yet the PRONAFICE (designed to make Mexico an industrial power by the year 2000) specifically conceded that the business sector would be the *principal agent* of economic development.

Was the struggle between de la Madrid Hurtado and the business elite during 1983–1985 purely ephemeral—as many have implied or assumed? Francisco Baez Rodríquez's study stood apart from other works on the de la Madrid Hurtado period in his insistence that there *were* substantive differences between the administration and the business elite, even though these differences were definitely not to be found in the discussion over the *Plan Nacional*; Articles 25, 26, and 28; or PRONAFICE. He drew a subtle yet powerful distinction, regarding de la Madrid Hurtado, that is worth bearing in mind in understanding the tensions between the state and the private sector through most of 1985:

> At the outset his was not a neoliberal project in the prevailing style of those under the monetarist yoke in many of the Southern Cone countries in the 1970s. Nevertheless there had been a clear return to orthodox schemes that did give sovereignty to the market. But the market that he had in mind was an ordered one, reconstructed with direction from above. It was a liberal model, but with a state presence that would intervene in the basic areas of the economy to maintain an equilibrium. This was a model that would carry through the reordering of the economy, while defending the productive apparatus wherever possible (Baez Rodríquez, 1985, 338).

Baez Rodríquez's analysis was consistent with the observed tension between the state and the business organization such as the CCE and Coparmex. The documents promulgated by the administration constituted no threat to these groups, but de la Madrid Hurtado's less than fulsome embrace of the theories of neoliberalism did.

Nor was this difference of perspective limited to ideological jousting. There were several real clashes involving the material interests of the groups. One of the larger clashes involved a conflict between private sector producers of synthetic fibers and Somex. Somex built a new state-owned plant, Finacril, which boosted national synthetic fiber production by 41 percent in May 1985. Somex argued that Mexico's production of such fibers was inadequate and that along with increasing production for the domestic market, the new plant could export any unsold production. Somex correctly maintained that it was preferable to export refined and semiprocessed petroleum products (such as synthetic fibers) rather than crude oil.

The three-member cartel that controlled private production fought bitterly to block the plant, claiming that the three companies were already operating with 50 percent excess production capacity. Somex and research agencies of the government strongly denied this claim. Other research claimed that the synthetic fiber cartel sold its products at "prohibitive" prices. If this probable claim were true, the private-sector cartel had much to fear from a state-owned plant that sold its products at competitive prices.

The administration was finally persuaded by the industrial associations. (In this case the Camara Nacional de la Industria Textil [National

Association of the Textile Industry] played an outspoken role.) Finally, SEMIP assured the private sector that once the plant was in operation, the state would privatize it (Zuniga, 1984, 22–23). The struggle over Finacril was instructive, for it demonstrated that the de la Madrid Hurtado administration in its first three years *continued* to use the power and leverage of the state to promote some state-led development. In these years, the administration was more prone to adopt the ideological perspective of the groups and the business associations than had any previous government since the 1940s. Yet there still lingered an element of the old state-led perspective that had dominated Mexican development policy for forty years. Thus, in the early years of this administration a *real*, if often subdued, struggle continued between the state and the private sector.

The private sector was clearly the aggressor in this struggle. The business offensive took two forms. One, which Matilda Luna has defined as the "technocratic," sought to work within the PRI to eliminate the tripartite elements of the state apparatus (the public, the private, and the social sectors). The business elite sought a bilateral relationship in which the private sector had the power to review all economic decisions to be taken by the public sector. The private sector not only demanded and received more extensive privileges of "consultation" regarding public sector decisions; the private sector also gained new power to condition the decisionmaking process within the public sector (Luna, 1988). Of particular concern to the technocrats (who served in numerous new consultative committees and commissions in order to guide the decisionmaking process) was that such decisionmaking be based on rigorous technical criteria rather than on "populist" or "social" considerations. These technical critera were to be developed within a market-society context. To be eliminated was a process based in personal contacts by businessmen who had "peso" (weight) within the state apparatus. The technocrats sought a stable business-government relationship with defined rules and procedures. No longer would business accept an informal *pacto político* of consultation with the state and assurances that the state would protect the interests of the private sector. The *técnicos* would ensure that the state had no discretion in the matter. This new posture was very much linked to the bank nationalization. The *técnicos* sought an institutional structure in which an act of state autonomy, such as a nationalization, could no longer be possible.

The new business offensive produced another, and more obvious, tactic. The business elite split into the technocrats and the right-wing populists. The populists, some of whom were drawn from Coparmex, the CCE, and CONCANACO (the three business associations most critical of the state) believed that the way to accomplish the goals that they shared with the technocrats was to build a popular base in order to engage in an electoral struggle against the PRI. It was this initiative that fueled the resurgence of the Partidad de Acción Nacional (National Action Party, or PAN) in regional elections during de la Madrid Hurtado's administration. The PAN, in fact, won some elections and forced the PRI into embarrassingly obvious electoral fraud and political repression. Meanwhile, the populist Right reinforced the pressure that the technocrats were exerting from within.

The Policy Shift of 1985–1986

The pressure on the administration seemed to reach a critical mass sometime in late 1985. While the economic situation deteriorated, the PAN began to show unanticipated electoral strength. Oil prices plummeted in 1986. With export revenues falling and imports of manufacturing surging, the surplus in foreign trade—one of de la Madrid Hurtado's proudest boasts—nearly disappeared.

In late 1985 the administration undertook a fundamental change in its approach to both the conjunctural and long-term problems facing the economy. The most obvious signal came when the administration announced that Mexico would join the General Agreement on Tariffs and Trade (GATT) in 1986. The GATT decision was momentous for it signified the end of a political posture that Mexico had long held *vis-à-vis* international organizations. Mexico had long been maintained that the country should not be bound by agreements of international organizations lest national sovereignty be placed in jeopardy. This was the official argument for Mexico's refusal to join The Organization of Petroleum Exporting Countries in the 1970s. The GATT decision meant in broad terms that Mexico would abandon a development policy that had for forty years emphasized state intervention, the prioritization of the internal market, and import-substitution industrialization. Nationalist and populist policies regarding the control of the activities of transnational corporations and banks would have to be forfeited in order for Mexico to remain a member in good standing with GATT. Given Mexico's "comparative advantage" in low-wage manufacturing, the GATT decision also carried deep implications for organized labor. Unions would have to be curbed, as would payments connected with the "social wage" such a social security and public health.

The GATT decision was momentous because of what it entailed regarding *internal* politico-economic policymaking. From mid-year 1985 to mid-year 1986 a number of important changes occurred—all connected with the decision to turn Mexico into a market-dominated, export-led economy and society. Of note was the major debt renegotiation under way during this period. Sizable new funds ($9 billion) flowed into Mexico from the IMF, the World Bank, the U.S. government, and the private banks. All of this money was lent on the condition that Mexico adopt a new development policy of export promotion. Meanwhile, the government relaxed its laws mandating 51 percent Mexican participation in foreign investments. Henceforth, such investment might entail 100 percent foreign ownership—the matter was to be decided on a case-by-case basis. The privatization program, heretofore pursued listlessly, gained momentum. Structural change now became the watchword of the administration.

It was no simple task to understand the nature of the transformation that took place from mid-year 1985 to mid-1986. The government had already championed structural change, export promotion, privatization, and new possibilities for foreign investors. Yet these policies had not received the single-minded emphasis that they gained after mid-1985. Only with some hindsight could one understand that a fundamental watershed had been reached midway in the de la Madrid Hurtado sexenio. As Celso Garrido and Enrique Quintana noted, the economic crisis of 1985–1986 "eliminated the last attempts to make a gradual transition toward a new growth model" (Garrido and Quintana, 1988, 54). Having now made a full and unequivocal commitment to a policy of all-out export promotion, the administration pursued its new project with little or no regard for the presumed short-term costs of its achievement. Having firmly set its sights on a long-term transition, the administration seemed callously indifferent to the mounting social suffering recorded in Mexico from 1986 through 1988. A new intransigence and a more pervasive aloofness were readily to be found. A new era, defined by Enrique de la Garza as one of *savage reconversion*, had begun (de la Garza, 1988, 7).

Engineering Structural Change: The Export Promotion Policy

Whether it was known as reconversion, restructuring, structural change, modernization, or any other term, Mexico's new development policy had clearly become, by late 1985, one of export promotion. The ostensible logic behind the export promotion program was that of the "free market." But implementing this allegedly promarket policy required massive state intervention. Why, one might ask, if the market so clearly destined the Mexican economy to be a successful exporter of manufacturing products, should there be any government intervention whatsoever to promote exports? This was a fair and indeed logical question to ask. But it was not asked or answered.

Just as state intervention had formed the basis for Mexican industrialization in the 1940s, 1950s, and 1960s, so, too, would the state play the central role in orchestrating a new turn toward the global market. Unquestionably, the export promotion program entailed the withdrawal of state intervention from numerous areas of the economy, particularly from the parastate industries and the social sector. Yet export promotion required as much, perhaps even more, state intervention than had any previous major development program. This was perhaps the greatest irony to be found amidst the tragedy of the de la Madrid Hurtado sexenio.

There were only two new elements to the program. First, the intellectual architects of the program claimed fulsome allegiance to the pristine principles of the free market. Second, the beneficiaries were an exceedingly small band of national groups and transnational corporations—certainly no more than 100. The outlines of the dichotomous nature of Mexico's new political economy were becoming painfully, if still only vaguely, clear by 1988: for the 100 export-oriented industrial behemoths, the state; for the rest, the market. To be sure, structural change entailed much more than export promotion—for example, new high–technology forms of production, such as computer-aided design and manufacture, were to be introduced into the commanding heights of the productive apparatus of the nation. Yet the crowning achievement of the structural change program was to be a fully modernized, globally competitive *export* sector, which would provide Mexico with the means of becoming an intermediate industrial power in the late 1990s.

The Export Promotion Policies

Information regarding the specifics of the export promotion program has been relatively limited. As mentioned, the *Plan Nacional de Desarrollo* proclaimed that the administration was committed to export promotion (Poder Ejectivo, 1983, 83–106, 190–199). Some commentators dismissed these declarations as examples of the time-honored "wish list" approach to economic planning. But when PRONAFICE was published in 1984, it suggested that there might be some serious commitment to export promotion (Gomez Chinas, 1987, 109–140). However, no funds were allocated for the export promotion policies until April 1985 when the Programa de Fometo Integral de Exportaciones (Integrated Plan to Promote Exports, or Profiex) was created to underwrite some of the costs of putting PRONAFICE into effect.

From the decision to create Profiex came the restructuring of Nafinsa and the Banco de Comercio Exterior (Bank for Foreign Trade, or Bancomext). Nafinsa was given a new mandate—export promotion. Bancomext, which had long been part of the state apparatus, was thrust into the foreground. Under the 1986 *Programa de Financimiento Integral para la Reconversion Industrial*, these two development banks received more than a doubling of their budgets in order to spearhead the reconversion–export promotion program. Together they were allocated roughly $10.5 billion—roughly 5 percent of the GDP—to devote to new projects (Rodríquez and Moro, 1987, 8–9). Bancomext's role was increased to the degree that its budget was roughly three-quarters of that of Nafinsa.

Many other programs followed in 1986 and 1987, the most notable of which was the Secretaría de Comercio y Fometo Industrial's (Secretary of Commerce and Industrial Promotion, or Secofi) *Programa de Concertación con Empresas Altamente Exportadoras* (Program of Support for High-Export Firms). Secofi's new program to assist exporting companies was specifically designed to aid only 100 high-export manufacturers—11 parastates, 27 transnationals, and 62 companies owned by the national groups.

Behind these major programs stood the *programas de rama* (sector programs) that Secofi had quietly begun early in the de la Madrid Hurtado administration. Prior to formal entry into GATT, the *programas de rama* were key elements of industrial policy. The sector programs were designed to "pick winners"—to locate what were thought to be emerging sectors or new industries that would allow Mexican industrialization to expand internationally. First and foremost among the sector programs was the auto industry.

The auto sector program seemed quite successful in the sense of luring major U.S. and Japanese automakers into locating large auto parts plants in the north. Along with these plants, that produced items such as engines and transmissions, a broad range of small-parts producers commenced or expanded production under the program. Many of the smaller auto parts producers were located within the *maquiladora* industry, but others operated in the interior of the nation and produced for the internal market. The auto sector program emphasized state-of-the-art manufacturing technologies—at least in the largest factories owned by the major auto transnationals. Thus, while the laser beam set the adjustment for metalworking tools and robots moved within the plant, outside the peasants goaded their oxen and used a sixteenth-century plows to scratch the soil. (The robot and the laser, of course, had to be imported.) The loosely articulated theory behind the emphasis on high-technology methods of production assumed that there were "spill-over" effects in manufacturing technologies. This meant that Mexico's antiquated manufacturing plants could indirectly benefit from having some of the world's most modern (and most capital-intensive) auto plants. Evidence confirming this assumption does not seem to be readily at hand.

The *programas de rama* were designed to be both import substituting and export promoting. Emphasis was placed on a high (and rising) local content. Firms that were eligible for assistance from Secofi had to export a considerable percentage of total output (approximately 20 percent in many cases). For qualifying firms all manner of subsidies were available. Plant sites were set up within industrial parks where water, sewage, power, railheads, and roads were provided. Tax holidays of five years or longer were common, and land rents in the industrial parks could be waived for several years. The industrial parks often provided housing for workers and in some cases low-level technical training for the work force. Water, sewage, electrical power, and petroleum products were sold to the new firms at highly subsidized rates. The qualifying firms could receive their imported inputs free of tariffs in many cases, and their exports were exempt from export taxes. To the extent that it was possible, the government stood willing to offer technical and production assistance and advice to qualifying firms.

Along with the auto industry, which received by far the most support from Secofi, the government emphasized several other sectors, the most important of which were petrochemicals, pharmaceuticals, and computers. The pharmaceutical program seemed to make unsatisfactory progress, but the computer industry blossomed. By 1988 the government believed that the Mexican computer industry would be a leading sector in its bid to find a niche in the world market of manufactures (World Bank, 1989, 20).

In 1986 the *programas de rama*, which had been a major focus of the administration, began to be phased out. The reasons for this, in spite of what appeared to have been some progress in the area of industrial development, were twofold. First, the sector programs were very obviously elements of a broader industrial policy and would therefore likely become targets of Mexico's competitors within GATT. They could easily charge that Mexico had engaged in unfair trading practices to promote its exports. Second, the World Bank, which increasingly played a role in the determination of Mexico's industrial policymaking after 1985 (as will be discussed in the following section), was totally opposed to Secofi's sector programs on the grounds that they amounted to statist intervention.

It is possible to perceive two phases of the export promotion program. First, from 1983–1985 the policy was pursued primarily by way of the direct effects of the *programas de rama*. The second phase, overlapping with the first, began with the Profiex program in April 1985. From this moment the export promotion program became broader, more institutionalized, and seemingly more coherent. Rather than making use of tax subsidies, which had been a linchpin of previous industrial programs, the private sector relied on the provision of *working capital* from the state—up to 50 percent was provided.

Profiex opted for (1) the permanent undervaluation of the peso against foreign currencies, (2) the elimination of barriers to the access of foreign exchange for exporters, (3) the simplification of import and export permits, and (4) a subsidy allowed on the importation of machinery and equipment to be used in production for exports (Ortiz Wadgymar, 1987, 7). Exporters would now receive "drawbacks"—quick repayment for certain value-added taxes and export taxes paid on finished products. In March 1986 the benefits of the Profiex program were extended to "indirect exporters"— that is, to companies that did not export but sold a considerable percentage of their products to companies that did. As mentioned, in 1987 the *Programa de Concertatción con Empresas Altamente Exportadoras* began at Secofi. This special program essentially linked together and institutionalized the multiplicity of new benefits that companies could receive from various government programs. Approximately one hundred companies qualified for this program. Secofi selected and provided the most beneficial package of assistance available. It functioned as a broker to its special clients. Further support came in February 1987 when the Banco de México began to cover exporters' foreign currency risks.

Policy-based Lending in Mexico

Before turning to an evaluation of the export promotion program, let us briefly survey the role played by the World Bank in the 1985–1986 shift toward all-out export promotion and *hyper-laissez-faire*. Beginning in the early 1980s the World Bank underwent a major transformation. From the close of the World War II until the 1980s, the World Bank had extended project loans—that is, loans for specific programs such as dams, roads, and housing. During the decade of the 1980s, however, the fastest growing component of World Bank lending came from policy-based loans. These loans, some known as structural adjustment loans, extended new funding to Third World nations *if* they would follow the policy of laissez-faire. In practice, the policy-based loans attacked the state's role in the Third World. Their specific objectives very much paralleled the major changes that occurred in Mexico under de la Madrid Hurtado—privatization, deregulation, elimination of subsidies and price controls, opening up to foreign investment, elimination of domestic content regulations, weakening or elimination of unions, reliance on private sector investment as a motor force driving the economy, and so on.

Officially Mexico did not receive a structural adjustment loan (nor was the crucial role of policy-based lending publicly understood) during the de la Madrid Hurtado period. (The administration succeeded in keeping secret its increasing commitment to World Bank intervention.) Nonetheless, beginning in 1986, Mexico became the foremost client of the World Bank and its chief recipient of policy-tied loans. The World Bank commenced a period of very intensive interaction with the Mexican government. Indeed, it would be no exaggeration to state that Mexico had become *the* test case for policy-based lending throughout the entire Third World.

Policy-based lending is highly interventionary because in exchange for badly needed hard currency that the recipient government can spend on whatever it would prefer, the borrower must agree to very deep, fundamental changes in the structure of the political economy of the nation during a three- to five-year period. It appears that policy-based loans force the surrender of a quotient of national sovereignty to the World Bank. Certainly a nation can, under these loans, engage only in practices that follow the new *hyper-laissez-faire* model. States may not plan and prioritize areas of their economy; the market will do this for them, they are told. Essentially, states must negotiate their own withdrawal from the economy, leaving behind only a watchman apparatus of courts, schools, the military, an infrastructure, and little more. The World Bank prioritizes foreign trade, arguing that poor nations can and must export their way out of poverty. It demands that the state do everything possible to facilitate the transformation of the economy into an export-led model.

The World Bank's role in Mexico's restructuring was even larger because of "cross-conditionality." This term describes the fact that in the 1980s the World Bank would continue lending only if the *conditions* under which IMF funds were lent were fulfilled and *vice versa*. Further, cross-conditionality could also involve the renegotiation of private bank debt; such renegotiations were *conditioned* on the recipient country's agreement to meet the stipulations of World Bank policy-based loans. Thus, for the first time in its existence, the World Bank granted funds that were "conditional"—as the IMF had done for decades. But the conditions of the World Bank were much more interventionary, much longer lasting, than was any package of conditions ever assembled by the IMF—at least in Mexico's case.

When not writing for public access, the World Bank was brutally frank on such matters:

The Bank has transferred increasing amounts of resources to Mexico through policy-based and sector adjustment loans in the context of an adjustment-oriented framework that was supported by the 1986–1987 commercial financing package; it has become Mexico's largest single source of new money. Six Bank Loans in trade, exports, agriculture, and industry were linked to the multi-facility financing scheme, providing drawdown conditions for the parallel money and growth facilities that were mobilized fully in March 1988. The Bank also put up guarantees of U.S. $750 Million. In addition, the Bank facilitated Mexico's efforts to issue securitized bonds [for example the zero-bond scheme] for retiring old debt in January 1988. The Bank's strategy supported primarily policies designed to open the economy (World Bank, 1989, 45).

From mid-year 1986 to mid-1988 the World Bank lent a total of $5.7 billion of new funds to Mexico—nearly $1 of every $10 the World Bank lent was then going to Mexico (World Bank, 1989, 43). Of particular importance to the World Bank was the opening up of the economy to direct foreign investment. The pressure that the World Bank exerted to eliminate Mexico's 1973 law limiting foreign ownership to 49 percent of an enterprise was unremitting. The World Bank was fully committed to the "free flow of capital" argument. It was, at best, indifferent to matters of national concern (enshrined in the Mexican Constitution) that excluded or limited foreign ownership of land, natural resources, power production, and other basic areas of the economy. The World Bank disagreed with the Mexican state's right to declare certain areas of the economy strategic and priority. Their watchword was transparency (all areas of the economy must be treated in the same way).

Just how interventionary policy-based loans are can be best understood by citing the World Bank itself. Here the Bank offered a summary of the "conditions" that were to be met for the $500 million industrial sector policy loan that Mexico received in May 1989:

The proposed Industrial Sector Policy Loan will support a program geared toward deregulating the Mexican industrial sector. It will support policy changes to be initiated in 1989 that will encourage more efficient allocation of resources in the industrial sector and stimulate sustainable industrial growth, based on market forces rather than on the use of discretionary policy instruments. The program will emphasize: (i) deregulation of the industrial sector programs [the *Programas de Rama*]; (ii) further improvement in the trade regime; (iii) establishing more open direct foreign investment and technology transfer regimes and improving the environment for R & D; (iv) relaxing barriers to entry and reducing the cost of doing business; and (v) implementing regulating changes to improve the provision of trucking services. An attempt will also be made to review and implement initial measures aimed at increasing labor mobility (World Bank, 1989, 13).

What was the relationship between the very enhanced role of the World Bank in lending to Mexico from 1986 onward and the shift that the de la Madrid Hurtado administration made at that time toward a new export-led development growth model? Dependency theorists would argue that here we have a clear-cut case of internal policy shifts being determined by external factors. This conclusion, while possible, pays scant attention to the fact that the industrial and financial groups had been urging the Mexican state to make just such a shift since the early 1970s. Furthermore, a dependency perspective would of necessity put little weight on the fact that the administration had since 1983 taken a series of steps that would gradually move Mexico in the direction that the neoliberals, both in Mexico and at the World Bank, urged. The conclusion to be drawn is that the shift in internal Mexican policymaking from mid-1985 to mid-1986 was not so much due to the pressure exerted by the World Bank (and other international forces) as it was a meeting of the minds of the administration neoliberals with those from the outside who urged such policy shifts. In this meeting it was the Mexican government that shifted, not the World Bank. Consequently, the leverage exerted by external factors was exceedingly important during this crucial period. Nonetheless, internal policy changes arising from forces internal to the Mexican social formation—above all the rising weight of the neoliberal ideology that the industrial and financial groups championed— had set the stage for this threshold step.

The Export Promotion Program and the Import of Manufactures

Hector Hernández Cervantes, the neoliberal head of the Secretaría de Comercio y Fomento Industrial, had been the cabinet's outspoken advocate of Mexico's entry into GATT during the José López Portillo administration. It was through his secretariat that virtually all aspects of the export program were concentrated and/or coordinated. It is therefore very fundamental to note that in 1988 he defined structural change (such as privatization and destatization) *and* export promotion as constituting a *new growth model* (Hernández Cervantes, 1988b, 531). By defining structural change as being inextricably linked to export promotion—with these two policies constituting the fundamentals of a *new growth model*— Hernández Cervantes was officially articulating the most profound shift in economic policymaking that had occurred in fifty years.

There can be no quarrel with the long-advocated idea that Mexico's capacity as an exporter must be enhanced. Nevertheless, a critique of the export promotion program is warranted because this program is

Table 6.5: Mexico's Manufacturing Trade
($ U.S., billions)

Year	Exports	Imports	Balance
1981	$3.316	$20.218	$(-)16.902
1982	2.944	11.871	(-) 8.927
1983	5.452	6.617	(-) 1.165
1984	6.986	9.122	(-) 2.136
1985	6.432	11.297	(-) 4.865
1986	7.840	10.196	(-) 2.355
1987	10.587	10.771	(-) .182
1988	12.300	16.572	(-) 4.272

Sources: Hector Hernández Cervantes, *Aperatura Comercial y Modernización Industrial* (México: Fondo de Cultura, 1988), p. 113; Bancomext, "Sumario Estadístico," *Comercio Exterior* 33, no. 5 (May 1983), p. 200, and 39, no. 3 (March 1989), p. 265.

premised on the advocacy of export promotion as an integral part, perhaps the most important single part, of an emerging *new growth model*.

As can be seen in Table 6.5, the ratio of manufacturing exports to manufacturing imports rose from .17 in 1981 to nearly 1.00 in 1987. The Mexican government was not hesitant to trumpet this change as the most obvious sign of the success of the state's project to construct a new growth model. A second look at the data, and the underlying conditions that gave rise to the change in the manufacturing trade balance, reveals the essentially Pyrrhic nature of this victory.

Mexico's real gross domestic product increased very little between 1981 and 1988 (between 1982 and 1988 *total* growth was minus 0.5 percent, while expansion from 1981 to 1982 was 8.1 percent). In 1981 manufactured imports came to $20.2 billion—nearly twice the level of such imports in 1987. Most of the net improvement in the trade balance in manufactured products came not from the expansion of exports but rather *from the contraction of imports*. Imports fell for three reasons. First, after 1981, the excess capacity in industry cut the demand for intermediate goods and machinery. Second, although the de la Madrid Hurtado government touted its new commitment to *laissez-faire* from the outset, it continued to use a combination of import licenses and prohibitive tariffs to keep manufactured imports at levels substantially below those attained under López Portillo. This state of affairs did not change fundamentally until 1987, when a relatively thorough liberalization of the tariffs commenced. The result of this policy shift was to be seen in the 1988 import figures. The gains made between 1983 and 1987 now appeared to be lost.

Third, probably the most significant factor in altering the trade balance in manufacturing since 1982 was the near collapse in government investment. That is, public investment in infrastructure had fallen from 5.5 percent of GDP in 1982 to 2.0 percent in 1988 (Benitz and Cruz, 1988, 25). State infrastructure investments could be achieved only by importing heavy equipment and parts—a situation that caused the "improved" manufacturing trade balance to take on a new meaning. The infrastructure needed to support industry had been allowed to deteriorate. Short-term alignment in the balance of payments was momentarily achieved at the expense of a fundamental weakening in the industrial base (and therefore the underlying base for manufacturing exports) of the economy.

In 1988 the groups pattern of investment in plant and equipment was notable. Domestically produced capital goods expanded at an annual rate of 9 percent. Meanwhile, *imports* of such items soared—the rate of increase was 51 percent (Acosta, 1989, 26). This was an important indication of what a recovery might bring: imports of machinery and equipment would soar—as they did in 1988, only more so—thereby pushing the manufacturing trade balance into deep deficit.

In closing this discussion of the structural impediments to export promotion, as viewed from the perspective of Mexico's propensity to import manufactures, it is important to mention one remaining point. As long as Mexico remains wedded to the model of debt-led development, a very large surplus in merchandise trade will be necessary to compensate for debt servicing expenses. At this point in time, there is simply no indication whatsoever that such outflows can be covered to any significant degree by sufficiently expanding manufacturing exports.

The Recent Record on Manufacturing Trade: Exports

As can be seen from Table 6.5, there has been a rapid increase in Mexico's manufacturing trade exports. They have far outstripped all other indicators of macroeconomic growth. The data, however, warrant further interpretation. To many observers, the most important element in explaining the "export miracle" has been the collapse of the internal market. It is argued by Eduardo Gitli, and others, that the groups, the transnationals, and the parastate firms have long been in the habit of searching out export markets in order to maintain sales only when the internal market is weak (Gitli, 1987). These observers maintain that should there be a recovery in Mexico, the export miracle will collapse because the profit margin on domestic production is higher. Furthermore, it has often been pointed out that the increase in manufacturing employment in the export sector has been *slightly less than* the decrease in manufacturing employment for the internal market. Mexico in the 1980s experienced a slow process of deindustrialization.

A second point to consider is that the Mexican government has spent massive sums of money—unfortunately existing data are not sufficient to generate a reliable estimate of the total—in order to provide an environment conducive to the export of manufactures. What has been the cost/benefit ratio of the export promotion program? To compute it precisely would be a daunting enterprise fraught with methodological difficulties. In 1988 manufacturing exports were $9.42 billion greater than in 1981 (see Table 6.5). If one were to assume (not unreasonably) that one-half of the rise in manufacturing exports came from the switching of production from the internal to the external market due to the depression of the 1980s, only $4.7 billion of net new manufacturing production for export was realized in 1988 (over that attained in 1981). The likelihood that the accumulated value of the state's export promotion program at least equals that of the net new manufacturing export figure is disturbingly high.

Indeed, what would seem to be an unimpeachable source, the undersecretary of the Treasury, Francisco Suárez Davila, stated that overall financial support for the export promotion program—including programs to reduce the foreign indebtedness of corporations in the hope that they would then expand output—came to $2 billion in 1982 and $8 billion in 1988 (Ortiz Rivera, 1988b, 13). His figures apparently included state investments made to support the export promotion programs that were funded by the World Bank and credits extended from the U.S. Export-Import Bank. Suárez Davila's data were not presented with any precision. His figures may have included state outlays that could not be strictly tied to the export promotion program. Furthermore, some of the massive funding that has come from the World Bank may raise export capacity in *future* years. Nonetheless, it remains most unlikely that the cumulative net increase in manufacturing exports since 1981 will significantly exceed the value of the sum of funds that the state has allocated for export promotion in those years. One-half of the cumulative increase in manufacturing exports since 1981—*over and above* the baseline export level of $3 billion per year established in 1981—would amount to $37.7 billion. Straight-line projections from the $2 billion figure for 1982 to the $8 billion figure for 1988 would predict that $36.5 billion had been allocated to export promotion by the state. By this crude method the net *cumulative* benefit from the export promotion program would be a trivial $1.2 billion, or $171 million per year from 1982 through 1988.

Whatever the precise figure may be, it seems all but certain that it is a relatively small amount. Nevertheless, the export promotion program must be measured against the imports needed to sustain the program.

Not only has there been a continued need to import machinery, equipment, and advanced technology, but matters appear to have worsened regarding the propensity to import. The export boom has been concentrated in a very narrow range of products, with automobiles, motors, and parts accounting for 29 percent of total manufacturing exports—up from 13.6 percent in 1981 (Bancomext, 1983, 200; 1988, 548). The growth in auto-related exports accounted for 36 percent of the total growth of exports from 1981 to 1988. Yet even in this most successful area of production, auto-related imports *cancelled out 55 percent* of the value of exports (Bancomext, 1988, 548). Numbers such as these suggest that the estimated figure for the net benefits of the export program ($1.2 billion for the years 1982–1988) should be cut by more than one-half (due to imports needed to support manufacturing exports).

Placed in a proper dynamic context, however, it is likely that the tendency has been and will be to *reduce* whatever small net benefits may have been derived from the export promotion program. Careful students of Mexico's export industries have noted that those industries that have performed above the average of all export industries are relatively few. Two studies using different years (1980–1986) and (1983–1987) noted that export growth has been led by a handful of industries—six in one study, seven in the other (Gitli, 1987, 416–417; Unger and Saldana, 1988, 6). Kurt Unger found that all of these leading export industries were "internationalized"—their production relied upon productive "chains" that transcended the nation. They were not industries that derived primarily from a national comparative advantage. Rather, they were industries located in Mexico as part of an international productive process (Unger and Saldana, 1988). Thus, local content of parts and other inputs would tend to be low. In two export industries cited by Unger and Saldana, local content levels were 40 percent for film products and were below 6 percent for 62 percent of the output of the touted computer industry (Unger and Saldana, 1988, 22, 39). Transnational ownership or co-production arrangements in computers tend to be all but universal. (Mexican-owned firms, which may also be operating with co-production agreements, have only 6.6 percent of the computer export market.) The percentage of local content will vary from industry to industry and over time. This percentage may well be increased by subsequent Mexican legislation that impacts upon the export industries. Nonetheless, the high incidence of "internationalized" industries (which process products made in more than one nation) suggests that the export promotion program will be *structurally* impaired by the high import propensity of the industries that are leading the export boom.

A further structural impediment arises from this situation: Transnational corporations will in the longer term repatriate their earnings, thereby undercutting some of the gains made in merchandise trade through outflows in the capital account. Habituated as they have been to high profits, low outlays for technology, and captive markets, Mexican businessmen are unlikely candidates for the export promotion program. Most, by all accounts, suffer from the "reluctant exporter" syndrome and have little interest beyond "switching" existing plant, equipment, and products from the domestic to the international market during the current depression. It therefore seems unlikely that in the future the existing predominance of the transnationals in the most dynamic areas of the export sector will be displaced by the national groups.

Export Promotion Through the Prism of Theory

The speed and scope of the restructuring–export promotion program that the state has increasingly imposed on the economy have not allowed for much of a theoretical assessment. One such effort by Patricia Olave in late 1987 ambivalently asserted that given the obvious weaknesses of the program a number of "questions" remained (Olave, 1987). A broader attempt at assessment in early 1988 appeared as a special issue of the bi-monthly review *El Cotidiano* (El Cotidiano, 1988,). Thirteen economists analyzed the program of industrial reconversion without attempting to strike an overall balance regarding the macroeconomic effects of the new growth model. The emphasis was on description rather than analysis.

More interesting from a theoretical perspective has been the work of José Valenzuela and Arturo Huerta. Valenzuela, in the widely cited work *El Capitalismo Mexicano en Los Ochenta* (Mexican Capitalism in the 1980s), viewed the success of the restructuring–export promotion program as problematic. Mexico, it seems, may well become a nation with a new *patrón de acumulación*—a secondary exporter nation. But because the export promotion program is obviously antipopular, it may not work (Valenzuela, 1986). Valenzuela's ambivalence may have been justified, yet it does not help much in understanding the dynamics and direction of policy changes in Mexico.

More helpful was a short article by Valenzuela and Arturo Huerta. They argued that there were two possible paths to the secondary exporter model. One was a neoliberal model that emphasized transnationalization—this was the model of "savage restructuring" or "forced subordination." The other was a "nationalist-development model" that gave rise to a renewed form of state monopoly capitalism. In this model, state subsidies were directed toward the export sector, but such benefits were inordinately channeled toward *nationally owned* firms. The second model was "progressive" in that it would develop the forces of production in Mexico and expand and "deepen" the industrial base (Huerta and Valenzuela, 1985, 56–57).

These ruminations, while interesting and often insightful, unfortunately do not deal with the "demand side" of the Mexican economy. If the restructuring is to be either that of "forced subordination" to the needs and objectives of the transnational corporations in the first instance (and the groups in the second) or secondary exports based in the nationalist development model, *both* remain, as defined by Huerta and Valenzuela, *antipopular* projects. Can an antipopular growth model be sustained? It should be stressed that during Mexico's years of strong economic expansion, the distribution of income changed dramatically. Both those at the top and those at the bottom received relatively less, while a new middle class was created in the 1950–1980 period. In a relative sense more was shifted from the top toward the second, third, and fourth deciles than from the lowest 30 percent upward (see Chapter 3). As mentioned, from 1983 through 1987 a dramatic shift in income occurred: The top 10 percent had 33.5 percent of the income in 1983 and 36.6 percent in 1987. Meanwhile, in 1988 the bottom 80 percent received merely 46 percent of the total income. Can such results sustain a growth model? Certainly not in the Keynesian paradigm in which growth is (for the most part) determined by demand. In the Keynesian paradigm the fact that the massive redistribution of the 1980s has been accompanied by the worst depression of the twentieth century is not accidental. In this interpretation the secondary exporter model is not a *growth* model; rather, it is a recipe for the transnationalization and deeper disarticulation of the productive apparatus of the Mexican economy.

The Pacto de Solidaridad (PSE)

In November 1987 the trade unions appeared to be ready to oppose the previous five years of wage decompression. But a threatened general strike evaporated with the new policy of the *Pacto de Solidaridad* (the Solidarity Pact). With inflation standing at roughly 159 percent in 1987 (even higher than that achieved in the tumultuous days of 1982), the economic cabinet turned to a new plan. The *Pacto* was a tactical agreement among the economic elite, the state, and labor to (1) maintain prices on government-controlled products, (2) essentially allow the private sector to follow its conscience in price setting, and (3) limit wage increases to very small increments that would be periodically arranged. The *Pacto* was to be renewed through March 31, 1990.

The *Pacto* had three principle economic effects, and one important political impact. First, the rate of inflation certainly declined. The government claimed it had fallen to "only" 52 percent for 1988 (Acosta, 1989, 24). Second, wages rose only 23 percent in the course of the first year of the *Pacto*, meaning that real wages fell another 29 percent. Third, the exchange rate was essentially stabilized, which at least temporarily put an end to the cycle of massive devaluations which had rocked Mexico throughout the sexenio. The great economic failure, of course, was that the *Pacto* did nothing to revive economic growth. The country marked time. If anything, the *Pacto* seemed to exhibit a more organized and smoother way to redistribute income upwardly, but it achieved little else.

Fourth, the *Pacto* and the selection of President Salinas de Gortari signaled continuity in the state's program to dismantle the state. Most importantly, the *Pacto* showed that de la Madrid Hurtado and Salinas de Gortari were willing to put the entire corporatist apparatus of the state into play in order to ensure that profit margins could be restored by way of further cuts in the real wage. The *Pacto*, in essence, constituted a no-strike pledge by labor. All lingering doubts that the CCE and other key business associations had maintained regarding the administration were swept-away by the *Pacto* (Márquez, 1988, 16). The *Pacto* served to split the economic elite's support for the PAN. The radicals (reduced to a small band of ideological purists) were left to support the PAN. The bulk of the business elite (including most former radicals) regrouped around the PRI. Once the election had been held, the strong showing of the populist leader Cuauhtémoc Cárdenas tightened the bond between the economic and the political elite.

De la Madrid Hurtado prided himself on his consistency while trying to distance himself from the often erratic behavior of Presidents Echeverría and López Portillo. And consistency there was—consistent error of analysis and execution and underneath a consistent, even relentless, determination to redistribute income upwardly. Perhaps what was often regarded by observers as the administration's greatest strength—consistency—was in fact its most damning weakness.

Notes

1. There is some reason for caution regarding the reliability of official data sources. For example, the government reported the downturn in GDP in 1983 as -7.6 percent, -5.3 percent, and finally -4.2 percent in its final revision (Ros, 1987, 70; IDB, 1985, 306; Vidal, 1988, 40). While skeptical of the revision process and cognizant of the political motives that may well have guided it, there is no other recourse than the usage of such data.

2. See *Nexos*, July 1983, for the comments of twelve Mexican social scientists regarding the crisis of 1982–1983 (Nexos, 1983, 15–40).

3. The Banco de México placed the ultimate inflow arising from the renegotiation at $9.1 billion (Banco de México, 1988, 443).

4. The buildings and communications systems that mushroomed throughout Mexico to facilitate trading on the exchange can be viewed as "investment" stimulated by the stock market's growth.

5. This section draws on a disparate, heterodox body of ideas that can be termed the "overinvestment/underinvestment" model. Hopefully, this term is faithful to a line of analysis that the Left-Keynesians and neo-Marxists of the Monthly Review School have attempted to demonstrate in the past forty years. Regarding this body of thought, see John Bellamy Foster's "Accumulation and Crisis" and "The Issue of Excess Capacity" (Foster, 1986, 74–127).

6. The table is not precisely equivalent to a relative share distribution of national income because it includes foreign borrowing as public sector income *and* the payment of interest on the international debt plus the remittances of income to foreign investors (thus the interest is counted twice). Also included is wage labor income from Mexican nationals working abroad. Excluded (properly), but of interest in computing the income shares of Mexican nationals, is income received on assets held abroad (such as income from capital flight), which would buoy the data in column 9 by as much as 2 percent (of *total* income) from 1980 onward.

7. In Mexico, the rate of exploitation (or rate of surplus value) is defined as GDP minus wages divided by wages. In computing the rate of profit in industry, one would normally deduct interest payments made by the firm because they would be a cost of doing business. What, however, of the massive interlocked groups in Mexico? Deducting the interest payment of an industrial firm that "borrows" from a banking entity within the "group" obviously creates some methodological problems. Until such time as the theoretical literature on the question of the measurement of the (Marxian) rate of profit clarifies such fundamental issues as these, works centering on the profit rate can only be considered as indicative.

8. Methodologists will undoubtedly recoil from the preceding attempt to intermingle elements of the Keynesian and classical Marxist paradigms. Yet until crisis theory develops further—particularly in its analysis of disarticulated peripheral-capitalist social formations such as Mexico's—those who seek to employ the fundamental insights of macroeconomic theory regarding ruptures in the accumulation process will be left with the inelegant task of combining disparate paradigms in order to present a more composite synopsis of such ruptures.

References

Acosta, Carlos (1989). "Logros Económicos." *Proceso*, no. 652 (May 5), pp. 24–26.

Aguilar, Alonso (1975). "La Fase Actual del Capitalismo Mexicano." *Estrategia* 1, no. 2, pp. 2–23.

——— (1983). *Estado, Capitalismo y Clase en el Poder en México*. México: Editorial Nuestro Tiempo.

——— (1988). "La Venta de Empresas Paraestatales en México," *Estrategia*, no. 82 (July-August), pp. 7–30.

Aguilar, Martha (1988). "Cuenca del Pacífico." *El Financiero*, October 3, p. 83.

Alcocer, Jorge, and Isidoro Cisneros (1985). "Los Empresarios, Entre los Negoicios y la Política." In Jorge Alcocer (compilador). *México: Presente y Futuro*. México: Ediciones de Cultura Popular. pp. 195–222.

Alvarez, Alejandro (1987). *La Crisis Global del Capitalismo en México*. México: Ediciones Era.

Ayala, José (1979). "La Empresa Pública y Su Incidencia en la Acumulación de Capital en México." *Investigación Económica* 150 (October-December), pp. 401–430.

Ayala, José, and José Blanco (1981). "El Nuevo Estado y la Expansión de las Manufacturas." In Rolando Cordera (compilador). *Desarrollo y Crisis de la Económia Mexicana*. México: Fondo de Cultura, pp. 13–44.

Ayala, José, José Blanco, Rolando Cordera, Guillermo Knockenhauer, and Armanda Labra (1979). "La Crisis Económica: Evolución y Perspectiva." In Pablo González Casanova and Enrique Florescano (coordinadores). *México Hoy*. México: Siglo Veintiuno Editores, pp. 19–96.

Baez Rodríguez, Francisco (1985). "La Crisis y la Política." In Pablo González Casanova and Héctor Aguilar Camín (coordinadores). *México ante la Crisis*. México: Siglo Veintiuno Editores, pp. 337–348.

Banamex (n.d.). *Mexico Statistical Data: 1970–1980* . Mexico: Offset Setenta S.A.

Banco de México (1980). *Inforamción Económica, Producto Interno Bruto, Cuaderno 1970–1979*. México: Banco de México.

——— (1988). *The Mexican Economy, 1988*. Mexico: Banco de México.

Bancomext (1983). "Sumario Estadístico." *Comerico Exterior* 33, no. 5, pp. 199–208.

——— (1988). "Sumario Estadístico." *Comerico Exterior* 38, no. 6, pp. 547–556.

Barenstein, Jorge (1982). *La Gestión de Empresas Públicas en México*. México: CIDE.

Barker, Terry, and Vladimir Brailovsky (1983). "La Política Económica Entre 1976 y 1982." *Investigación Económica* 166 (October-December), pp. 273–317.

Basave, Jorge, Julio Mogel, Miguel A. Rivera Rios, and Alejandro Toledo (1982). "La Nacionalización de la Banca." *Teoría y Política*, nos. 7–8 (December), pp. 47–63.

Benitez, Rodolfo, and Noe Cruz (1988). "La Inversión Pública y Privada Esta en su Nivel Más Bajo." *El Financiero*, December 5, p. 25.

Bennett, Douglas, and Kenneth Sharpe (1982). "The State as Banker and Entrepreneur." In Sylvia Ann Hewlett and Richard Weinert (eds.). *Brazil and Mexico: Patterns of Late Development*. Philadelphia: Institute for the Study of Human Issues, pp. 169–211.

——— (1985). *International Corporations Versus the State*. Princeton, N.J.: Princeton University Press.

Bernal Sahagún, Víctor (1980). *Pensamiento Latinoamericano: CEPAL, R. Prebisch y A. Pinto*. México: Instituto de Investigaciónes Económicas, UNAM.

Blair, Calvin (1964). "Nacional Financiera." In Raymond Vernon (ed.). *Public Policy and Private Enterprise in Mexico*. Cambridge, Mass.: Harvard University Press, pp. 194–238.

Blanco, José (1985). "Política Económica y Lucha Política ante la Crisis." In Pablo González Casanova and Héctor Aguilar Camín (coordinadores). *México ante la Crisis*, vol. 1. México: Siglo Veintiuno Editores, pp. 399–435.

Boltvinik, Julio, and Enrique Hernández Laos (1981). "Origen de la Crisis Industrial." In Rolando Cordera (compilador). *Desarrollo y Crisis de la Economía Mexicana*. México: Fondo de Cultura, pp. 456–534.

Boltvinik, Julio, and Fernando Torres (1986). "Concentración del Ingreso y Satisfacción de Necessidades en la Crisis Actual." *El Economista Mexicano* 19, no. 2, pp. 15–45.

Bonilla, Arturo (1984). "La Política Económica Actual." In Arturo Bonilla (compilador). *La Política del Estado Mexicano*. México: Instituto de Investigaciónes Económicas, UNAM, pp. 1–31.

Bortz, Jeffrey (1985). "Salarios y Ciclos Largos en la Economía Mexicana." *Coyoacan*, nos. 17-18, pp. 87–100.

——— (1987). "El Ciclo del Salario en México." In Jesús Lechuga (compilador). *El Dilema de la Economía Mexicana*. México: Ediciones de Cultura Popular, pp. 141–156.

Bravo, Luis (1987). "Comparmex and Mexican Politics." In Silvia Maxfield and Ricardo Anzaldúa (eds.). *Government and Private Sector in Mexico*. San Diego: Center for U.S.-Mexico Studies, pp. 89–103.

Bravo, Víctor (1979). "Determinantes Externos del Cambio Organizacional en las Empresas Estatales y Privadas." In Viviane de Márquez (compiladora). *Dinámica de la Empresa Mexicana*. México: El Colegio de México, pp. 293–320.

——— (1982). *La Empresa Pública Industrial en México*. México: Instituto Nacional de Administración Pública.

Brett, A. E. (1983). *International Money and Capitalist Crisis*. Boulder, Colo.: Westview.

Brothers, Dwight (1973). "El Financiamiento de la Formación de Capital en México." In Leopoldo Solís (compilador). *La Economía Mexicana*, vol. 2. México: Fondo de Cultura, pp. 189–218.

Brothers, Dwight, and Leopold Solís (1966). *Mexican Financial Development*. Austin: University of Texas Press.

Business Week (1979). "Mexico's Reluctant Oil Boom." *Business Week*, January 15, pp. 64–74.

Cabral, Roberto (1981). "Industrialización y Política Económica." In Rolando Cordera (compilador). *Desarrollo y Crisis de la Economía Mexicana*. México: Fondo de Cultura, pp. 67–100.

Camarena, Margarita (1981). *La Industria Automotriz en México*. México: Universidad Nacional Autónoma de México, IIs.

Carmona, Fernando (1973). "La Situación Económica." In Fernando Carmona and Alonso Aguilar (compiladores). *El Milagro Mexicano*. México: Editorial Nuestro Tiempo, pp. 13–102.

———— (1978). "La Política Económica." In Alonso Aguilar and Fernando Carmona. *México: Riqueza y Miseria*. México: Editorial Nuestro Tiempo, pp. 175–242.

———— (1980). "Comentarios." In Alonso Aguilar (compilador). *Capitalismo Atrasado y Dependencia en America Latina*. México: Universidad Nacional Autónoma de México, pp. 186–202.

Carrillo Castro, Alejandro, and Sergio García Ramírez (1983). *Las Empresas Públicas en México*. México: Miguel Angel Porrua.

Casar, José L., and Jaime Ros (1984). "Comercio Exterior y la Acumulación de Capital." *Investigación Económica* 167 (January-March), pp. 75–91.

Casar, María Amparo, Gabriel Gaspar, and Edmundo Jacobo (1988). "Los Empresarios y el Estado." In Celso Garrido (coordinador). *Empresarios y Estado en America Latina*. México: CIDE, pp. 207–230.

Casar, María Amparo, and Wilson Peres (1988). *El Estado Empresario en México: Agotamiento o Renovación?*. México: Siglo Veintiuno Editores.

Ceceña Cervantes, José (1982). *La Planificación Económica Nacional en los Países Atrasados*. México: Universidad Nacional Autónoma de México.

Centro de Estudios Contables (1973). "Es Justo Nuestro Sistema de Impuestos?" In Leopoldo Solís (compilador). *La Economía Mexicana*. México: Fondo de Cultura, pp. 56–62.

CEPAL (Comisión Económica para America Latina) (1979). *Principales Rasgos del Proceso de Industrialización y de Política Industrial de México en la Decada de los Setenta*. México: Naciónes Unidas, Consejo Economico y Social, 79-6-293-60.

———— (1981) *Notas Para el Estudio Económico de America Latina, 1980*. México: Naciónes Unidas, Consejo Económico y Social.

Chávez, Elias (1986). "El Director del IEPES Exalta el Dominio Privado." *Proceso*, no. 492 (April 7), pp. 22-24.

CIEN (Centro de Estudios Nacionales) (1988a). "Las Finanzas Públicas: 1982–1988." *CIEN 100* 9, no. 2, (September), Entrega 218.

———— (1988b). *La Economía Mexicana 1988, Analisis Añual*. México: CIEN.

Cline, Howard F. (1963). *Mexico, Revolution to Evolution, 1940–1960*. New York: Oxford University Press.

Conchiero, Elvira Antonio Gutiérrez, and Juan Manuel Fragosa (1979). *El Poder de la Gran Burguesia*. México: Ediciones de Cultura Popular.

Cordera, Rolando (1979). "Estado y Economía en México." *Economía de America Latina*, Semestre no. 3, pp. 101–125.

———— (1980). "Estado y Ecomonía: Aputes para un Marco de Referencia." In Nora Luistig (ed.). *Panorama y Perspectivas de la Economía Mexicana*. México: El Colegio de México, pp. 429–478.

Cordera, Rolando, and Carlos Tello (1981). *México: La Disputa por la Nación*. México: Siglo Veintiuno Editores.

Cordero H., Salvador, Santín, Rafael, and Ricardo Tirado (1983). *El Poder Empresarial en México*. México: Terra Nova.

Córdova, Arnaldo (1974). *La Política de Masas del Cárdenismo*. México: Ediciones Era.

———— (1977). *La Formación del Poder Político en México*. México: Ediciones Era.

Cruz Serrano, Noe (1988). "Se la Desprendido el Estado de 55 Empresas." *El Financiero*, August 25, p. 49.

Cypher, James (1979). "The Internationalization of Capital and the Transformation of Social Formations." *Review of Radical Political Economics* 11, no. 4, pp. 33–49.

———— (1980). "Relative State Autonomy and National Economic Planning." *Journal of Economic Issues* 14, no. 2, pp. 327–349.

———— (1988a) "The Political Economy of Mexico's Restructuring." Paper presented at Western Social Science Association Conference, Denver, Colo., April.

———— (1988b). "Debt, Economic Crisis Undermines Mexico's PRI." *Dollars and Sense*, no. 142 (December), pp. 8–11, 21.

———— (1988c). "The Crisis and Restructuring of Capitalism in the Periphery." In Paul Zarembka (ed.). *Research in Political Economy*. vol. 11. Greenwich, Conn.: JAI Press, pp. 45–82.

———— (1989). "The Debt Crisis as 'Opportunity.'" *Latin American Perspectives* 16, no. 1, pp. 52–78.

Davila Jimenez, Gerardo (1982). "La Política de Precios y Subsidios" In Héctor González M. (compilador). *El Sistema Económica Mexicano*. México: La Red Jonas, pp. 228–249.

De la Garza, Enrique (1988). "Desindustrialización y Reconversión en México." *El Cotidiano*, no. 21 (January-February), pp. 2–8.

De la Madrid, Miguel (1987). *Cambio Estructural en México y en el Mundo*. México: Fondo de Cultura.

Dietz, James (1988). "Technological Autonomy, Technological Culture and Linkages: A Strategy of Development." Paper presented at Western Social Science Association Conference, Denver, Colo., April.

Dietz, James, and James Street (1987). *Latin America's Economic Development*. Boulder, Colo.: Lynne Rienner.

Eatwell, John, and Agit Singh (1981). "Se Encuentra 'Sobre Calentada' la Economía Mexicana?" *Economía Mexicana*, no. 3, pp. 253–278.

El Cotidiano (1988). "Pacto y Reconversión." *El Cotidiano*, no. 21 (January-February), pp. 1–97.

El Financiero (1988). "El Ingreso Real de los Mexicanos se Redujo." *El Financiero*, November 23, p. 19.

Estrategia (1982). "La Crisis y la Nacionalización de la Banca." *Estrategia*, no. 48, pp. 1–30.

Evans, Peter (1979). *Dependent Development*. Princeton, N.J.: Princeton University Press.

Fitzgerald, E.V.K. (1985). "The Financial Constraint on Relative Autonomy: The State and Capital Accumulation in Mexico, 1940-1982." In Christian Anglade and Carlos Fortin (eds.). *The State and Capital Accumulation in Latin America*. Pittsburgh: University of Pittsburgh, pp. 210–240.

Foster, John Bellamy (1986). *The Theory of Monopoly Capitalism*. New York: Monthly Review Press.

García, Theres, and Noe Cruz (1988). "El Estado Optar Solo por Regular la Economía: SEMIP." *El Financiero*, December 1, p. 33.

Garrido, Celso, Edmundo Jacobo, and Enrique Quintana (1987). "Crisis y Poder en México." *Estudios Sociológicos* 15 (September-December), pp. 528–539.

Garrido, Celso, and Enrique Quintana (1988). "Crisis del Patrón de Acumulación y Modernización Conservadora." In Celso Garrido (coordinador). *Empresarios y Estado en America Latina*. México: CIDE, pp. 39–60.

Gitli, Eduardo (1987). "Exportaciónes Manufactureras, Fuga Hacia Adelante." *El Cotidiano*, no. 20 (November-December), pp. 414–420.

Gollás, Manuel (1979). "Estructura y Causas de la Concentración Industrial en México." In Viviane B. de Márquez (compiladora). *Dinámica de la Empresa Mexicana*. México: El Colegio de México, pp. 265–292.

Gómez Chiñas, Carlos (1987). "La Política Comerical de México." In Jesús Lechuga (compilador). *El Dilema de la Economía Mexicana*. México: Ediciones de Cultura Popular, pp. 109–140.

González, Eduardo (1981). "Empresarios y Obreros: Dos Grupos de Poder." In Rolando Cordera (compilador). *Desarrollo y Crisis de la Economía Mexicana*. México: Fondo de Cultura, pp. 638–665.

González Gary, Oscar (1985). "Poder y Presiónes de la Iglesia." In Pablo González Casanova and Héctor Aguilar Camín (coordinadores). *México ante la Crisis*, vol. 2. México: Siglo Veintiuno Editores, pp. 238–294.

Goodman, Mike, and George Reasons (1979). "Oil—The Rush to Development." *Mexico: Crisis of Poverty, Crisis of Wealth*, special supplement, *Los Angeles Times*, July 15, pp. 15–16.

Guadarrama, José (1988). "Preven Grave Rezago Industrial si Persiste el Estancamiento en el Desarrollo Tecnológico." *El Financiero*, November 25, p. 70.

Guadarrama, José de J., and Noe Cruz (1988). "Estudia el Gobierno Ceder Rubros Estratégicos a la Iniciativa Privada." *El Financiero*, October 3, p. 24.

Guillén, Arturo (1986). *Problemas de la Economía Mexicana*. México: Editorial Nuestro Tiempo.

Guillén, Héctor (1984). *Origenes de la Crisis en México*. México: Ediciones Era.

———— (1988). "De la Crisis Financiera a la Austeridad Hayekiana en México." Universidad Nacional Autónoma de México, IIEc, Mimeo, pp. 1–47.

Hamilton, Nora (1982). *The Limits of State Autonomy*. Princeton, N. J.: Princeton University Press.

Hansen, Roger (1971). *La Política del Desarrollo Mexicano.* México: Siglo Veintiuno Editores.

Hernández Cervantes, Héctor (1988a). *Aperatura Comercial y Modernización Industrial.* México: Fondo de Cultura.

———— (1988b). "Lineamientos de la Política Comercial Actual." *Comercio Exterior* 38, no. 6, (June), pp. 528–531.

Hernández Laos, Enrique (1985). *La Productividad y el Desarrollo Industrial en México.* México: Fondo de Cultura.

Hernández Rodríquez, Rogelio (1984). "Antonio Ruiz Galindo: Una Expresión del Pensamento Empresarial Mexicano." *Estudios Políticos* 3, no. 1 (January-March), pp. 35–46.

———— (1988). *Empresarios, Banca y Estado.* México: FLACSO.

Hinojosa, Oscar (1983). "El Plano Satisfizo a Todos." *Proceso,* no. 344 (June 6), pp. 10–11.

Huerta, Arturo (1985) "Economía Política de la Transición Capitalista." In Jorge Alcocer (compilador). *México: Presente y Futuro.* México: Ediciones de Cultura Popular, pp. 37–62.

———— (1986). *Economía Mexicana: Más allá del Milagro.* México: Ediciones de Cultura Popular.

———— (1987). "El Estancamiento del Sector Industrial." *El Cotidiano,* no. 19 (September-October), pp. 290–301.

Huerta, Arturo, and José Valenzuela (1985). "Economía Política de la Transición Capitalista." In Jorge Alcocer (compilador). *México: Presente y Futuro.* México: Ediciones de Cultura Popular, pp. 37–62.

Huss, Torben (1987). "Proyectos Empresariales y Reestructuración del Capitalismo Mexicano." *Economía Informa* 159, pp. 11–30.

IDB (Inter-American Development Bank) (various years). *Economic and Social Progress Report.* Washington, D.C.: IDB.

INEGI (Instituto Nacional de Estadística Geografía e Informática) (1985). *Estadísticas Historicas de México,* vols. 1 and 2. México: SPP.

———— (1986). *Encuesta Nacional de Ingreso-Gasto de los Hogares.* México: SPP.

Jacobs, Eduardo (1981). "La Evolución Reciente de los Grupos de Capital Privado Nacional." *Economía Mexicana:,* no. 3, pp. 23–44.

Jacobs, Eduardo, and Wilson Peres (1983). "Tamaño de Planta y Financiamiento." *Economía Mexicana,* no. 5, pp. 79–110.

Kalecki, Michael (1969). *Theory of Economic Dynamics.* New York: Augustus M. Kelly.

King, Timothy (1970). *Mexico: Industrialization and Trade Policies Since 1940.* Oxford: Oxford University Press.

Labastida, Julio (1972). "Los Grupos Dominantes Frente a las Alternativas de Cambio." In Jorge Martínez Ros and nineteen others. *El Perfil de México en 1980,* vol. 3. México: Siglo Veintiuno Editores, pp. 101–164.

Loaeza, Soledad (1985). "Las Clases Medias Mexicanas." In Pablo González Casanova and Héctor Aguilar Camín (coordinadores). *México ante la Crisis,* vol. 2. México: Siglo Veintiuno Editores, pp. 221–237.

Lomas, Emilio, and Ruben Alvarez (1988). "En Unos Meses Más se Duplicará la Produción de Petroliferos." *La Jornada,* November 3, p. 26.

Looney, Robert (1985). *Economic Policymaking in Mexico*. Durham, N.C.: Duke University Press.

Luna, Matilda (1988). "La Derecha Empresarial." *El Cotidiano*, no. 24 (July-August), pp. 72–77.

Luna, Matilda, Ricardo Tirada, and Francisco Valdés (1987). "Businessmen and Politics in Mexico." In Silvia Maxfield and Ricardo Anzaldúa, (eds.). *Government and Private Sector in Contemporary Mexico*. San Diego: Center for U.S.-Mexico Studies, pp. 13–44.

Lustig, Nora (1988). "La Desigualidad Económica." *Nexos* 11, no. 128 (August), pp. 8–11.

Machado, Jorge, Wilson Peres, and Orlando Delgado (1985). "La Estructura de la Industria Estatal." *Economía Mexicana*, no. 7, pp. 123–135.

Manzo, José Luis (1988). "Patrón de Acumulación y Excedente Petrolero." In Celso Garrido (coordinador). *Empresarios y Estado en America Latina*. México: CIDE, pp. 61–70.

Márquez, Alfredo (1988). "Conflictos y Acercamientos en la Relación Estado-Empresarios." *El Financiero*, November 8, p. 16.

Martínez del Campo, Manuel (1985). *Industrialización en México*. México: El Colegio de México.

Martínez Nava, Juan (1982). *Conflicto Estado Empresarios*. México: Editores Nueva Imagen.

Morera, Carlos, and Jorge Basave (1981). "La Crisis y el Capital Financiero en México." *Teoría y Política*, no. 4, (April-June), pp. 75–124.

Mosk, Sanford (1950). *Industrial Revolution in Mexico*. Berkeley: University of California Press.

Nacional Financiera (1978). *La Economía Mexicana en Cifras*. México: Nafinsa.

Nafinsa-CEPAL (1971). *La Política Industrial en el Desarrollo de México*. México: Nafinsa.

Navarrete, Ifigenia (1967). *Los Incentivos Fiscales y el Desarrollo Económico de México*. México: Universidad Nacional Autónoma de México.

Nexos (1983). "La Crisis de México." *Nexos* 6, no. 6 (July) pp. 15–40.

Niblo, Stephen (1988). *The Impact of War: Mexico and World War II*, Occasional Paper no. 10. Melbourne, Australia: La Trobe Univesity, Institute of Latin American Studies, pp. 1–39.

O'Connor, James (1973). *The Fiscal Crisis of the State*. New York: St. Martin's.

Olave, Patricia (1987). "Apertura Exterior: Un Proyecto Viable?" *Momento Económico*, no. 31 (November) pp. 7–9.

Ortega Pizarro, Fernando (1983). "Un Pobre Manejo Administantivo Causa de la Vulnerabilidad de Pemex." *Proceso*, no. 346 (June 20), pp. 6–11.

―――― (1988b). "El Auge de las Exportaciónes se ha Dado en un Contexto de Baja Inversión Privada." *Uno Más Uno*, September 30, p. 13.

Ortiz Mena, Antonio (n.d.). *Desarrollo Estabilizador: Una Decada de Estrategia Económica*.

Ortiz Rivera, Alicia (1983). "El Gobierno Reprivatiza y Reagrupa Sus Empresas." *Proceso*, no. 340 (May 9), pp. 9–12.

―――― (1988). "Un Grupo Muy Comodo Negocio el Pacto." *Uno Más Uno*, May 19, pp. 1 and 14.

Ortiz Wadgymar, Arturo (1987). "La Política de Comercio Exterior." Seminario Sobre la Economía Mexicana, IIEc. Mimeo. pp. 1–16.

Pellicer de Brody, Olga (1978). *Historia de la Revolución Mexicana: 1952–1960,* vol. 23. México: El Colegio de México.

Pereyra, Carlos (1979). "Estado y Sociedad." In Pablo González Casanova and Enrique Florescano (compiladores). *México, Hoy.* México: Siglo Veintiuno Editores, pp. 289–305.

Perzabal, Carlos (1979). *Acumulación Capitalista Dependiente y Subordinada: El Caso de México (1940–1978).* México: Siglo Veintiuno Editores.

Poder Ejecutivo, Federal (1980). *Plan Global de Desarrollo, 1980–1982.* México: SPP.

_____ (1983). *Plan Nacional de Desarrollo, 1983–1988.* México: SPP.

_____ (1984). *Programa Nacional de Fomento Industrial y Comercio Exterior, 1984–1988.* México: SPP.

Polanyi, Karl (1944). *The Great Transformation.* Boston: Beacon.

Poulantzas, Nicos (1978). *Classes in Contemporary Society.* London: Verso.

Prebisch, Raúl (1950). *The Economic Development of Latin America and Its Principal Problems.* New York: United Nations.

_____ (1981). *Capitalismo Periferico, Crisis y Transformación.* México: Fondo de Cultura.

Puga, Cristina (1984a). "Los Empresarios Mexicanos ante la Catástrofe." *Estudios Políticos* 3, no. 1 (January-March), pp. 47–57.

_____ (1984b). "Empresarios y Política en México." In Salvador Cordero H., and Ricardo Tirado (coordinadores). *Clases Dominantes y Estado en México,* México: Uiversidad Autónoma de México, IIs, pp. 185–203.

Ramírez, Carlos (1988). "1983–1988: Informe de la Crisis." *El Financiero,* November 25, pp. 54–56.

Ramírez, Gilberto, and Emilio Salim C. (1987). *La Clase Política Mexicana.* México: EDAMEX.

Ramírez Brun, Ricardo (1983). *Estado y Acumulación de Capital en México,* 2nd ed. México: Universidad Nacional Autónoma de México.

Rangel, José (1988). "La Inflación como Recuperación de la Ganancia." *El Cotidiano,* no. 23 (May-June), pp. 3–9.

Razónes (1982). "Que Pasa en Estes Seis Años?" *Razónes,* no. 69, (August 23-September 5), pp. 14–17.

Reding, Andrew (1988). "Mexico at the Crossroads." *World Policy Journal* 5, no. 4 (Fall), pp. 615–650.

Revista Expansión (various years). "Las 500 Empresas Más Grandes de México." *Revista Expansión,* (August).

Rey Romay, Benito (1984). *La Ofensiva Empresarial Contra la Intervención del Estado.* México: Siglo Veintiuno Editores.

_____ (1987). *México 1987, el País que Perdimos.* México: Siglo Veintiuno Editores.

Rivera Rios, Miguel Ángel (1986). *Crisis y Reorganización del Capitalismo Mexicano.* México: Ediciones Era.

Robinson, Joan (1956). *The Accumulation of Capital.* London: Macmillan.

Rodríquez, Jesús, and Alfonso Moro (1987). "México: Situación Económica en 1986–1987." *La Batalla* no. 19 (November-December), pp. 5–12.

Rodríguez Garza, Francisco (1983). "Reflexiónes en Torno al Pensamiento Económico Latinoamericano." *Teoría y Política*, no. 9 (January-March), pp. 35–68.

Ros, Jaime (1987). "Mexico from the Oil Boom to the Debt Crisis." In Rosemary Thorp and Laurence Whitehead (eds.). *Latin American Debt and the Adjustment Crisis*. Pittsburgh: University of Pittsburgh Press, pp. 68–115.

Ruiz Dueñas, Jorge (1982). *Sistema Económico, Planificación y Empresa Pública en México*. México: UNAM-Azcapotzalco.

Ruiz Durán, Clemente (1985). "El Perfil de la Crisis Financiera." In Pablo González Casanova and Héctor Aguilar Camín (coordinadores). *México ante la Crisis*, vol. 1. México: Siglo Veintiuno Editores, pp. 183–206.

Saxe-Fernández, John (1988a). "Festin Desnaciónalizador." *Excélsior*, March 22, pp. 7, and 11.

————— (1988b). "Exorcismos Políticos." *Excélsior*, June 14, pp. 7–8.

————— (1988c). "Batalla por la Nación," *Excélsior*, August 16, pp. 7–8.

Secretaría de Gobernación (1988). *Reestructuración del Sector Paraestatal*. México: Fondo de Cultura.

SEPAFIN (Secretaría de Patramonía y Fomento Industrial) (1979). *Plan Nacional de Desarrollo Industrial, 1979–1982*. México: SEPAFIN.

Shafer, Robert (1973). *Mexican Business Organizations*. Syracuse, N.Y.: Syracuse University Press.

SHCP (Secretaría de Hacienda y Credito Público) (1979). *Un Nuevo Valor a los Estimulos Fiscales*. México: SHCP.

Solís, Leopoldo (1986). *La Realidad Económica Mexicana*, 15th ed. México: Siglo Veintiuno Editores.

SPP (Secretaría de Programación y Presupuesto) (1978) *Información Económica y Social Basica* 1, no. 4 (March), pp. 114–117.

————— (1984). *Cuentas de Producción del Sector Público, 1975–1983*. México: INEGI.

Stockton, William (1986). "Mexico Tries an Open-Door Policy." *New York Times*. February 16, p. 4F.

Tamayo, Jorge (1987). "Las Entidades Paraestatales en México." *Investigación Económica* 182 (October-December), pp. 255–283.

Tello, Carlos (1976). *La Política Económica en México*. México: Siglo Veintiuno Editores.

————— (1984). *La Nacionalización de la Banca en México*. México: Siglo Veintiuno Editores.

Tokman, Víctor (1984). "Global Monetarism and Destruction of Industry." *CEPAL Review*, no. 23 (August) pp. 107–121.

Torres R., Blanca (1979). *Historia de la Revolución Mexicana: 1948–1952*, vol. 19. México: El Colegio de México.

————— (1984). *Hacia la Utopia Industrial*. México: El Colegio de México.

Toye, John (1987). *Dilemmas of Development*. Oxford: Basil Blackwell.

Trejo Reyes, Saul (1987). *El Futuro de la Política Industrial en México*. México: El Colegio de México.

Unger, Kurt, and Consuelo Saldana (1988) "Las Economías de Escala y de Alcance en las Exportaciónes Mexicanas Mas Dinámicas." San Diego: Center for U.S.-Mexico Studies, Mimeo, pp. 1–43.

Valenzuela, José Feijoo (1986). *El Capitalismo Mexicano en los Ochenta.* México: Ediciones ERA.

Vargas, Hugo (1985). "Las Alternativas de la Derecha," In Pablo González Casanova and Héctor Aguilar Camín (coordinadores). *México ante la Crisis,* vol. 2. México: Siglo Veintiuno Editores, pp. 342–354.

Vela González, Joaquin (1983). "Estudio Historico Sobre la Crisis en México: 1954–1983." *Teoría y Política,* no. 11 (July-December), pp. 69–98.

Vernon, Raymond (1973). "El Dilema de México." In Leopoldo Solís (compilador). *La Economía Mexicana,* vol. 2. México: Fondo de Cultura, pp. 574–589.

Vidal Bonafiz, Francisco (1985). *Las Empresas Estatales en el Desarrollo del Capitalismo Mexicano.* México: Universidad Nacional Autónoma de México, Area Posgrado de Economía.

———— (1988). "Durante Este Sexenio la Economía Permanecio Estancada." *El Financiero,* August 30, 1988, p. 40.

Villarreal, René (1976). *El Desequilibrio Externo en la Industrialización de México.* México: Fondo de Cultura.

———— (1982). "De la Industrialización Sustitutiva a la Petrodependencia Externa." In Héctor González M. (compilador). *El Sistema Económica Mexicano.* México: La Red Jonas, pp. 28–56.

———— (1988). *Mitos y Realidades de la Empresa Pública: Racionalización o Privativación?.* México: Diana.

Villarreal, René, and Norma Rocio R. Villarreal (1977). "Las Empresas Públicas." In Gerado M. Bueno (ed.). *Opciónes de Política Económica en México.* México: Editorial Tecnos, pp. 81–112.

Whitehead, Laurence (1981). "De la Bancarrota a la Prosperidad: Una Evaluación Política del Programa Mexicano de Estabilización 1976–1979." *Comercio Exterior* 31, no. 8 (August), pp. 908–916.

World Bank (1989). *Report on Proposed Industrial Sector Policy Loan.* Washington, D.C.: World Bank, Report no. P-4950-ME.

Zabludovsky, Gina (1980). *México: Estado y Empresarios.* México: Universidad Nacional Autónoma de Méxcio, ENEP-Acatlan.

———— (1984). "Proposiciónes para el Estudio de las Relaciónes Entre el Estado y Empresarios Durante el Periodo de Miguel Alemán." *Estudios Políticos* 3, no. 1 (January-March), pp. 22–27.

Zepeda, Mario J. (1988). "México 1987: El Año de la Economía Desigual." *Momento Económico,* no. 36 (May), pp. 3–5.

Zuñiga, José Antonio (1983). "La Rectoria del Fondo Monetario." *Proceso,* no. 344 (June 6), pp. 8–9.

———— (1984). "Finacril, Planta de Somex," *Proceso,* no. 399 (June 25), pp. 22–24.

———— (1988a). "Concluirá la Desincorporación de 702 Paraestatales este Sexenio Dice la SHCP." *Uno Más Uno,* June 13, p. 13.

———— (1988b). "El Sector Paraestatal Quedará Integrado por Solo 448 Empresas y Organismos al Terminar Este Sexenio," *Uno Más Uno,* July 15, p. 14.

———— (1988c). "Más de 395 Mil Trabajadores de la Industria Manufacturera Quedaron Cesantes Este Sexenio," *Uno M:aaas Uno,* November 4, p. 14.

Series in Political Economy
and Economic Development in Latin America

Series Editor
Andrew Zimbalist
Smith College

Through country case studies and regional analyses this series will contribute to a deeper understanding of development issues in Latin America. Shifting political environments, increasing economic interdependence, and the difficulties with regard to debt, foreign investment, and trade policy demand novel conceptualizations of development strategies and potentials for the region. Individual volumes in this series will explore the deficiencies in conventional formulations of the Latin American development experience by examining new evidence and material. Topics will include, among others, women and development in Latin America; the impact of IMF interventions; the effects of redemocratization on development; Cubanology and Cuban political economy; Nicaraguan political economy; and individual case studies on development and debt policy in various countries in the region.

Index

ABM. *See* Asociación de Banqueros Mexicanos
Accumulation process, 27, 63, 71–72
    and balance of payments, 78
    and capitalist-rentier state, 67
    and debt drain, 159
    and falling profit rate, 82, 83, 84, 166–167
    monetarist theory regarding, 171–172
    and nationalist-populist state, 11
    and privatization of parastate sector, 148, 149
    and sectoral imbalances, 81
Acerves Saucedo, Ángel, 150–151
Acumulación Capitalista Dependiente y Subordinada (Perzabal), 38(n2)
Aeroméxico, 150, 152
Agriculture, 6–7, 12, 23–24, 130, 188
    during Alemán administration, 54–57, 85(n2)
    during Ávila Camacho administration, 48, 53
    during Echeverría administration, 90, 95, 104, 105(table)
    during López Portillo administration, 114, 116(table)
    during Ruiz Cortines administration, 59
    during stabilized growth period, 66, 75, 83–84
    during war years, 42–44, 45
    See also Peasants
Aguilar, Alonso, 9, 33, 34–35, 149
AHMSA, 98
Alemán, Miguel, 20, 49, 52–53, 60, 85(n2)
    agricultural boom under, 54–57
    capitalist-rentier state under, 57–59
Allende, Salvador, 102
Altos Hornos de México, 51, 131(table)
Angeles Cornejo, Sarahí, 145
Argentina, 14
Asociación de Banqueros Mexicanos (ABM), 57, 85(n1), 104, 124, 139

Austrian School, 118, 136, 137, 176. *See also* Monetarist theory; Neoliberal state
Auto industry, 58, 68–69, 97, 98, 153, 193
    investment in, 164–165
    sector program for, 184–185
Ávila Camacho, Manuel, 20, 42–43, 45, 58
    industrial policies of, 46–49, 53, 55
Ayala, José, 80, 81

Baez Rodríquez, Francisco, 178–179
Bahías de Huatulco, 162
Balance of payments, 6, 56, 59, 60
    during Echeverría administration, 93, 106
    and export promotion program, 191
    and IMF stabilization program, 107
    during López Portillo administration, 117
    and stabilized growth model, 73–78, 80
Banco de Comercio Exterior (Bancomext), 183–184
Banco de México, 45–46, 197(n3)
    and debt crisis, 119, 120, 121, 123, 175
    during Echeverría administration, 92, 94, 100
    and export promotion program, 186
Bancomext. *See* Banco de Comercio Exterior
Banks, 11, 12, 23
    and Canacintra, 85(n1)
    and currency speculation, 118
    during Echeverría administration, 94, 96, 100, 102, 103
    and General Agreement on Tariffs and Trade, 181
    middle class deposits in, 121
    and Multiple Banking Law, 108
    nationalization of, 27, 48, 87, 120–126, 163, 177, 178, 180
    and parastate sector, 128, 139
    and relative state autonomy theory, 29
    as source of investment funds, 51–52, 75, 78, 100, 108

DATE DUE